BROTHA VEGAN

OF RELATED INTEREST

A. Breeze Harper, editor
Sistah Vegan
Black Women Speak on Food, Identity, Health, and Society
(New Tenth Anniversary Edition)
248 pp, 978-1-59056-145-4

Aph Ko and Syl Ko
Aphro-ism
Essays on Pop Culture, Feminism, and Black Veganism from Two Sisters
202 pp, 978-1-59056-555-1

Aph Ko
Racism as Zoological Witchcraft
A Guide to Getting Out
168 pp, 978-1-59056-596-4

Alycee J. Lane
Nonviolence Now!
Living the 1963 Birmingham Campaign's Promise of Peace
216 pp, 978-1-59056-506-3

Letters to a New Vegan
Words to Inform, Inspire, and Support a Vegan Lifestyle
148 pp, 978-1-59056-504-9

BROTHA VEGAN

BLACK MEN SPEAK ON FOOD, IDENTITY, HEALTH, AND SOCIETY

OMOWALE ADEWALE
Editor

A. BREEZE HARPER
Series Editor

Lantern Publishing & Media • Brooklyn, New York

2021
Lantern Publishing & Media
128 Second Place
Brooklyn, NY 11231
www.lanternpm.org

Some of the chapter "Reprogramming the System" by Kimatni D. Rawlins was adapted from "Fit Fathers, Devoted Dads," by Kimatni Rawlins, published in *Running, Eating, Thinking: A Vegan Anthology*, edited by Martin Rowe and published by Lantern Books, NY, in 2013.

The poems "Grab Them" and "Cultural Co-Opting" by Donald Vincent are reprinted from *Convenient Amnesia* by Donald Vincent, published by Broadstone Books of Frankfort, KY, in 2020. They are used with permission.

The publisher would like to acknowledge the work of Stephanie Araujo in conducting the interviews on behalf of *Brotha Vegan*, and to thank Brighter Green for its sponsorship of this book.

Cover Design: EastRand Studios (www.eastrandstudios.com/)

Notice: This book is intended as a reference volume only, not as a medical manual. The information given here is designed to help you make informed decisions about your health. It's not intended as a substitute for any treatment that may have been prescribed or recommendations given by your health-care provider. If you suspect that you have a medical problem, we urge you to seek competent medical help.

Printed in the United States of America

LIBRARY OF CONGRESS CATALOGING-IN-PUBLICATION DATA

Names: Adewale, Omowale, editor.
Title: Brotha vegan : black male vegans speak on food, identity, health, and society
/ Omowale Adewale, editor.
Other titles: Brother vegan
Description: Brooklyn, NY : Lantern Publishing & Media, [2021]
Identifiers: LCCN 2020054293 (print) I LCCN 2020054294 (ebook) I ISBN
9781590565988 (paperback) I ISBN 9781590565995 (epub)
Subjects: LCSH: Vegetarianism--United States. I Veganism—United States. I
African-American men—Social life and customs. I African-American men—Health.
Classification: LCC TX392 .B755 2021 (print) I LCC TX392 (ebook) I DDC
613.2/62—dc23
LC record available at https://lccn.loc.gov/2020054293
LC ebook record available at https://lccn.loc.gov/2020054294

CONTENTS

APPRECIATIONS

Omowale Adewale

S istah Breeze. Thank you for your vision. A debt of gratitude to Stephanie Araujo. Young Sis, you are a light.

To the white folks at Lantern Publishing & Media for not getting in my way, but clearing a path: Martin Rowe, Rebecca Moore, Brian Normoyle, and Emily Lavieri-Scull. Thank you.

Thank you, EastRand, for your work and patience. Y'all are dope!

Mom, Dad: Everything I do is an apprenticeship under you.

Mama Asantewaa, I'm sorry. You are a great mentor.

Francis Peña, you are the most consistent Brother I know.

To my firstborn, Rayne, you are always centered in my heart.

Aziza, you are already great.

Chisore, you are my young champ for life.

To my womb Brothers, Wendell and Christopher, I love y'all vegan journey.

Nadia Muyeeb, you are my guiding force, Queen. Thank you for pushing me.

To the Brothers who submitted and contributed their voices, you helped make this. Thank you: Anteneh Roba, M.D.; Anthony Carr; Baba Brother-D Aammaa Nubyahn; Brandon Morton; Bryant Terry; Charles McCoy; Donald Peebles; Dr. Ietef "DJ Cavem" Vita; Milton Mills, M.D.; Eric Adams; Fred "Doc" Beasley II; Jae Yahkèl Estes, XVX; Kevin Jenkins; Kezekial McWhinney-StLouis; Khnum "Stic" Ibomu; Kimatni Rawlins; Malcolm ("malc") Jones; Michael Barber; Mutulu Olugbala a.k.a. M-1; Ra-leek Born and Ra-tru Born; Richard Rogers; Scott Bernard; Stewart Devon Mitchell; Donald Vincent; Lord Cannon; and Torre Washington. ✺

PREFACE

A. Breeze Harper

Fifteen years ago, having gone on a plant-based Afro-Kemetic diet after reading Queen Afua's *Sacred Woman* in an attempt to deal with fibroids, I became interested in how Black women who identified as vegans saw their choices. The books and arguments I had read by white people on veganism tended to assess the issue through the lens of the mistreatment of nonhuman animals. Not only was it evident that Black women were largely absent from these discussions, but it was clear that our focus on our health and on decolonizing our bodies from the consequences of systemic racism was not being acknowledged by mainstream veganism.

I realized that I needed to hear from other Black women about their experiences with veganism, and how and what they thought about it as an identifier. I started the Sistah Vegan Project in 2004, and over the next several years, I placed a call on forums and list-servs for Black girls and women to tell me their stories. In 2010, I gathered some of the poems, essays, and biographies that I received into an anthology, and *Sistah Vegan: Black Female Vegans Speak on Food, Identity, Health, and Society* was published in 2010. (A tenth anniversary edition, with a new foreword reflecting on the decade and what I have learned since then, was published in September 2020.)

Sistah Vegan showcased some of the many issues that animate the lives of Black vegan women across this country, and beyond: gender, sexuality, health, diet, racism, body image, the environment, class, family, work, parenting, Afrocentric spirituality, and animal advocacy. Once the book was complete, I had hoped to start its companion volume, *Brotha Vegan*. However, I had recently become a parent and was in the middle of a Ph.D. program. As the years went by, and I birthed three more kids and began my own consulting business, the possibility of my compiling and editing *Brotha Vegan* receded.

Under the leadership of Omowale Adewale, however, *Brotha Vegan* has finally been published. In this book, two-dozen Black-identified vegan men and a boy talk about the realities of their lives and their commitment to the plant-based lifestyle. This volume is as diverse, challenging, and insightful as *Sistah Vegan*, and will, I hope, inspire and provoke as many readers as the earlier book did and continues to do.

I'm pleased that one of my original discussions, with DJ Cavem, a.k.a. Ietef Vita, is in *Brotha Vegan*. Ietef is an organic, veganic gardener and hip hop artist who raps about liberation through decolonizing the body with a vegan diet and growing your own food. He encapsulates the intersectional, multi-dimensional, and layered approach that many contributors to *Brotha Vegan* illustrate.

When I conceived of *Brotha Vegan*, I hoped it would countermand the notions that, first, veganism and animal rights is a construct by and for those who identify as girls and women; and that, second, particularly in terms of their manifestation in the colonization of the Americas over the last four centuries, eating meat and hunting animals are fundamental to the "appropriate" way to perform masculinity. I also thought it would be interesting to examine issues of gender and racism, and the stereotypes, narratives, and internalized ways of thinking about masculinity that operate within different subsets of the Black community. This was especially important given that Black men have been negatively stereotyped throughout this country's racist history as *hypersexualized* and *natural predators*.

In her 2007 book, *Black Masculinity and the U.S. South: From Uncle Tom to Gangsta*, Professor Riché Richardson, currently associate professor of African-American literature in the Africana Studies and Research Center at Cornell University, explores some of these stereotypes of Black masculinity. Her work inspired me to start thinking about what alternative masculinities might be possible—especially through the models of plant-based eating and animal rights. I've already touched on how veganism is usually associated in mainstream America with white people, and white women and girls especially. Black vegan men are, therefore, the antitheses of what might be "expected" of men (particularly heterosexual men), and doubly antithetical to expectations surrounding Black men.

In encountering artists like Ietef and Supanova Slom, who is the son of Queen Afua and who also is a hip hop artist, the subtler and richer insights of Black men and food come into sharper relief. Supanova Slom's song "Sugar Crack" questions the history of the sugar industry and examines how so many Brown and Black indigenous people were enslaved to harvest cane sugar, and then re-enslaved by it in the sugary drinks and salty junk food that predominate in spaces of *food apartheid* within many communities of color in the United States. Of course, sugar cane is vegan—at least, in its raw form before it is often refined through animal bone char. However, it has a long history in chattel slavery and suffering, and it is linked to hypertension and diabetes, which disproportionately affect Black and Brown indigenous communities that do not have access to a whole-foods, plant-based diet.

Much of this book was created before the emergence of COVID-19 and the widespread demonstrations against police brutality and systemic racism following the murder of George Floyd in Minneapolis, Minnesota, on May 25, 2020. However, the material in *Brotha Vegan* clearly speaks to these times. The pandemic and Floyd's murder (and others), as *Brotha Vegan* demonstrates, have revealed profound inequities: in the food system that denies people access to food that might support their immune system; in employment and health, where many people of color are in professions considered essential and are unable to work from home; in the criminalization of Black men and the carceral state; and in the disposability of Black people's lives.

The contributors to *Brotha Vegan* offer a critique and an alternative not only to Black masculinity, and to masculinity as a whole, but to these current models of racism and exploitation. *Brotha Vegan* shows how these issues are not separate from the food system, politics, education, and climate change but intrinsic to why they are so bad and how they might be remediated. The anthology makes abundantly clear that if any of us are going to have a future worth living, we will need multi-dimensional approaches and many solutions that don't involve ceding more power, privilege, and resources to those who already have too much. It gives voice to a spectrum of Black men—such as trans and gay men—who are working to change a system that has oppressed them and denied them the right to be fully human. Finally, *Brotha Vegan* models a set of discourses and multi-generational engagements that benefit not only the wellbeing of Black men and communities of color, but society as a whole. ☀

A. Breeze Harper
—July 2020

INTRODUCTION

Omowale Adewale

In 2018, I was invited by A. Breeze Harper and Lantern Publishing & Media to edit an anthology of writings by Black men as a companion to Breeze's 2010 volume, *Sistah Vegan*. *Sistah Vegan* has become a hugely influential staple in the Black vegan community, and for years Black women have talked to me enthusiastically about the book and what it's meant to them. My goal with *Brotha Vegan* is simple: to showcase an incredible cast of Black men from all walks of life, and to have their writings resonate with Black men the same way *Sistah Vegan* seems to have resonated with so many Black women. I also hope this book encourage readers to find or revisit *Sistah Vegan*. Both books are a symbiotic response to Black people's struggle in America, as vegans and those transitioning to veganism.

Brotha Vegan also aims to create a set of core ideas of Black veganism and a caucus of Black vegans to dissect and process veganism within society. For a long time, Black vegans and vegetarians have felt ignored by and marginalized within multiple communities. Black people, much like other communities of color and oppressed people who experience poverty, have been conditioned into believing that obtaining meat is the ideal and the goal; we have considered the consumption of meat primary to our aspirations. *Brotha Vegan* offers an opportunity to help change this dynamic. With its rich and diverse contributions, the anthology presents multiple variations on what freedom feels like in the Black context.

Significantly, *Brotha Vegan* provides theories manifested *by* Black people *for* Black people during a time when we are revisiting Black liberation: its importance, realities, and strategies. In this book, I share my own purpose for founding Black VegFest and how and why it became so attractive to the Black community in such a short span of time.

Even though much of the groundwork for this anthology was undertaken at the end of 2019 and in the earliest months of 2020, it would be impossible to present this collection of essays, poems, and interviews without taking into account the events of 2020—a year when

Black liberatory action became palpable in the streets and online, death disproportionately met our community through COVID-19, and where the Trump administration continued to impact our livelihoods.

Brotha Vegan is, therefore, of the moment, and yet emerges from a recognition that the Trump administration is only the latest version in a long line of oppressive regimes throughout the history of the United States. Yes, today's racial hatred is explicit, but more people are learning and finally understanding that it is an outgrowth of systemic racism and implicit bias. That is why, as you read this anthology, you will see on the page the many layers of trauma with which Black men and Black people have had to grapple. That trauma is not discrete or separable, just as the liberation that is required is not only Black liberation, but complete liberation drawn from the Black experience in the United States.

Brotha Vegan also explores less violent interactions between humans and animals, healthier ways of eating, Black trans safety, the role of the Black man in the family, and reimagining masculinity. We learn about growing herbs and plants, intracommunity connections between children and elders, advice on strengthening intimate relationships, and how to address the climate crisis. Some essays examine white veganism and how white people often miss the scope of racism and how the entire oppressive system rests on top of Black people.

Whatever the subject matter, however, *Brotha Vegan* is unapologetically Black. What do I mean by that? I mean that *Brotha Vegan* gives the information necessary to the Black community without thinking about how white people, or, for that matter, any other community might receive it. In the last several years, documentaries, websites, and books (such as *Sistah Vegan*) have shown that veganism and the Black community are not mutually exclusive. The information that folks need is more accessible; people are more open to learning about animals and their misery; society as a whole is understanding oppression and what solutions are available; and more and more Black people are interested in going vegan. Today, many of us recognize that animals are more than just options on our plate. It is out of this sense of what is possible that I hope *Brotha Vegan* sparks a liberatory movement in the Black community.

Finally, *Brotha Vegan* not only presents an analysis of veganism from a Black perspective; it offers a profound rethinking of the meaning of veganism. The activists, doctors, teachers, artists, and thinkers in this book have come to this lifestyle in many different ways. They recognize that the vegan community has very different potential than the average community. People in the vegan community can understand that, yes, there's going to be racism within their community, *and* yes, there is also ableism and speciesism. But to consider all the different struggles that exist in the world, and to work to piece together conversations with others about these layered issues, is both exciting and scary. I hope *Brotha Vegan* sparks discussions on all the topics raised in these pages, so that when you finish this book, you think to yourself: *I want to speak with someone about what I just read.*

Brotha Vegan is a debriefing, a logbook, and a manual of inspiration. It's the book I've been waiting my whole life to see; an effort that goes beyond self-expression or bookselling to learning, going vegan, and dismantling all oppressive systems.

Much practical work needs to be done. Individuals will transition at their own rate, and I feel very strongly that you can't change that individual nature in anyone. But people will want to change if you give them good information, with decent options and solid alternatives that are accessible, and *Brotha Vegan* fulfills that task as well. In presenting this anthology during an unstable time, the onus is on me, the other writers in this volume— and you, the reader—to bring the pulse of the Black man to the fore. In this practical sense, therefore, I give you a rebellion in print through a praxis of unapologetically Black vegan intersectionality. ✹

1

A BLACK LESBIAN VEGAN SAVED MY LIFE

Donald Peebles

People come into our lives for a reason during a season. People come into our lives to teach us valuable lessons. People come into our lives: shining jewels, gems, pearls, diamonds, and emeralds. People come into our lives to impart their wisdom. People come into our lives with the grace of God/Spirit.

This person who came into my life for a reason was Monalisa McCombs.

I met Monalisa at Unity Fellowship of Christ church in the East New York section of Brooklyn. Although we were not friends at first, I was always intrigued by her. She was a tall, light-skinned, and proud Black lesbian Assemblies of God woman, with long black locks. I observed her always arriving late to service when Bishop Zachary Glenn Jones or whoever else delivered the sermon. I liked her energy and spirit for some unknown reason.

Monalisa befriended me after hearing about my working on my Master's thesis on African-American soap opera history from her then-partner, Norma Jackson. Norma was a biracial chef with African-American and Italian-American roots. She sat with my friend Eric Fergerson and me on the Thursday night food pantry. She schooled us about the bestselling diet book *The Zone: A Dietary Road Map* by Dr. Barry Sears. She had so much energy and zest. I thought she was a health nut. I didn't understand what she was talking about until she introduced herself to Eric and me as Monalisa's partner.

Monalisa and I became closer when she interviewed me as one of the subjects for her documentary *Being Black, Proud, and LGBT in America*. I learned about her being a vegan who ate organic food and drank Smart Water. Her vegan lifestyle contrasted with my lifelong sedentary, fast food, and chip-loving lifestyle. We worked on the documentary during the wee hours and early mornings at her Flushing, New York, apartment, where she lived with her mother, Miss Marie. I mostly snacked on Pringles and other chips. She ate her organic popcorn and other snacks she purchased from her favorite health food stores, Westerly and LifeThyme Natural Markets.

I never understood fully why Monalisa befriended me. I was a lifelong overweight guy whose life revolved around food, weight, diets, and diabetes. My late paternal grandparents, Eugene and Sally Peebles, my father, Abdul Peebles (né Donald Sr.), and my uncle Ronald Peebles dealt with Type 2 diabetes. My maternal grandmother, Lucille McDaniel, had a stroke, developed Type 2 diabetes, experienced a foot amputation, and passed away from diabetic complications. I grew up as a picky eater who found fruits and vegetables nasty; instead, I enjoyed Friday night dinners at McDonald's with Grandpa. I was an emotional eater who found comfort in fast and junk foods like chips to cope with being teased, taunted, and bullied for my weight, stutter, and gender-nonconforming sexuality.

Monalisa took me with her to Westerly and LifeThyme whenever we hung out, either after church or after her ninety-minute workouts at the New York Sports Club on Seventh Avenue in Greenwich Village. At Westerly, she ordered green juices with extra sweetness from organic green apples and sampled wheatgrass at the juice bar. She also bought numerous soups. At LifeThyme, she ordered vegan cookies, raw food, and air-popped popcorn with sea salt and nutritional yeast. I was always self-conscious because I felt like the Black brotha and the Latina bakery sistah at LifeThyme knew that I was not into anything organic, raw, or vegan.

Monalisa spent money on me to try all those foods, but I found most of them bland, boring, and nasty. She also gave me a free PETA Vegetarian Starter Kit. Although it was great to learn about vegetarian and vegan celebrities, I was still not convinced. I craved my McDonald's, Wendy's, and other fast and junk foods. I even ate the Wendy's value menu of a bacon cheeseburger, French fries, and a soft drink in front of her in her car. I didn't realize how I disrespected all her efforts at introducing me to veganism.

Everything changed when I was diagnosed with Type 2 diabetes in 2011. I went into complete shock and denial. It was the source of my fatigue during my Vendor Services Representative job at an advertising and marketing company. I didn't know what to do. I had assumed it was inevitable for me to inherit Type 2 diabetes from three of my grandparents, my father, Uncle Ronald, and my maternal uncle, Barry McDaniel. But somehow I never thought I would have been diagnosed with it. My company had a health fair where a nutritionist, whose name I don't recall, offered her services. She was an expert in raw foods. I was not about to eat raw vegetables of any sort. I took her information but buried it in my dresser drawer.

I decided to experiment with vegetarianism in 2012. I bought fruits and vegetables whenever I saw them from my Latino peeps at a produce stand on 91st Avenue and Sutphin Boulevard in Jamaica, Queens. I often bought forty dollars' worth of produce, only to throw most of it out after letting it spoil in my refrigerator. I also shopped at Trader Joe's for my bagged salads and other favorite items. Monalisa preferred shopping at Whole Foods, Westerly, and LifeThyme because she valued everything organic. I found Trader Joe's more affordable and reasonable, and it worked for me. I tried eating "chik'n tenders" from Trader Joe's and having a Sunday dinner at Vegetarian's Paradise 2 in the Village, but I wasn't feeling the taste of tofu, soy, seitan, and other mock meat ingredients.

I researched vegetarianism by watching documentaries—such as *Simply Raw*; *Forks Over Knives*; *Fat, Sick & Nearly Dead*; *Super Size Me*; and *Food, Inc.*—on YouTube. I caught the 1990 episode of *The Phil Donahue Show* on which Lisa Bonet, Raul Julia, River Phoenix, and John Robbins spoke about vegetarianism at a time when it was unpopular. I attended the Green Festival at the Jacob Javits Convention Center, took home some samples, and purchased a book or two to introduce myself fully to vegetarianism and veganism. I also lined up to enter the New York City Vegetarian Food Festival. When I finally got inside, I felt so disconnected that I had to leave, wishing I had the money to purchase a Vitamix blender. Despite my eagerness to learn and change, I was still not convinced, so my vegetarian journey was short-lived.

In 2015, a high-school classmate of mine named Aida Feliz Vicuna gave me information about veganism on Facebook. She snail-mailed me a book, *Eat Vegan on $4 a Day* by Ellen Jaffe Jones. Unfortunately, I still wasn't convinced about eating a vegan diet on so little money. I was working at Dollar Tree on Coney Island and living in a post-homeless shelter transitional home in the East New York section of Brooklyn. I had survival on my mind. Veganism was not an option in a home where food was constantly stolen out of the refrigerator by other former homeless-shelter residents, their girlfriends, and their baby mamas. Veganism was not an option in a home where there was straight-up negativity every day, all day.

On Sunday, April 22, 2018—Earth Day—I decided to give up meat after watching the documentaries *Vegucated*; *Food, Inc.* (again); and *Simply Raw* (again) on YouTube. I was more optimistic about being a vegan, although I found it hard to give up cheese. I ate lots of mock meats and vegan junk food. I had fun attending the New York City Vegetarian Food Festival on the weekend of May 17–18, 2018. I became acquainted with vegan and plant-based people in real life and on social media. I began going to some of the quarterly vegan and veg-curious meet-ups facilitated by Brooklyn Borough President Eric L. Adams at Brooklyn Borough Hall with my Brooklyn Public Library colleague and birthday twin, Venus Hunter. I couldn't wait to attend Black VegFest in Brooklyn after hearing founder Omowale Adewale discuss it at one of the meet-ups. I attended the first annual Black VegFest on a rainy Saturday afternoon on August 11, 2018, with my best friend, Ra Shawn (Da Professor) Chisolm, who was veg-curious. I had an excellent time eating vegan food, watching presentations and cooking demonstrations, supporting numerous vendors, and meeting other vegans of all colors. Black VegFest made me proud of being an African-American/Black male vegan without feeling as if I'd lost all my Black cultural cred.

Some family members and Brooklyn Public Library colleagues had mixed to negative reactions to veganism. There were challenges, such as finding vegan and/or veg options at restaurants and other stores in the East Flatbush/Brownsville neighborhood for breakfast and lunch. Prepping for lunch and dinner in the rooming house I lived at in Jamaica was kind of difficult. However, I found myself able to manage despite other tenants dominating the shared kitchen and living room. I worried about eating vegan on the Fourth of July and Thanksgiving with family members and friends. It was not as bad as I thought it might be, because I was able to enjoy my black-bean burger and fries at Johnny Rockets and my Lightlife Vegan Smart Dogs at home on the Fourth of July. I was able to enjoy the meatless sides at Thanksgiving while my uncle and aunt, Larry and Karin McDaniel, and cousins Tenaya and Tamia ate their non-vegan meals. I enjoyed the black-bean burger and fries at Dallas BBQ while Ra Shawn and Christian Williams, another friend of ours, had their respective meals.

As soon as it looked like I had passed Thanksgiving with flying colors, I fell off the vegetarian wagon. I was packing to move for a week, when a visa-visiting girlfriend of a tenant dominated the kitchen, making it difficult to prep and enjoy my meals. I relapsed into eating McDonald's, Popeye's, Little Caesar's Pizza, bad Chinese food, and other junk. My taste buds absorbed the salt, sugar, fat, and grease. My seven months of vegetarianism was shattered . . . or so I thought.

I moved into my new one-bedroom apartment at Alvista Towers at the end of 2018. I was relieved to finally have my own food sanctuary to prep for my vegan meals and dishes.

My vegan life was revived when I enrolled in Bellevue Hospital's Plant-Based Lifestyle Medicine Program on Wednesday, January 26, 2019. I enjoyed my appointments with dietitian Lilian Correa, health coach Krisann Polito-Moller, and physician Gaurav Sharma. My health has improved, although I still have lots of work to do with reversing blood pressure, diabetes, cholesterol, and obesity. I'm learning a lot from my time in this program—the innovative brainchild of Eric L. Adams and Dr. Michelle McMacken.

I am finally coming to terms with the ways food has affected my life, health, and wellness. I still need to give up my addiction to chips of all kinds, though.

Although I am no longer friends with Monalisa at this present time, I want to express my gratitude to her for helping me to open my eyes about veganism. We all must show gratitude to people who paved the way to our successes, achievements, and accomplishments. I wasn't mentally and spiritually ready to embrace veganism during our friendship; I know now how veganism is a mental, spiritual, and ethical choice. Monalisa sparked this in me, but I was too blinded, clouded, and distracted to get the lesson, jewelry, and wisdom. I totally get it now—thirteen years later.

People come into our lives for a reason during a season.

We never know who God/Spirit sends into our lives.

I am proud to proclaim how a Black lesbian vegan saved my life. ✿

2

BROTHERHOOD

An Interview with Bryant Terry

Brotha Vegan: *Please tell us about yourself.*

Bryant Terry: I'm a James Beard Foundation Award–winning chef, educator, and author known for my activism to create a healthy, just, and sustainable food system. Since 2015, I have been the Chef-in-Residence at the Museum of the African Diaspora (MoAD) in San Francisco, where I create public programming that celebrates the intersection of food, farming, health, activism, art, culture, and the African Diaspora.

I'm a Black man, and my primary focus as an activist is addressing the public health crisis among African-Americans that is partially driven by what we eat. A large part of my work is about helping my people *remember* that our traditional diets are replete with nutrient-dense dark-green leafy vegetables, protein-rich legumes, vitamin-packed fruits, and the like. When we move beyond the reductive way that people imagine African-American cuisine (i.e., antebellum survival food eaten by enslaved Africans and/or the comfort foods that Black folks most often enjoy on holidays and special occasions), we will find that traditional Black diets can play an important role in our journey to liberation. When one considers that for thousands of years traditional West and Central African diets were predominantly vegetarian—centered on staples like millet, rice, field peas, okra, hot peppers, and yams— and that many pre-colonial African diets heavily emphasized vegetables, plant-based diets celebrating the food of the African diaspora are perfectly fitting.

BV: *What is the food of your birthplace and where do you live now?*

BT: I was born and raised in Memphis, Tennessee. My people are from there so that place rooted and raised me to be all that I am today. My fondest memories are gardening with my paternal grandfather and cooking with my maternal grandmother. I was invited to teach cooking to young people at a program based in Oakland, California, in the summer of 2003. Within the first week, I knew I wanted to live there. I didn't so much choose the place, as the Bay Area chose me. The far-left politics, beautiful weather, and food justice community all made the town feel like my spiritual home. Also, my wife's family lives in Berkeley, so it's nice living so close to loved ones.

BV: *Tell us about your wife.*
BT: My wife is a brilliant, beautiful, and bout it-bout it organizer, philanthropist, and artist. She's also a fantastic mother to our daughters. One of the things I admire most about my wife is her unwavering commitment to building grassroots movements for social change.

BV: *How would you describe your politics?*
BT: I'm a radical food justice activist. My work is deeply inspired by programs of the Black Panther Party in the late 1960s and '70s that addressed the intersection of poverty, malnutrition, and institutional racism—their grocery giveaways and Free Breakfast for School Children Program. For those who don't know, food justice is a movement to ensure that everyone is afforded the human right to healthy, safe, affordable, and culturally appropriate food. I'm simply using my national platform to a) bring light to the economic, physical, and geographic barriers that many people in communities across this country have to accessing good food; and b) work to build power in those communities so those most impacted can create solutions to food injustice.

BV: *Why and how did you become a vegan?*
BT: I grew up an omnivore. My family owned farms in rural Mississippi and kept gardens in Memphis, so I always had the freshest local food that was grown and cooked by people I love. When I got to high school, I started eating a lot of fast and crappy food because that is what many of my buddies on the football team were eating. I began to move toward a more compassionate and healthful diet when I was in tenth grade, after hearing the song "Beef" by the hip hop crew Boogie Down Productions. I learned a lot about the ethical, health, and environmental reasons for maintaining a vegan diet from Rastafarians and

other Black elders who used to shop at the health food store in downtown Memphis. I think it's important to note that my path was non-linear. When I studied abroad in France in the late nineties, it was challenging maintaining a strict vegan diet. I share that to encourage self-compassion and remind folks that we are humans trying to do the best we can in this life.

BV: *How do you develop your recipes?*
BT: Many people build altars, visit gravesites, and reminisce with photos to engage with loved ones who have passed. For me, recipe creation is a praxis where I honor and bring to life the teachings, traditional knowledge, and hospitality of my blood and spiritual ancestors by making food. I approach recipe development as a collagist—curating, cutting, pasting, and remixing staple ingredients, cooking techniques, and traditional Black dishes popular throughout the world to make my own signature recipes. In addition to Black food, my family eats a lot of Chinese, Japanese, and Vietnamese food at home. It is easy getting ample vegetables, since they are so prominent in those cuisines.

BV: *What is your go-to meal when you're not in the mood to cook and no one's around to help you prepare?*
BT: I keep a stash of locally made mushroom tamales in my freezer so I can pull them out whenever I want an easy meal. I just sauté some dark leafy greens to go with them, serve them with a good-quality salsa, and grub.

BV: *Why do you think Black vegfests are important?*
BT: We need spaces that celebrate and center our food cultures. Maintaining diets mostly comprised of vegetables isn't new to Black folks. When you look at many of the traditional diets throughout Sub-Saharan Africa, the Caribbean, and the American South, they are largely vegetable-based. In addition to that, there is a thread of Black-led food and health activism throughout the twentieth century. We are standing on the shoulders of many individuals (and organizations) who have long understood the connection between diet and overall health and well being. One of the keys to Black folks' getting free is remembering these legacies and putting them into practice.

BV: *What advice would you give to Black men who see your life as an example?*

BT: Determine what your definite major purpose in life is. Create daily habits that move you closer to that goal. Read autobiographies and biographies from accomplished people to learn from them. Fight to dismantle all systems of oppression. Remember that you rise by lifting others.

BV: *Finally, what does brotherhood mean to you?*

Brotherhood is recognizing there's no separation between self and other, and that everyone and everything is interconnected. ❁

3

REPROGRAMMING THE SYSTEM

Kimatni D. Rawlins

When my two daughters ask me why I decided to go vegan, I think back to dinner time when I was growing up in the 1970s in Camden, New Jersey. Keeping the fridge and cupboards stocked was problematic for my mother, so my two younger sisters and I would take a vote on what was ideal based on the limited ingredients. Three days out of seven we had "breakfast for dinner," since there was always a carton of eggs, milk, pancake mix, and a few slices of bacon lying around. On special days, we would have BLTs on toasted Wonder Bread—yes, that white bread that turns into paste when wet—layered with mayonnaise and a yokey fried egg. Other nights, my mother would serve fried liver with mashed potatoes or white rice or macaroni.

Over the years, my mother worked feverishly on her nursing degree to help my sisters and me escape the immense poverty, minimal education, and debilitating crime of a city that seemed bent on self-destruction. There were no shopping malls, movie theaters, or recreation centers for us kids to escape to. There were, however, bullying, fights, drugs, and free blocks of government cheese that we used to make grilled sandwiches that hardly melted under the heat. Food stamps played an integral role in our food choices and level of nutrition. When times were tough we survived on mayonnaise sandwiches; when times were good we ate out at McDonald's and Roy Rogers.

Although Mom made us eat Quaker Oats and corn and peas (the kind that came in frozen bags), our diet mostly consisted of foods that were fried or made with enriched white flour. The only physical activity available to my mother was the dreaded long, weekly walks from the grocery store with heavy bags of sugar, Kool-Aid, and every fattening snack imaginable. She also roller-skated, which burned calories. Yet we certainly didn't look at any of these activities as exercise, and the foods were what my mother could afford. None of us knew they had the potential to cause heart disease, diabetes, and colon cancer.

I was introduced to a healthier diet by my father. My parents split up shortly after I was born, when they were teenagers. After serving in the Vietnam War, my father found himself in Washington, DC, where he became a strict vegetarian (vegan by today's standards). When I visited him in the summer and on holidays I inexorably took on this strange pattern of eating. Protein shakes, vitamins the size of grapes, gluten, tofu, soy milk, millet, and fruits and vegetables of all colors, shapes, and flavors replaced the crap I was used to eating. The change was so devastating that I would always break out with rashes when I switched diets. My father said it was the poisons detoxing from my body. Yep, he was officially "mad" in my book. Looking back, he was absolutely right. A former boxer, Pops was lean and muscular and always practiced what he preached.

My father never explained his reasons for becoming a vegetarian and how it led to healthier digestion, growth, and living. He also never showed me how to read labels, and he certainly didn't expound on the nutritional benefits of a meatless and dairy-free diet. My two sisters from my father's side and I would look at each other sideways and just eat the stuff. We also rode bikes, walked to the zoo, swam, went camping, and practiced yoga. My father was fervently in tune with the mind–body connection and even made us meditate.

Each fall, I would return to Camden leaner and stronger than when I left. My mother encouraged me by purchasing a cement weight set that I employed to work out five days a week. By the age of twelve I was without doubt the strongest kid in the neighborhood. This was useful on the treacherous streets of Camden. Back then we played basketball and football, raced each other on foot, and biked or walked everywhere. Our families didn't have the luxury of modern transportation. Every kid in Camden was fit. More important, there were so many bullies looking to pick a fight that speed was a common necessity for escape. I considered myself a peacemaker and saw no moral victory in fighting . . . until later in high school.

High school was a pivotal time for me. My mother moved us out of Camden and into the suburban neighborhood of Voorhees, where the education was much better. Soon, I was living out the prototypical story of the kid from the city who goes to school in the burbs and makes good. I performed well inside the classroom and out, and gradually developed into one of the top athletes in New Jersey. I won state titles in track and field, excelling in the 100- and 200-yard dash, hurdles, and the long jump. As a 205-pound running back I led my high-school football team to a conference title and a spot in the Group Championship game. I was racking up accolades and awards, as well as recruitment visits from Division 1 collegiate football programs. It became clear that I would become the first member of my family to attend a Division 1 university, and on a scholarship, no less.

Although I went on to play for North Carolina State and later transferred to the Georgia Institute of Technology, my story soon became one familiar to many college students: heavy drinking began to play a major role in my educational and athletic development. Thinking back, I believe I took in some booze and even an occasional blunt every day of the week. Oftentimes, I went on the field still intoxicated from all-night binges. My focus eroded and my athletic skills diminished. On top of that, the coaches were stuffing us like factory animals. I grew to 225 pounds of pure muscle while chowing down on meat, potatoes, and cheese dishes. Inevitably, I lost my love for the sport and simply showed up in order to graduate.

Afterward, I started working in various fields in the automotive industry, where my old man had made his career. He published *African-Americans on Wheels* automotive magazine, pivotal since his company was the only diverse media outlet in the auto world at the time. Who would have thought, a vegetarian entrepreneur breaking into the upper echelons of big business?

Eventually, I ventured out on my own and founded Automotive Rhythms Communications, a lifestyle automotive media and marketing portal. This allowed me to travel the globe assessing new automobiles and motorcycles, as well as cuisines that were new to me. Here I was, a kid from Camden, staying in a five-star hotel in Paris and being given the opportunity to try foie gras, frogs' legs, and snails. Unfortunately, with all the traveling and hosted dinners came more eating and drinking to unprecedented levels. By the end of a night, I would typically have consumed nine glasses of wine and a few Johnnie Walker Blacks and sometimes Blues, which typically cost $50 a glass. *How much better could it get?* I thought. This disastrous lifestyle continued for ten more years.

One morning in 2011, at the age of 35, I walked into the bathroom, stepped on the scale, and discovered that I weighed more than 250 pounds, but was devoid of most of my muscles. I was as chubby as a beaver. I looked in the mirror. My face was thick and my skin as dry as a raisin. When I went to the closet, I noticed that I now wore size 42 jeans and 3X shirts. How had this happened? Well, I didn't exactly exercise twice a day like I had back at Georgia Tech, but I still played basketball, flag football, and weightlifted. I had even cut back on the partying and drinking. But my daily diet was only slightly better than what I had grown up with, except that I had given up beef and pork. Nonetheless, chicken cheesesteaks, wings with blue cheese, sugary drinks, chips, and other snacks ran my life. To top it off, I was driving everywhere, since Automotive Rhythms always had a fleet of vehicles in the driveway. Why ride a bike when a $100,000 Mercedes-Benz awaited? But enough was enough, and I decided to make a permanent lifestyle change.

The very next day, I signed up for the Men's Health Urbanathlon, a nine- to eleven–mile run through the streets of Chicago, New York, and San Francisco. Training for the event required four days of running activities, alternating between distance and sprints, and two days of strength training. I decided to run the Chicago race first because I wanted the chance to climb the hundreds of stadium steps at Soldier Field—where my hero, the running back Walter Payton, played—as part of the course. By the time race day came around five months later, I had lost twenty-five pounds, toned up quite a bit, and stopped drinking alcohol completely. Additionally, I had progressed from not being able to run a mere mile without breathing heavily to checking off eight, ten, and twelve miles without hesitation or strain. Best of all, I had dropped four waist and two shirt sizes. It felt good to be trim again.

Since most of what I had been taught by public educational institutions regarding food was wrong, I set out to educate myself by reading a book a week, watching documentaries such as *Forks Over Knives*, and attending seminars and health conferences. Slowly, light was being shed on the childhood eating habits I had learned from my father. Once I understood that we must eat whole foods from the earth to meet the balance of vitamins, minerals, and phytonutrients our bodies need, I went on a mission to rid myself of all meat, dairy, and processed foods. My next challenge was running a full marathon while operating on vegan fuel. Once I completed that task, I knew I would never turn back. More important, I got down to my high school weight of 202 pounds, could still bench my max of 405 pounds when I trained for four months, and regained my sprinting capabilities, which helped me run a 21-minute 5K at age forty.

But it wasn't enough that I was getting healthier; I needed my wife and two daughters, ages nine and six at the time, to be healthy, too. I began to make subtle changes, replacing fattening snacks with celery and hummus, sodas with fresh kale and pineapple juice, or a strawberry smoothie made with coconut milk. Dinner time now involved whole grains, such as brown rice, millet, and quinoa, and cruciferous veggies like spinach, broccoli, and collard greens. With sadness, I realized how costly the healthier organic path to eating could be, and understood why my mother couldn't nourish us as she wanted to. My wife and I also began involving the kids in as much physical activity as possible, including swim class, soccer, dance, and family bike riding. Now my younger daughter likes to hit the punching bag with me.

Even that wasn't enough. I looked around me and saw all the fast food, sugary snacks, and excessive Internet and television use that have supplanted home-cooked meals and active living to a point where obesity and lethargy are accepted as the norm. For that reason, I founded Fit Fathers, an inspirational and life-enhancing movement to help families focus on their wellbeing and that of their children. The program offers fitness workouts and routines, recipes for wholesome meals, nutritional food-shopping advice, childhood activity integrations for busy parents, recommendations on degenerative-disease prevention and fitness-friendly places to travel, and of course encouragement to keep mothers and fathers on top of their game. Now I am a certified fitness trainer as well as certified in plant-based nutrition from T. Colin Campbell's eCornell.com program.

So when my daughters ask me why I and our family decided to go vegan, I tell them that it is the best food in the world and that our bodies need nourishment from foods that grow from trees, roots, and plants rather than foods that are born. We love animals and they deserve to be free, just as we humans do. Over the years, I have learned to distinguish between eating as an omnivore and as a herbivore, and ultimately chose the better path. But I have no regrets about the manner in which I was raised. It has shaped me into the person I am today and allows me to engage with those who currently live the life I used to. The journey toward health and happiness is waiting for us; sometimes we just need a little encouragement from those who have run the same path and completed the journey.

Since I adopted a plant-based diet, my vegan education has deepened and expanded. Through Fit Fathers, I have instituted an annual "nomadic journey," in which a group of us visit places around the world in search of mental, physical, and spiritual reconnection. We have traveled to Machu Picchu, Peru; Kenya's Maasai Mara; Cambodia and Vietnam; Nepal and Japan. In doing this, I am externalizing my intellectual and personal interest in the many philosophies and cultures of the world. In my research and travels, I have always discovered that at the heart of every culture's cuisine—the staples that a civilization has depended on for centuries—is a legume and/or a grain.

So, I have eaten kale, spinach, cabbage, tomatoes, beans, potatoes, avocados, rice, and millet in Kenya; in Ethiopia, we sampled wheat, barley, chickpeas, lentils, and injera (a flatbread made out of teff flour). My trip to Egypt was marked by visits to the Pyramids of Giza and the Sphinx—manifestations of the ancient African kingdom of Kemet. I had a personal connection to this place, since my father had introduced me to the Kemetic world as a child, and he and my mother had named me after the deity Ma'at, who judged the level of a man's truthfulness during the time he was alive. I returned from Egypt with the recipe for koshari, Egypt's national dish, which contains lentils, chickpeas, macaroni, onion, brown rice, and spices.

The central part of the Fit Fathers program also continues to grow. In my experience, men in general—but Black men in particular—don't shop for food and don't like another man telling them how to be healthy. I see it as my role as a Black man and a father to break this pattern. I first tell those in the Fit Fathers program that what they thought was a healthy diet isn't necessarily the case ("You mean grilled chicken isn't healthy?!). I then break down some of the ingredients they should definitely be buying, and then we go on shopping trips together. I show men how to work from the outside of the grocery store (where the fresh fruits and vegetables usually are) through to the interior aisles, and to keep away from rich, white, boxed foods.

I also make real to them the journey to healthy eating in terms of the sacrifices they may have to make. It's a shameful fact that healthier foods are often more expensive. This is partly a function of the fact that the U.S. government subsidizes meat and dairy rather than promoting healthier products. It's partly the result of systemic economic disparities between African-Americans and other communities. Nonetheless, I point out to them that when I stopped drinking I saved $500 a month, which allowed me to spend money on nutritious food. I also remind them that bulk items (like grains and beans) are often cheaper and last longer.

I let them know that another sacrifice they may have to make is that they may lose some of their friends. When I began my plant-based journey, some friends thought I was judging them for not adopting my lifestyle. They stopped inviting me on their trips or wanting to socialize with me. As a student of human psychology, I can see that they took my lifestyle as a threat, and that, even though I didn't brag about the changes that were happening to me, my silence on the subject was somehow intimidating. But you cannot be responsible for other people's reactions to what you know is the right thing for you, your family, and your community. As a result, therefore, I now center myself within a new cadre of friends who are either supportive of my mission or are part of the Fit Fathers community.

Since I entered my fifth decade, I have become acutely aware of the need to maintain my overall wellness, and this has meant visiting the doctor. Here, too, men in general are falling down; we are not going to the doctor as regularly as we need to. Black men are particularly resistant, at least partly because of the abuse they historically suffered at the hands of the medical profession (for instance, the notorious Tuskegee syphilis experiments). Black men worry that we will be similarly violated.

It is true that if you follow the three pillars of the Fit Fathers method (exercise, optimal nutrition with an emphasis on plant-based food, and a positive mental state), you may avoid unnecessary medications and expensive surgeries later on. However, it's still necessary to receive regular check-ups from your doctor, especially for conditions such as colon and prostate cancer. Black people are twice as likely to suffer from prostate cancer as white people; and colon or colorectal cancer is the third leading cause of cancerous deaths among American men and women, accounting for 50,000 deaths annually.

This is why, on my forty-fifth birthday in 2019, I had my first colonoscopy. Being Black in the United States typically means increased risks for heart disease, diabetes, high blood pressure, colon cancer, and prostate cancer due to traditional food habits, heightened levels of sedentary behaviors, and lower levels of income. However, I refuse to be cast into a script that is not indicative of the evolutionary choices I've made. I eat a plant-based diet consisting of five to seven servings of fruits and vegetables daily and religiously take in whole greens, legumes (beans), seeds, and nuts.

This is key, since the World Health Organization, the World Cancer Research Fund, and the American Institute for Cancer Research have determined that processed meats are correlated to various cancers; and that red meat specifically, along with a lack of dietary fiber and exercise, is one of the main culprits for initiating colon cancer. Drinking alcohol and smoking tobacco will not help your cause either. Thankfully, I have made wise decisions that have led to the prevention or elimination of these carcinogens.

It is up to all of us who have this knowledge to change the negative consequences to our individual health, our families, and society at large that result from Americans being some of the sickest people in the world. We have too many tools at our disposal not to change: "Moderation applies to healthy things, not to carcinogens," says Dr. Neal Barnard of Physicians Committee for Responsible Medicine. "And processed meats are indeed carcinogens." This is why we must cut out the hot dogs and bacon and increase our servings of quinoa, Swiss chard, and chickpeas.

The American Cancer Society used to advise people to get colonoscopy screenings from the age of fifty, but it has recently lowered that age suggestion by five years. The procedure involves taking a special laxative preparation to liquefy the stool and expel it from the body. (The formula costs $85, even under insurance, which is surely a disincentive to those who cannot afford it, and may need it most.) You are required to fast on water the day prior to the examination. In the examination itself, you are placed under anesthetic, and an elongated flexible tube with a camera on one end (called an endoscope) is inserted in the anus to the place where the endoscopist can observe your colon. If they find polyps in the wall of the intestine, the endoscopist will cut them out on the spot and send them to a pathologist for a biopsy. If the polyps are cancerous, you will be advised of treatment options.

My results revealed no polyps, and I was told to come back in ten years. I'm glad I took the exam—not only for peace of mind, but because Black men and women are more susceptible to this disease, and to polyps, than other races. We must do what we can to remain healthy for ourselves and our families. My mother was one of five brothers and sisters, all of whom have passed away. Half of these family members passed away in their late thirties due to chronic diseases based on their lifestyle. We grew up thinking that being aged forty was old. Now, we know from studies of populations who live in the Blue Zone (parts of the world, such as Okinawa in Japan and Sardinia, with the most centenarians) that we should be living much, much longer.

As a result of the death of George Floyd in May 2020, we are seeing a resurgence of awareness of some of the systemic problems that exist in the United States when it comes to the oppression of Black people: the implicit biases are becoming explicit.

My county's health department asked Fit Fathers to produce ten online videos (half fitness, half vegan cooking) to help our residents continue to focus on their health to help reduce the comorbidities that have exacerbated the consequences of contracting the novel coronavirus. We also partnered with Neal Barnard and Physicians Committee for Responsible Medicine to reach urban communities with free nutritional classes, so that people could fortify their immune systems with healthy food. Although we were prevented (as were so many of us, because of social distancing restrictions) from working directly with community members due to the COVID-19 pandemic, we nonetheless celebrated a virtual version of our *7th Annual "Fit Fathers Day" Celebration* on Father's Day in 2020. Viewers throughout the United States, and from as far away as Japan and Jamaica, were able to join our interactive workout.

To become a vegan in this society requires retraining your brain, being willing to be an outlier, and doing the research to make sure you're not programmed to a system that is holding you down or keeping you back. There are many such systems in this country, and the food system is as debilitating as any other. That is why, on Juneteenth, Fit Fathers in collaboration with the African-American Health Program (AAHP) put together a program on the Internet that praised the liberty of good health through exercise and vegan nutrition. With cooking demonstrations and fitness programs, we celebrated the wealth and freedom of extending our lives through wellness. ✸

4

NO GRAVE BUT THE SEA

A Poem by Jae Yahkèl Estes, XVX

In Loving Memory of Willie D. Estes, Jr. (1/23/1961–5/15/2018)

Dedicated to my father; who showed me that
Black fatherhood does not have to be absent,
Black masculinity does not have to be toxic,
and Black spirituality does not have to be colonized.

they say that loose lips sink ships
yet we both managed to somehow stay afloat
traversing the middle passage of an earthly existence
born breech baptized by great tribulation
a victimless mandatory minimum life sentence
commuted time served enslaved inside warm cells
broken vessels forged of seaworthy melanin skin
and bones
and breath
and blood
soaked years building arks deferring dreams
flooded from sunken eyes tearing
tearing hypertrophied muscles wearing
as we wade in waters polluted awash torrential purple rains
sluicing golden hours amidst a multitude of mudslides
hemorrhaging crimson sins into rocky rapids

rolling tides of debilitating phantom pains until calm armageddon comes
and goes
and ebbs
and flows
through white whale waves serenading sleepy sober saints
singing softly spoken spells seducing sacrificial seventh sons
sailing sandy shores secretly seeking sacred sunsetting sites
their hidden treasures remain drowned beneath cascades in holy reverie
while the inevitable forever weathers an everlasting comforting
ancient maps whisper stay the course for better or for worse
synchronize your hallowed compass to navigate us back ✾

5

PRESERVING THE FUTURE

An Interview with Brandon Morton

Brotha Vegan: *Tell us who you are and what you do.*

Brandon Morton: I'm currently in my final year studying at Bronx Community College in partnership with the New York Botanical Garden for a degree in horticulture. I'm also going to obtain another certificate for propagation with the New York Botanical Garden. I also volunteer with a couple of different gardens—one being the garden on East 12th Street in Manhattan. I do some composting with them now whenever I have free time, using *bokashi*, which is an anaerobic, fermented, organic method from Japan. I am also learning Korean natural farming and other farming practices to stay diverse.

BV: *When did you first go vegan, and how did that begin?*

BM: It actually happened in the military. I wanted to get myself in shape and so started to look at eating a bit healthier so I could give myself the best chance to pass basic training, which was in South Carolina in 2011. I was still eating meat at the time. I realized that the food I was being served in training had a bunch of preservatives in it. I had pretty much gotten backed up and didn't make a bowel movement for about a month, which was very dangerous. That made me pay attention to my digestive system. I slowly found myself just not wanting to eat meat, because I wasn't digesting properly. In 2013, I went pescetarian, and a year or so later made the full transition. I did it gradually. I didn't want to place myself in a box. I wanted to make it easy.

Although I went vegan initially for health reasons, I never went back, because I saw how my body responded to it. And it just brought me closer to life. After wanting to eat better, I saw differently how things grow and what enabled them to grow. I began to ask why things tasted good and why everybody didn't grow things that tasted good. I started to eat organic foods and saw the difference in the colors and the care of the farm that grew it. Once I *saw* the difference, it was very hard to consciously go against that knowledge.

I've not looked back since then. In addition to studying horticulture, mycology, and farming, I'm growing my own food with the space that I have. I live in an apartment, which doesn't have much space, but I can grow edible flowers and mushrooms. It's made me realize that with just a few dollars you can grow your own food. It may not be able to feed you around the clock, but it definitely keeps some money in your pocket.

BV: *Why did you get into horticulture?*
BM: When I started to eat healthier, I began to experiment with cannabis and other medicinal plants that are frowned upon, and these plants opened my eyes to really *see* and pay attention: that you could treat plants differently and get a different outcome. I found out that all tomatoes aren't colorless and tasteless; that you could grow them with fewer inputs and get improved results. And I really wanted to feed myself and was tired of paying for food. It's expensive to buy organic produce, and there's no reason why it should be more expensive—especially when there are fewer inputs and you're getting better quality. I discovered that horticulture was a valuable skill; I loved to do it, and the more I learned about plants, the more I realized they were literally teaching me about life.

BV: *How so?*
BM: The more I've learned about plants in nature, the deeper and more exciting the rabbit hole becomes. You just keep on going. Fungus and plants run the world. Without them, there are none of us. In fact, 96 percent of all plants on Earth have a symbiotic relationship with fungus. They cannot grow without fungus, because the fungus makes the nutrients available to the plant. There are hundreds of thousands of species of plants that we know about, but whose properties we're still unaware of. Fungi, which include mushrooms and yeasts, make up one of the phylogenetic kingdoms that people forget about—especially in regard to eating and veganism. There are 1.5 million kinds of mushrooms, and counting, and we haven't even researched them all. All those proteins and vitamins, including B_{12} and other complexes, that we lack in our diet, we can get them from mushrooms and plants.

BV: *When did you realize that you first wanted to grow marijuana or CBD?*

BM: It was in 2012 or 2013. I was in California, and I had only tried street cannabis, in New York. The way the Californian cannabis looked and smelled—it literally took me one experience to realize: *Whoa! This is something different.* Since then, I've worked on a couple of cannabis farms, and I have my medical card. I've been to over a hundred dispensaries, and this led me into managing a dispensary, and then working on a grow.

I was employed at a wellness center in California. It had a shop with recreational marijuana upstairs and CBD downstairs. I ran the CBD shop. Previously, I'd been interested in the recreational side of cannabis use because it seemed fun. However, I remember one day an old lady came into the store with fingers that were cut or dislocated. They looked like someone had run over them with a car. She couldn't even hold the pen or the clipboard for the paper she had to sign.

It wasn't possible for me to mention the cannabis shop upstairs, because at the time it was illegal. But I wanted to give this lady something to experience. So I took a relatively weak lotion from the counter with CBD oil in it and rubbed it on this lady's hands. I then began to show her around the store. I asked if she wanted to hit a vape pen, but she didn't want to do that. Fifteen to twenty minutes later, as she was about to leave, she grabbed the clipboard and picked up a pen. "Oh my God," she said, "I can move my fingers!" And she started to cry.

It was unbelievable. And that was when I was like, "What the fuck just happened?!" I'd never seen that happen before. I have a friend whose neighbor had a gaping wound on her hand that wouldn't close. My friend applied CBD salve, and slowly, week after week, the open wound closed up and sealed. Later, I helped the grandmother of a friend of mine who now has a CBD company in New York. His grandmother was dying of pancreatic cancer, and I processed cannabis for her to make it into concentrates to keep her alive. We brought her cancer cell count from 960 to dormant; when she stopped the doses of cannabis concentrate, her cancer cell count rose.

After witnessing things like this, I didn't need to be convinced of the power of marijuana. I saw how real it was—and how it has so many different uses and in so many different areas.

BV: *Could you explain the difference between marijuana and CBD?*

BM: CBD and THC are chemical compounds (cannabinoids) inside cannabis resin (trichomes). Take a look at the cannabis plant: it's green, and has that recognizable leaf form. When the plant is in flower, you'll notice the plant glistening, and the leaves feel sticky. Those are called glandular trichomes, and they're microscopic, mushroom-like. If you collect the trichomes into a mass, they form a resin, and that's where all the compounds are. These are called cannabinoids.

THC—tetrahydrocannabinolic acid—is the compound that most people know is associated with the feeling of being high, or euphoria. CBD—cannabidiolic acid—is another compound. These aren't the only compounds in the plant; they're just the ones that have been studied the most and the ones we know can be synthesized in our body and make us feel a certain way. In fact, there are over eighty compounds that combine and give you what's called "the entourage effect" of feeling high.

CBD used to be known as the compound that made you feel relaxed, relieved pain, and had anti-cancer properties; THC was known only as a psychedelic. However, some studies have shown—and this will flip people on their heads—that CBD is psychoactive as well. It's just not as strong as THC. CBD will deliver a head high, but nothing even comparable to THC. CBD can be isolated just like THC, but the molecules differ in their size and their structure and in what they do for you.

The distinction *between* highs is what has allowed CBD to be legalized and THC not—because CBD means you're controllable. However, if ten to fifteen years ago we'd had the science we do today, we would be having a different fight. Because if the authorities knew that CBD gets you high as well, those of us who want legalization wouldn't have had any leeway. CBD is the compound that was able to give cannabis a platform in order to be legal, with some medical data behind it.

BV: *Are you an advocate of legalizing recreational marijuana?*

BM: I am. I've always been open about my use of psychedelic plants, and I see marijuana as medicine *and* recreational. I look at it as something that grows from the earth, no different from a potato. I find it ridiculous that it has ever been seen as anything other than something that can nourish us in some kind of way.

When I moved back from California, I looked like some crazy jungle guy—talking about plants and so on. But I wasn't gonna hide. I've never shied away from talking about it. I like to educate people and share as much information as I can. I feel good that I stuck to my guns, especially to see it become what it is now. I want to empower people to grow it; and if I learn anything new, and I have a platform, I'll share that knowledge with one person or a hundred.

BV: *What do you feel the impact would be if recreational cannabis were legalized?*

BM: I think it would open a lot of opportunity for many people. For one, it would allow people to use medicine without looking over their shoulder and feeling like they're criminals. For instance, if you were living in California in 2011, you could take cannabis with no worries. However, if you went to visit your family in another state, and you were a medical patient with a card to prove it, you couldn't use the medicine that was helping you deal with your condition. You'd just stepped into a whole other world where you could go to jail and lose your livelihood for doing something that was legal one state over, or even across the country.

Apart from rationalizing the laws, legalizing marijuana would encourage a bunch of businesses to open. Like any market, the market will become oversaturated; there'll be closings and consolidation; and then it'll find its level. You'll have big cannabis companies— like you have Coors, Budweiser, and Amstel—and then you'll have your small ones, like the producers of craft beers. There'll be boutique cannabis for connoisseurs, and then ordinary cannabis for your everyday consumer who wants to alleviate some light pain or wants to generate a small buzz.

State by state, city by city, people will start growing themselves and taking the initiative to see what the plant does on its own. Using will become more open, and I think that more people will start to talk to one another. Groups will start intermingling that usually don't: whether it's recreational users or medical practitioners. It'll bring people together.

Another benefit is that legalization won't allow the police to target African-Americans and minorities, and over-police neighborhoods and tie people up in jail for years—all for something that grows out of the ground.

BV: *What has been the impact of the criminalization of marijuana for Black men?*

BM: I was born in Coney Island in Brooklyn, New York. I live there now, and didn't leave Coney Island until I was eighteen or nineteen, when I went to the West Coast. I've seen how the police treat people from a multitude of different backgrounds, and not just in neighborhoods with one ethnicity; it's obvious that we're being targeted. When New York City's mayor said that the city would begin to decriminalize weed and wouldn't arrest people for marijuana possession or use unless they were actively selling it, I saw that that wasn't true for everybody. In Coney Island, people were harassed for smoking cannabis; whereas in Williamsburg, it's like a party.

BV: *You're right. I live in Williamsburg, and here white folks are smoking it everywhere. Like cigarettes.*

BM: So, you're being profiled. You either have to look like a member of corporate America or you have to have a different-colored skin in order not to be seen as a drug dealer or a user in a negative way. Or you can be the same person, and smoking a joint in Coney Island will have a different result from lighting up in Williamsburg. I still think African-Americans will be harassed no matter which neighborhood we're in, and that's partly because there's such a stigma connected with African-American males and smoking cannabis. I've seen people arrested for smoking a joint. A friend of mine had a cop stick his hand in his coat pocket to grab a joint—just because he smelled it. He didn't even see him smoking it. My friend lost his job and had to move to California.

We're still being targeted, and we're not safe. We're just held to another standard and not treated equally, and that is the reality. The same thing would go for African-American women, I'm sure. But you see a lot of it with the men.

BV: *Black men are seen as a threat.*

BM: If we dress in urban wear and we're smoking, we're a threat. I honestly think it will require the law to change and the old white lawmakers who are alive now to pass on so that this younger generation can take control. It's much more liberal. But that's the reality. Now, as an African-American trying to make it in the cannabis industry, I'm gonna be careful when I say this, because many people in California were open to me and gave me opportunities, and didn't even make me feel that the color of my skin was a concern. But looking back, I can see how I had to leave the cannabis industry and come all the way back to New York to educate myself and truly be *in* it.

Part of that education was learning about my own family. I hadn't realized that my family was from the South. On my dad's side, my family had been on the land since the late nineteenth, early twentieth centuries. My grandmother, who passed away about ten years ago, had a mother who was enslaved. So we had a deep history in the South, and I now understand that this has always been a part of my identity; it just skipped a generation because I'm in New York.

I think a lot of other African-Americans are beginning to comprehend that this heritage is in us: that we're farmers. We have a calling. It's funny that I ended up living in New York City, and even though nobody handed me a plan or told me to be interested, I nonetheless ended up coming right back to what my family has been doing for so long.

I think that's a reality for a lot of Black people. You have to teach yourself. Nobody's gonna help you out, because if you get an opportunity and begin to get into it, they're going to see you as competition. I had to help myself. I'm not complaining: it's empowering. But that's why I want to help people along the way.

BV: *What are your short- and long-term goals?*
BM: My first goal is to place myself on a cannabis farm and practice organic, regenerative permaculture for cannabis. That would mean something that's ecological, sustainable, healing to the environment, and self-sufficient. Permaculture is permanent culture— setting up a system that can support itself even after someone leaves, and that takes nothing from the environment. That's happening, and that's how I want to grow cannabis.

But my goals are much bigger, and that's why I'm studying mycology and soil science. I want to introduce cannabis via permaculture, because unsustainable farming practices as a whole are one of the major causes of climate change. Minerals are leaching into the waterways; fewer trees mean that less carbon is being fixed in the soil; and so forth. I want to show companies like Corona—the beer company, which has invested $4 billion in cannabis—that growing cannabis doesn't have to follow Big Ag, that there's another way. I want to introduce permaculture on a commercial level. Because we could have craft cannabis and organic farming all we want, but if the people who are feeding the masses aren't growing anything responsibly, we're not doing much. Those are the people's minds we have to change.

I want to start off with a farm that will allow me to practice this form of regenerative agriculture and scale it up. Then I'd like to incorporate that into a more diverse business, because I like to cook and to grow and to educate. I began a business in 2020 called Earth Eater LLC, which is going to be an umbrella company for farming, education, and research. I'm looking to relocate permanently to grow food, cannabis, and fungus for production—organic and regenerative—and hold classes and turn the land into a place that people can visit and be interactive and see how food is grown. I have some family land in Virginia, where I might start some side projects. That's a long-term goal. It may happen faster than I think, but that's what I've been leaning toward.

BV: *What are you working on at the moment?*
BM: As a side project, I'm working on wild-crafting organisms. I don't want to pay for the starting material for the products, so I'm finding out how to grow them myself. For instance, kombucha is a "symbiotic culture of bacteria and yeast"—or, SCOBY. Now, if you don't know how to make the SCOBY, you have to get it from a company. I'm learning how to harvest these organisms in the wild and create these cultures on my own.

I'm also growing plants, looking at soil under microscopes, and developing my skills in mycology and botany, so I can learn more and be a more efficient grower and make things better. I do my vermicomposting in a shoebox, and I also have my homegrown kombucha and the *bokashi* projects: so aerobic and anaerobic fermentation respectively.

Finally, I read an article a year ago about an experiment conducted in Japan in which researchers introduced a pulse electromagnetic frequency into a couple of different species of mushrooms. They found that a certain voltage increased the size and yield of the mushrooms. You can see how those applications might help people. In fact, I have a friend who's a biologist and has access to the same equipment the Japanese researchers used, so I'm planning to try to repeat that experiment. I contacted a company I met at a mycology festival in August, and am gonna ask if they'd donate some mushrooms for this experiment. If not, I'll cultivate the mushrooms myself and bring them to the lab.

BV: *One argument for veganism is that it could solve world hunger. There's enough food in the world, but so much of it is wasted.*

BM: Absolutely. Nothing has to go to waste. Everything natural can be broken down by microbes—although you need to put it in the right place. For instance, if you throw a banana on a tree pit you might think, *I'm feeding that tree pit*. Not really. That banana has to be broken down by microbes first to make its nutrients available in the form that a plant can take. But if you put the banana in a compost system with a bunch of different waste, now its energy is being utilized the right way. If we were just smarter about where we put our waste, we could literally turn our scraps back into food.

Here's another for instance: You could buy an oyster mushroom, take a tissue sample, replicate it, and spread it on coffee grounds on cardboard. There are hundreds if not thousands of coffee shops, and lots of cardboard around. These are sources of nitrogen for the mushrooms to get nutrients off, but it's being thrown away every day. People on the street who are starving could be eating these mushrooms. We are literally throwing food away every single day. ☀

6

LIVING IN THE WOUND AND ATTEMPTING TO HEAL

Omowale Adewale

In April 2020, I will start my eighth year as a vegan, although the transition to veganism has taken twenty. Between 1993 and 1995, I went to high school in West Palm Beach, Florida. I was no older than sixteen when, during a routine visit to the doctor, I was told that I had high blood pressure. Everyone was stunned. When I told my older brother, Wendell, who'd called me to find out how I was doing, he recommended that I no longer eat any meat.

Not eating meat wasn't an entirely new concept to me. My mother, Cleo, had abstained from meat at times during my childhood and had dragged me to health festivals for years before I turned veg. She provided a healthier way of living than my grandparents and what I saw in the world, and there were many conversations about food in my household. I even remember finding the definition of *veganism* in the dictionary as I was looking into vegetarianism, but veganism seemed too difficult at the time. Nonetheless, I've always listened to Wendell, and he's never tried to steer me wrong—especially with something that's serious. He was the catalyst, and I stopped eating animals there and then.

Now, like many people, I didn't become vegetarian the proper way, because I wasn't eating healthy meals. Back in the 1990s, going vegetarian or vegan was rare, and because Wendell and I lived in different states, I didn't have a support system. I was a teen and into sports, so I wanted to work out and bulk up. My base for at least the first few years as a vegetarian was rice slathered with butter, processed grains, bleached white flour, and sodium-laden cans of greens and beans. However, even at fifteen years old, I had the mindset of "I can get by without eating any animals."

Like many people, I approached this new lifestyle from a health perspective. As time passed, and I became more knowledgeable and began to talk to others about it, I formulated the philosophy I now utilize to help people transition to veganism. I trained in bodybuilding and track and field between 1995 and the early 2000s, and started to eat more fruits and more fresh vegetables to encourage a healthier way of eating. I asked myself critical questions: *Is this helping me? Is this working? Is it possible for me to be as healthy as anyone who's eating meat? Can I still gain muscle?*

In 1996, I moved back to New York City. Although I was using diet and trying to avoid medication, I still battled high blood pressure. Hypertension, or high blood pressure, isn't always the "silent" condition we think, and it can impact your brain and cause severe migraines. When I suffered my first migraine, I literally fell asleep hoping that sleep would suffocate that pounding in my brain. However, when I awoke, the pounding was still there. For years, my headaches worsened, and I became frightened of them. I began to take hydrochlorothiazide, which are pills that thin the blood and encourage water: I ended up urinating all the time. It was one of the pains that taught me to be conscious of other people's pain or inability to cope with pain.

Doctors also prescribed me aspirin, sometimes at 800 mg. I'd stock up on it because aspirin muted my migraines almost instantly. Doctors began offering me other kinds of pills, some of which had worse-sounding side effects than insistent urination. I didn't want to take them, but I needed to write, to attend school, to go to work, and had been organizing regularly since 1998—so I required fast remedies. Although there were mentors in my life for organizing, politics, and work, there weren't any for my health. Because my family was poor and working class, I never had a regular doctor. Medicaid makes it so that health-care providers can drop you easily, depending on where you reside. During the 2000s, I lived in Brooklyn, the Bronx, Queens, and Harlem. I picked up prescription medicine and saw doctors in each of these boroughs and even more neighborhoods. You cope how you cope. I would never hope this for anyone. You need a relationship with your health-care provider.

By 2013, I'd been a vegetarian for twenty years. I was being interviewed on the subject, when I was asked, "Why aren't you vegan?" At that stage, I'd stopped drinking dairy some years before—although I was still ingesting a lot from cakes, pizza, and other products, and I struggled to stop eating eggs. The interviewer's question really made me think. I hadn't needed to eat animals for years, but I was at that stage boxing and doing Mixed Martial Arts (MMA), and I was still worrying how I was going to perform. *Would I be strong enough?*

Shortly after that conversation, I decided to go vegan, but this time my transition was for ethical reasons: I didn't consume animals. In that first week, as I began conducting more research and getting more information on veganism, I began to experience physical withdrawals. I was spitting up, sometimes vomiting, and blowing my nose a lot more. In fact, my nose was running profusely. I thought, *What is going on?* So much mucus was pouring out of my body!

When I was a vegetarian, I was never totally sure of my health. In fact, I'd never admitted that I was lactose intolerant, like most Black people. After only two weeks as a vegan, I could finally breathe in and out of my nose, which had been exceedingly difficult before. I noticed my sinus issues and my bronchitis going away, for good. I could recognize that my ethics were impacting my health in a much better way than they had over the previous twenty years.

FROM MY FAMILY TO THE COMMUNITY

When folks talk about trying to transition to veganism, it often sounds difficult and makes me want to help and support them. When I first stopped eating meat and told my family, they weren't surprised: "Well, he's easy to please! He's okay with rice and cornbread and green beans." So, whereas other households might have thrown a fit, I was in a home where it was relatively smooth sailing.

In addition to having abstained from meat herself for a time, my mother was always resourceful and nurturing. She provided hands-on learning and really took the lead on teaching me history, culture, and community. She encouraged me to create and make my own meals and be with her in the kitchen. She also took me to places where I learned history and culture. She was a former Black Panther Party organizer when she was a teenager, and so we attended many demonstrations and protests. We marched in support of the family of Yusuf Hawkins, who was murdered by racist white teens in Howard Beach, Queens, in 1989.

We attended rallies for Black workers' rights as well as cultural celebrations, such as the International African Arts Festival and the West Indian Labor Day Parade, held respectively in Brooklyn's key Black neighborhoods of Bedford-Stuyvesant and Crown Heights. I gained enormous value from hearing her talk about what she'd done and knew, and she's been my foremost educator. Without that connection to her history and her work, which became my springboard, I'd be lost in the world.

Parents don't always acknowledge their impact and the things that we, their heirs, hold close to our heart. My parents gave me a complete sense of being and an understanding of how to use my voice for others, and exposed me to political thought and organizations. They showed me genuine love and helped me appreciate in a personal way what my responsibility was to myself *and* my community. That community has poured itself into my mind and body—strengthening me and making me stand up for myself and them.

My father, Everton, kept a lot of activities simple by taking me to some of his favorite places. More important, he contributed a kind of love that taught me that love *lives* in men. He gave my brother and me hugs and kisses on the cheek, which communicated to us that it was appropriate for men to express affection. Although my parents separated when I was seven, my father said *hello* and *goodbye* with love. Through him, I understood how to unravel and understand masculinity more. I utilize his example in terms of how I communicate. Even today, I always ask myself: *How do I communicate from a place of masculinity? How do I understand what is masculine, and how do I educate other young men who misunderstand masculinity, or think that everything has to be masculine?*

The nature of Black masculinity is an evolving conversation in the Black community, which sometimes points the finger at men—occasionally with justification, but also excessively. The question is, How do we decide what is justified and what is excessive? It's complicated for a lot of Black men to open up and recognize that femininity also lives within us. For instance, I didn't learn about misogynoir—a combination of misogyny and racism that Black women experience—until I was much older. I learned about it and other terms mainly at social justice gatherings and in neighborhood discussions. They have become quintessential to being Black in America.

G.A.ME

By the time I had my first-born in 2001, I was failing at Hunter College but picking up with my outside studies in community organizing from the Uhuru Movement. I learned more about politics and government after leaving school. I was fortunate to join the staff of New York State Assemblywoman Aurelia Greene. Carolyn Jones, my mentor and the district office manager in Assemblywoman Greene's office, was a strong critic who wanted me to excel; she even allowed me to attend college while I was working full-time.

For twenty years, Assemblywoman Greene made it her business to address constituent issues with respect and patience. The difficulty was communicating to her that our community's goals needed to be unapologetically Black and Brown. She almost never heard me. I realized after my mentor left the office for a better-paying job that not everyone recognizes talent underneath their noses. Nonetheless, I was grateful to Carolyn Jones for picking my resume and bringing me in. I soaked up a lot of hard lessons and, even though the end was abrupt for me, it was the best job I'd ever had. From 2002 to 2008, I worked in that office as well as became the executive director of my not-for-profit organization, Grassroots Artists MovEment (G.A.ME).

G.A.ME is special to me. I've worked at numerous places over twenty years, but I've always been focused on my personal goals and what I thought the community was missing. Running a not-for-profit while you work somewhere else places an incredible onus on you. G.A.ME allowed my team and I never to have to wait to address local and national concerns, but to do so via political action, referral letters, talks with the health community, or the mobilization of artists.

G.A.ME organized concerts with Common and dead prez, and supported Rep. John Conyers' universal health care legislative initiative in 2004 and 2006 with testimony at congressional hearings on behalf of the artist community. With cofounder Francis Peña, G.A.ME helped bring doctors together to heal low-income workers and treat artists and other communities in New York City; transport medicine to Lagos, Nigeria; or simply to tell our story. We connected many cities and artists with one another with the objective of unionizing artists. With no one able to tell us what or how to do it, we ran centers to organize retreats for students and employed young people in our efforts to expand access to local healthy food in our community. By the time I was twenty-eight, I was running an international organization and traveling, teaching what I'd absorbed. I was always learning, even when I thought I knew it all.

G.A.ME has forced me to learn the back end of the office and the front end of organizing. When I talk about not-for-profits' weaknesses, it's from a place of solid experience and not because I didn't have other options. If you're organizing outside of a non-profit system, you need to think about who and what is handling the money. I can now teach classes on media and communications, funding, and mobilizing people. But I'm happy to have grown from that mode of thinking, because I'm not interested in educating people on how to develop not-for-profits. You cannot liberate minds or bodies by starting more non-profit organizations.

CREATING BLACK VEGFEST

Black VegFest had a number of origins. One was Ital, or Rastafarian food. Rastafarian culture is 100 percent Black culture, which emerged from a combination of Jamaican-born Marcus Garvey's message of freedom for all Africans throughout the Diaspora, and Ras Tafari's religious teachings during the 1930s. Rastafarians or Rastas interpreted Tafari's message as an extension of Garvey's, which simply translates to treating your fellow living beings as you would want to be treated.

Rastafarians weren't necessarily mobilizing people to follow the Rasta culture in the United States, although they share a pride with many Black people around the world because of Garvey's teachings of Black liberation. Rastas never labeled themselves vegans. They explained their lifestyle to people to clarify their practice, but they weren't about converting anyone.

Rastafarians would serve vegan stew and faux meats at the International African Arts Festival, which has been a Brooklyn cultural staple for fifty years. When you asked, Rastas would reveal the food was based on compassion, but they didn't insist on anyone eating the same. Instead, they gave information and never went in-depth about animal liberation. As

I think back to my exposure to Rastafarians at the African Arts Festival, I admire the fine line they navigated with an oppressed people. It taught me that you have to know how to communicate with the culture, and for that culture to see you in action.

I was also aware of a number of vegetarian or vegan festivals that were focused on healthy foods, or a combination of ethics and healthy foods. In the last few years, the vegan festival scene has grown enormously, especially because most vegfests now make it clear that vendors have to be 100 percent vegan. As well as scores of local food businesses to choose from, festival vendors can provide vegans with an oasis of non-animal foods, which is heaven for those of us who are often trapped in a food desert with nothing but fried, baked, or steamed carcasses to choose from. It's the main reason why many of us flock to vegan festivals. Amazing speakers educate us on a variety of different topics, from breaking down the science of the vegan diet to explaining how to eat cheaply as a vegan. Experts tie everything together and guide transitioning vegans to a new lifestyle. Performers play instruments, sing, dance, rap, and a lot more. There's a great variety of different vegan festivals spanning the calendar year.

Vegan festivals made sense to me, and I did benefit from each one I attended: I was able to compare the differences in focuses on animal advocacy versus product excellence. However, the central issue as I saw it was that everybody I contacted or who contacted me about their vegfest was white. Not all of the festivals and events were white-run, but white-run festivals dominated the food-consumption scene, as they do most industries in the U.S. In my experience, white vegans are generally focused on encouraging people to go vegan for the animals; however, they often dismiss oppression elsewhere. By being so white or devoid of Blackness, such festivals claim that animals need to be centered—thus, not only not tackling Black issues but essentially ignoring them. These white festivals bend over backward to make white attendees, speakers, and vendors comfortable at everyone else's expense. The performers and speakers are often white. I've found that white people give off a sense that they can make all cultural cuisine, without ever securing the livelihoods, wisdom, and practices of folks who have lived the culture.

Black businesses barely vended at these places until more Black-run vegan festivals jumped on the scene. I remember speaking at a vegfest in New York City—which is majority

BIPOC (Black, Indigenous, and People of Color)—and myself and another individual were the only Black people among the forty-plus speakers. That's a clear example of implicit bias. Furthermore, the conversations and the programs white organizers generally expect from Black speakers don't necessarily fit the needs of the Black community. However, as a speaker, you try to educate anyone interested in going vegan.

What were missing from all these vegfests were unapologetically Black conversations. The BIPOC community was not present in numbers, and this helped stoke the mistaken belief that Black people didn't want to go vegan. I felt the goal of going unapologetically Black would strike to the heart for many looking to make changes in their kitchen.

For me, a Black vegfest held a deeper aim than showcasing veganism to and within the Black community. Let me explain.

If you were to ask some Black men, *What would you prefer to be doing with your time?* the answers would be varied. Some would say, "I'm trying to grow twenty different species of plants for food and beauty, and I'm learning about new ways to strengthen human relations with animals such as bees, whom we understand to be in a symbiotic relationship with everything else on Earth." Others would say, "I'm discussing intra-community connections between children and elders," or, "I'm offering commentary and opinions on how to strengthen intimate relationships," or "I'm learning about science that relates to cooling and heating the planet." And still others would say, "I'm doing liberation work that I feel the white community needs to catch up on and fully embrace. I'm looking for them to go beyond firing or calling out racists to dismantle a racist system."

In short, what the Black populace has been attempting to cultivate—within the confines of the fraction of the space and resources that we actually need—is exactly what white communities cultivate for themselves and then promote throughout the media: loving families; wealth production via numerous industries; deeply rooted interfamilial and intergenerational prosperity; and, of course, healthy, educated, and cultured young people. It's a fact that white people have achieved this at the expense of all other organisms on the planet, which is why discussing social inequities and a lack of justice is not a luxury so much as a necessity. In the absence of true freedom, Black people cannot purchase property, grow food, and build wealth without a white person at the end of our happiness.

If justice or community development are dependent upon the goodness of white men and women, the thread of our enslavement continues, only in another name.

It is in this context that I saw that a Black vegfest was also not a luxury but a necessity. It could be a space where Black people discuss and educate each other on how we choose to eat and live within Black spaces; a space to explore family, food, and traditions outside of our conflict with oppressors; and a space to connect to the ancestral traditions that we shared and that were fractured by the Middle Passage and slavery.

A Black vegfest could help Black men and women fully accept our Black selves through our own lens and not through the lens of white supremacy, through which Black people have been fed and have digested all the lies about ourselves. A Black vegfest could showcase our love for and to ourselves, and make apparent to everyone else the contradiction and complicated difficulty of living *in the wound while attempting to heal*. A Black vegfest would be a surgical incision beneath sensitive tissue to repair critical damage, and enable us to find some peace, express some love, share good news, and move forward to our destiny. It would be a miraculous, beautiful, and powerful refuge within the unnatural system of white supremacy.

After speaking to a friend in a Black-owned vegan restaurant in 2013, I immediately saved the website blackvegfest.org and .com. However, it wasn't until five years later that I was able with my G.A.ME team to launch Black VegFest.

From a practical sense, the inaugural Black VegFest in 2018 aimed to accomplish a short list of goals: that if you bring a brand that is unapologetically Black, make it open to all Black people, and extend the same love to each one, the people will come. That August weekend, two thousand people attended our debut—destroying forever the myth that Black people aren't interested in veganism. Black businesses made a lot of money that day; for some, it was their largest take ever. Black people are always looking to support each other, because we know what it means when one of us does it for everyone Black.

My job during Black VegFest is to remedy issues non-stop, conduct interviews, and greet people. I normally speak for ten to fifteen minutes every Black VegFest to preface what folks might be missing about the entire festival. It's impossible for even a family to witness everything at Black VegFest. In exchange for our ethics of liberation for all beings, Black people cheered us and helped us return for the second Black VegFest in 2019. Here, we deepened the vegan discussion around intersectionality and developed a larger team of organizers. We held around thirty workshops and discussions that responded to criticism of whatever we missed in 2018.

We organizers want our community to be proud of us. I am prouder of my community for not making me a liar. Folks in Brooklyn resonate the most because we have centered Black people even when we've been taught to *not* center Black people anywhere. This was true with the first two Black VegFests.

In actuality, the biggest obstacle to the production and success of the Black VegFest came from New York City's inconsistent regulations. The New York Police Department did not want us to work with the New York City Housing Authority's (NYCHA) Kingsborough Houses, situated next to the historic Black settlement of Weeksville, in Brooklyn, where the 2019 Black VegFest took place. The city fumbled its rules and procedures. A few local businesses looked to capitalize off our excitement without paying for participation, but I was able to communicate with them without involving security to make sure that any misunderstanding was handled appropriately.

Because white people have a penchant for racism, being an unapologetically Black vegan festival also places a target on your back, which is why there aren't any explicitly culturally named vegan festivals. Some posted less-than-flattering comments on how Black VegFest was educating our community on veganism, and a segment of the white vegan community saw us as a threat to their current vegan campaigns. They contrived the notion that we were stealing limelight from animals, even though the last time I checked in with an animal they had no qualms about more people going vegan.

But being unapologetically Black means not apologizing for perceived infractions of protocols that do not serve Black people. It doesn't matter to me whether folks like how I express myself or what I have to say. I'm not interested in selling a fun story, or showing them a good time, or smoothing over my message so that white people will buy the book *and* the message and support me to be successful—if to do so requires my not raising certain issues or forgoing my principles. Black people in the United States have fought for freedom and raised our voices in the face of four hundred years of violence against us. The laws that have been passed to protect us—whether the Emancipation Act in 1863, the 1868 ratification of the fourteenth amendment, or the 1964 Civil Rights Act—were ignored, overturned, and routinely violated.

So, we Black people understand the importance of holding on to our rights. As far as I'm concerned, the complaints that we weren't engaging enough with animals was the white community barring us from communicating about veganism without their white talking points. I've started to believe that given the way some vegans flaunt their protection of animals, they don't actually care about them.

It needs to be stated directly that Black people are attempting to rescue our minds from historic brainwashing within the very institutions that we often credit for providing us with the degrees and the certifications we wave. Systemic racism is real and embedded in the school-to-prison pipeline, housing, employment, and institutional policies of all kinds. All white people have grown up with stereotypes about Black people, and they may be able to unlearn these. However, when access to positions of power, capital, agency, justice, and even the right to stay alive are continually denied to Black people, the solution is not for white people to stop being "accidentally" racist but for them to work with us to dismantle the system that allows that racism to exist.

It is out of that mindset that Black people have a deep understanding of how animals are taken advantage of, because we are able to understand intersectionality and approach veganism from a more ethical perspective. This was why I was pleased to speak at the City Council meeting when New York City passed its ban on foie gras in 2019. I was only a few-years educated about the abuse of geese and ducks, and during that year I learned even more. I had never realized that goose and duck livers were a "delicacy" and that foie gras was a product developed for the rich. No one will go hungry if we end this disgusting mutilation of animals.

Misanthropic white vegans may say they hate humans and love animals, but that's not a literal reality, as they at least love their fellow vegan comrades on the same battlefield of compassion, as well as members of their family. Vegan intersectionality has allowed me to focus on many different issues and lend compassion to all of them. I don't have to ignore the grief of factory-farmed animals, puppy mills, the horrible clubbing of seals, or the cruelty of foie gras in order to strive for Black self-determination. Even if you despair of and feel contempt for human behavior, you shouldn't want to allow oppression to spread to everyone who wants liberation. Support Black people regardless of whether you believe in their creed, theology, or what makes them seem different.

The notion that animals were absent from Black VegFest was, simply, a lie. At both Black VegFests, attendees brought their various animals—even though this wasn't necessarily legal (something I'm aware of). In fact, nothing is more vegan than being cited for having a chicken on the road! The irony is that New York City has hundreds of festivals and block parties per year where it's fine for a chicken to be present, except that chicken is dead and being eaten. Years from now, the fact that we allowed a *live* chicken on the road will not be considered crazy. Other attendees brought small domestic animals, and they greeted children with kindness. That's another lesson for the youth in our community. In the spirit of Harriet Tubman, we must never leave anyone behind.

THE BLACK VEGFEST EFFECT

When I walk around New York City and see people wearing Black VegFest shirts or they see me wearing one, a conversation ensues. Many people say, "I was there!" Some people love to post and share their photos and videos; others love the facts that Black people are teaching them, providing them with their favorite meal, or having a block party on the street.

Black VegFest has created opportunities beyond measure. One area has been regarding income streams, because Black businesses have found more value in themselves and vegan businesses have had to revamp their marketing plans to Black people. Black people can now sell to ourselves without a "buy Black" hustle.

We see our work in Black VegFest as an extension of what G.A.ME has been doing since 2003, with our Hip-Hop for HealthCare campaign. However, I sometimes wonder what work G.A.ME could have achieved had I become vegan earlier. That said, listening to the right mix of mentors throughout my life, rolling with the punches, and following a philosophy of "don't wait" on any help has brought me through the long way. I have to recognize that I needed to take a rugged approach, as it were, to learn to find a larger solution to our collective problems as Black people and a society. I knew that what I was doing was never just about me, but about trying to assist various subgroups in our community—such as Black disabled folks, who are without accessibility in our city; or the Black Trans community, who are deadnamed, purposely misgendered, and even murdered in our neighborhoods. G.A.ME and Black VegFest have done their best to make these communities feel safe and comfortable, although I'm certain we have a long way to go.

In 2020, G.A.ME and Black VegFest were challenged, like everyone, by the COVID pandemic. Nonetheless, we've kept organizing. Our first project after Black VegFest was our Senior Food Demos, so we could track down those most likely to have difficulty reaching a free or low-cost festival. Initially organized by Nadia Muyeeb, we prepared fruit pancakes, juices, and smoothies and worked with the seniors who lived in NYCHA's Brevoort Houses, which are closest to our G.A.ME office in Bedford-Stuyvesant. Mina Washington, a senior in her mid-seventies, became a good friend of mine. She doesn't eat meat, takes no pills, and walks without a walker.

Black VegFest faced the tough call of whether we would have our 2020 vegan festival, given concerns over Black injustice following the police murders of Ahmaud Arbery, George Floyd, and Breonna Taylor, and the real fear of COVID. Utilizing proper security guidelines through the Malcolm X Grassroots Movement (MXGM), Sala Cyril of the Little Maroons Childcare Cooperative donated PPE (personal protective equipment), and we organized via the leadership of LoriKim Alexander, Jillian Mariscal, and other women a Black VegFest focused on community awareness and de-escalation tactics.

CONCLUSION

Whatever I learn, I try to format it in a way that's usable to others. Veganism is the guiding floodlight. Veganism is about compassion, and, at the end of the day, Black people are fighting for the same thing everyone else is: compassion. When we organize on the street to protest police murder, then we're understanding compassion in a particular way.

Vegan intersectionality has enabled me to open up to other issues. By becoming aware of Black LGBTQIA+ folks through education and development and giving time to this community to speak out at protests, I've reached Black men to discuss masculinity. I can address the realities of being poor and working class and Black in the United States, and not truncate my vision of liberation for others. I don't need a straight pride parade or heterosexual movement to empower me, because my manhood is not being attacked and neither is my right to be a cisgendered, heterosexual Black man. The truth is that the police don't zero in on Black men for being straight or for being men. Black men are attacked because they present a threat as a Black person. Are we more of a threat to the white establishment than Black women? To the patriarchy, the answer is: *Yes, we are.*

Black men have a special opportunity to expand the leadership of Black liberation, but we sometimes poison the community with transphobia, homophobia, and misogynoir. Being transphobic, homophobic, and hating black women does not advance our liberation or our right to self-determination. Understanding this, I use my strength to advocate for those who are maligned and are even more marginalized in my community than I am. I've had police pull guns on me, and I have financial difficulties that stem from a lack of intergenerational wealth. Intersectionality creates a pathway toward accountability and a broader understanding of oppression. You can be oppressed and still aid others who are oppressed so there's some relief for the next day or the following year.

Ultimately, Black VegFest has allowed me to create a space for a wider audience of Black people, within a community hungry for solutions to how we can be our best selves, how we find our health, and how we save our planet from the harmful gas emissions that lead to climate change. This community—*my* community—seeks to understand the interconnectedness of bees, fruits, and the animals that eat the fruit, a relationship beyond domesticated animals or a general appreciation for nature. Animals exist in our world for myriad reasons that have nothing to do with our exploitation of them for nutrition, clothing, entertainment, and education. The last several years of internalizing veganism through this lens of intersectionality has been an arduous task that I am still processing in my home and inside my organization. ✺

7

THE ITCH BENEATH THE SKIN

An Interview with Kezekial McWhinney–StLouis

Brotha Vegan: *Who is Kez?*

Kezekial McWhinney-StLouis: I'm of Afro-Caribbean descent: my mother is Jamaican, my father is Trinidadian; both my parents are Black. I'm twenty-six years old, and, especially as a Millennial, I feel there's more potential to express who I am because I'm always evolving and changing. What I would have said about myself last year is completely different from how I would describe myself now. But I am a Black, queer, and trans vegan, currently living in Philadelphia with my little community of queer and trans vegans of color.

BV: *What is the appropriate conduct regarding addressing your gender?*

Kez: The pronouns I prefer to use are they/them. However, if I kind of know someone, I'll say, "If you must use binary pronouns, use the ones that you use for yourself, for me." However, if you see me drop something on the street, you don't need to know my gender definition to hand it back to me. But if you feel you must use pronouns, then just ask. What would feel uncomfortable, however, is if you met me with one of my cisgender friends, and you only asked me what my pronouns were, and not my friend's. Most of the time, it isn't necessary in ordinary conversation; and if it doesn't come up in conversation, it's not the end of the world.

BV: *What was your journey toward realizing your gender?*

Kez: Well, as I said, my journey is always evolving, but I remember from a very early age that I had a sense of gender as a kind of game of house that people were playing, in which you'd "disappear" into a role: "I'll be a mom," or "I'll be a wife." The older I got, and especially around puberty, I began to realize that people were way more serious about gender than I thought. And I had a series of major breakdowns. I could never put my finger on the reasons why I had these breakdowns. It was like an itch I couldn't scratch: an itch beneath the skin.

At that stage in my life, I didn't have an outlet to know anything else. I would see some trans people on television, such as *The Jerry Springer Show* or *Maury*, and think to myself, *Oh, this person is actually a man*, but of course it was in a negative light. I then came across Thomas Beatie, who was the trans man who became pregnant, and who claimed to be the world's first pregnant man (which wasn't true). Again, I didn't grasp the notion of being transgender yet, but Thomas Beatie made a distinct impression on me.

Because of my breakdowns, I went to an alternative high school, and a gender non-conforming friend of mine told me about the term *genderqueer*. I remember looking it up on one or two websites that discussed the subject, and something in their explanation made a lot of sense to me. And that's where I settled, and I've been evolving from there since.

BV: *When did you internalize relating more toward men?*

Kez: It wasn't so much about relating toward someone else; it was more how I wanted my body to be. I wanted my body to be a particular kind of way that it just naturally was not. I am addressed as a man, and I can understand that. I'm more of a feminine person, and I still felt more comfortable being seen as a more feminine man, because that's how I was. I understand the narrative of gender dysphoria—where we have to grapple with internal pain because our brains register us as different from our bodies and we have to transition. But the hardest struggle for me truly is acceptance from the outside. It's the fact that sometimes I can't properly express myself in ways that other people would understand.

For instance, it's like the discussion about whether you're Black or not. Sometimes, it's hard to explain to someone who isn't Black every little detail of my life that's conglomerated into making me who I am as a Black person. Because the beginning and end of any identity I may have isn't only pain and oppression, and I may not want to describe myself in those terms: i.e., "I know I'm Black because I was discriminated against in this way." Instead, I may want to say, "I'm Black because of my culture, because I am beautiful and handsome," and so on. The same is the case with being trans. I don't want to express myself in a way that leads others to think: *I'm sorry for this trans person.* I want to say, "I'm a wonderful human being." Or, "I'm out here doing whatever I want to do!"

BV: *How would you describe the difference between binary and non-binary?*

Kez: Binary identity can encompass either a binary cis or a binary trans person. Both are people who are fully and solely men or women. In other words, they feel they are a man or woman 100 percent of the time, and feel that gender fully. I know that some don't get when people say they "feel a gender." But it's the same as if you've never had a stomachache; you'll never know what a stomachache feels like. A non-binary person, however, which is how I would mainly identify myself, is someone who isn't fully and solely either a man or a woman. A non-binary person can be someone who feels *both* a man and a woman, or *neither* a man nor a woman, or is someone who can even move between gender identities, or be all of these things.

So, there's a lot to learn! The Internet doesn't always contain the full or correct information. My advice would be for people to attend events or talk to people who are more knowledgeable in these areas. They'd be happy to explain them.

BV: *Were your parents supportive?*

Kez: When I first came out, my father struggled with it at first. Both of my parents are fundamentalist Christians, and they were ignorant on LGBTQ+ issues. My father reacted by quoting Bible verses; voices were raised and there was an argument. But in retrospect, he handled it—and is still handling it—much better than I ever thought he would. I know he loves me, no matter what.

My mother was cautious at first. I framed my coming out more as a fact that I was struggling with my identity and that I wanted to know why I was struggling so much, and that this was why I was having a lot of breakdowns. She said, "You know what? I've seen you struggle a lot, and, if this is the reason, then, baby, I'm here for you, whatever you need. But I still don't necessarily understand everything that's going on." My mother had to do a lot of trying to figure things out in her mind.

My brother did a 180—to the moon! He used to be homophobic, transphobic: the whole nine yards. And he'd often debate people about how it was wrong to be gay and so on. When I came out, it was massively confusing to him. But almost a day later, he looked back at our life, and started to realize: *Wow! Truly, I never really had a sister.* And when everything fell into place in this way, he became my biggest supporter.

BV: *That's beautiful.*

Kez: Yeah, my brother is my best friend. I think what my coming out did was to open a door for him to know what it meant to him to be a man. He had to question what masculinity that wasn't toxic looked like—or even whether it even existed. He began to question himself and started to ask himself, *How do I create manhood into an image of what I want a man to be?* So, my coming out became a journey for both of us—because when one person transitions, the people around that person also transition, in a way.

So, my support system is my family. Both my mother and father are getting used to my transition. I understand that my father frames it as though he has lost a daughter. The thing is, *daughter* is a label; I have not died. But that's where gender is so powerful in people's lives, because when I was growing up I thought that if I wasn't being a woman, I had lost my humanity; that being a woman was a part of being human. So, when I transitioned, I went through a crisis: *How do I become a person again that isn't in this image of what I suppose me to be?* The conversation I'm having with my parents is very open, and it is to remind them that I'm the same child that I've always been, but I'm just more happy than I was before. And that's what really matters.

My new friends here in Philly, and my old friends, were all extremely receptive and supportive when I came out. It clicked for them as well. Even my coworkers, or those in my life right now who don't know or understand that I'm trans, are also supportive, because I'm visibly gender non-conforming. I'm not really a masculine person, nor do I try to be. However, by recognizing me as a person—a good person—without fitting into a definition of what a traditional man should be (even without knowing that I'm trans), they're being supportive in a different way.

BV: *How is it dating and meeting new people?*

Kez: Meeting new people will always be strange, because most people assume that everyone around them is cisgender. They don't assume they're going to meet a trans person. So, when people first meet me they assume I'm just a more androgynous, cis man—perhaps bisexual. This makes me inherently uncomfortable because when people assume you're cis, they'll expect you to say or do certain things. Now, there are plenty of trans people who are gender-conforming and no questioning of other gender roles occurs. However, I didn't transition to go into another comfortable box and stay there. This makes me careful when I meet new people, and I tend not to get super close, unless I see them on a daily basis. But this could be applied to anybody. Most of us have something in us that we don't necessarily want to share: that you have to take care of your family because your parents can't, or your husband died, or your wife left you.

I don't have problems dating when it comes to being trans; I have problems when it comes to just being myself! I'm a very particular kind of person, with a particular personality, and this has nothing to do with me being trans. If somebody doesn't want to be with me because I'm trans, I don't think trans people should be with someone like that anyway: they should stay away. So, I don't waste my time. I mostly date within the LGBTQ+ community, because that's where I feel most comfortable.

But I struggle more as a vegan than I do with being trans. That's why I mostly go on first dates, and not on second ones.

BV: *How do you struggle as a vegan?*

Kez: Socially, whether dating or being with friends. Veganism to me is much like how feminism is to a lot of people. It's an ideology that says, *I do not tolerate this kind of bigotry against this particular marginalized group.* For instance, if somebody is bigoted toward gay people, I can be around that person and there may be other things we can talk about, but eventually I don't want to keep having that same conversation and not confronting them with why they believe it is OK to say what they say or act the way they do. The same is the case with those who are anti-Black. I'm visibly Black: I don't want to waste my time with people who are anti-Black.

So, with veganism, if I'm around people who are criticizing veganism or are actively harming vegans, unless they're receptive to learning then I'm going to call them out. I'm going to encourage them to be better or to change their behavior—at least around me. That's why I have quite a few friends who were either vegan when I knew them or have turned vegan. The same is the case with my brother: he turned vegan a few years ago, and we still have a lot of tough conversations. But when something comes up, at least I can bring up issues and ask questions and there isn't a whole derail. We keep it moving.

Finding people who are open to all of it can be very hard, especially when they're strangers. So, most of the time, the people that I tend to date are already my friends. Because then they know how I am.

BV: *Yes, you want people in your life to align with what you believe. They don't have to believe everything, but you want mutual respect and to find middle ground. So, this next question is very difficult: How have the murders of Black trans people affected you, and how can we protect and support them?*

Kez: So, this is my struggle. I'm what people would consider a trans-masculine person. I was assigned female at birth and am transitioning to the man side of the spectrum. Many of the murders are happening to Black trans women. There's a degree of separation, when I am not the main target. Yes, Black trans men and non-binary people are attacked, assaulted, and murdered. And, specifically, suicides among Black trans men are pretty high relative to the rest of the community. But for Black trans women, death is mostly in the form of murder; for Black trans men, the trauma is suicide and assault—although Black trans women are also assaulted. My aim is to figure out how I can best support Black trans people who are targeted.

The murders have deeply affected my family, because they are very concerned about me, all the time. Obviously, bathrooms are a big topic, so they talk about them. I'm transitioning into a Black man, which is a scary thought to people, especially to my family, because of how I will be perceived by police or others. And, especially, I'm a more effeminate man, so I'm sometimes mistaken for being a Black trans woman. That's how ignorant some people are. This is why it's so important to try to dispel a lot of the myths and misconceptions, when someone looks at you and reads you completely wrong.

The majority of the murders of Black trans women come from Black cis men. So, the struggle has to be to deal with homophobia and transphobia within the Black community, which is something I'm still healing from. I'm still trying to understand that bigotry internally: that I can either be Black or be queer and trans, but I can't be both.

This is not just an internal fight. It's important that, as a person who is "read" as a Black man, I feel that my own community engages in a genuine conversation about these issues. I understand that some people will never understand, and I'm not going to expend excessive amounts of time trying to make them, especially when they don't want to. But I'm going to call out people who think it's funny to make inappropriate comments. Everyone wants to be a comedian, and some people get real offended when they're told they're not funny. But they wouldn't be laughing if a white person made a racist comment. Now, being willing to call someone out takes some getting used to, but it needs to be done, whenever possible. More important are those people who are curious or want to understand, and don't know what to do.

We have to accept that there are all sorts of people in our community, and I've got to balance my specific experiences with theirs. I'm not a Black trans woman so I do not have that experience, but I have been hit on by Black men who think I am. And it is night and day from when they try to hit on me to when they exit the door and act differently in the wider world.

This leads me on to another question that I'm often asked: *What would you say to cisgender Black men who say that you're not equipped to represent Black men?* My response is to ignore it, because you could have the entire Internet at your disposal or a whole set of dictionaries and encyclopedias, and some of those who ask this question are never going to understand your answer because of their rigidity. As I transition, I'm read as a Butch, a cisgender Black man, or "just a woman." These people are not living the reality of my experience.

BV: *How do Black men protect Black women?*

Kez: If you see something, say something. If you make it part of your routine to call people on their statements or actions, it becomes easier. If someone calls a woman a bitch, you say,

"That's not cool." And if you call it out, someone else will do the same next time, and then it becomes part of the group dynamic.

In our communities we have slogans, such as "Protecting Black women, liberating each other," and so on. But I'm not entirely sure what these are supposed to look like—beyond buzzwords you can put on posters. So, I concentrate on the internal work and sharing what I have to share. When it comes to protection, I see people as family—the way I protect my brother, and he protects me, and I protect my mother. I'm always asking myself, *How I can take care of my own community?*

My advice is to try to mend the relationships you have and make them better, and do right by them. To return to that slogan: Black women are not an abstract concept; they're in your home and your neighborhood. Not every Black woman is a doll angel who never does anything wrong. We can hold one another accountable, and say that something she did isn't right, and still view her as a person and listen to her. You may not agree with what she says or how she says it; others may not do so either. But you can be more intentional about listening—to Black women and others—and go from there.

BV: *Do you feel welcome in the Black vegan cis community?*

Kez: I'm not gonna lie: I have reservations. There are some who don't get it, or are uncomfortable, or stare, or avoid me. Some of this I understand, even if I don't like it. But my main reservation why I don't feel welcome is because Black spaces can be especially patriarchal and gender normative. You know, "Black men do this," and "Black women do that." Then there's a strange battle between the genders, and some people make this persona their entire identity: what a Black man or a Black woman should be like. What makes this so frustrating is that 90 to 95 percent of the time, their gender self-identity doesn't matter—unless it's at the doctor's office or you need to breastfeed your children.

In the vegan Black community, where many spaces are very focused on health, I can find it difficult, because I didn't go vegan because I needed to eat more kale, or to get stronger! Most of the time when I go to events, or I'm among certain groups, the subjects are very focused on those things.

BV: *So why* did *you go vegan?*

Kez: When I was four years old, I saw a Shake 'n Bake commercial, where a headless chicken was running into the oven to be baked and then being put on the plate for the family to eat. I have no recollection of this, but my mother told me later that I said, "I don't want to eat birdies!" She said that, up to that moment, I hadn't known what I was eating, but then I realized that "chicken" meant actual chickens.

When I was young we'd travel to Jamaica, Trinidad, or Grenada to visit relatives. My grandmother in Jamaica had backyard farm animals, and I witnessed killing there. It was traumatizing for me, as I think it is for any child at that age, but we tend to get desensitized as we get older. I was a difficult child when it came to eating chicken in particular.

Around the time I was ten or eleven years old, I recall someone was running down the halls in school, saying, "You need to watch this video." It was a video from PETA [People for the Ethical Treatment of Animals] that showed the grounding up of male chicks. I was outraged, and I remember thinking, *I didn't know that was what McDonald's was doing.* There was a McDonald's a block down from my street, and I remember doing a lot of yelling at them. Even though I didn't know the word *boycott*, that's what I decided to do.

I did this off and on for many years, because I hadn't heard of vegans. I knew about vegetarianism because my uncle on my mom's side was Rastafarian. When he would come to visit us in the U.S., he would talk about the Ital lifestyle, and not eating certain animal products.

I absorbed all this information until I watched a Bite Size Vegan video on environmentalism. (This was before the release of *Cowspiracy*, I believe.) I thought to myself, *Wow, the world is ending. I need to take this vegan thing more seriously.* I typed in the words *Black vegan trans* into a Google search, and up came the name Pax Ahimsa Gethen, who is another Black, vegan, trans, non-binary person, who was an atheist and writing on veganism. I saw myself. This was going to be me in the future. I didn't know any of it was possible, and in every single combination!

So I've been on my vegan journey, on and off, for a very long time. When I found representation, that's when I felt I finally knew what I was doing, and when it made sense.

I wasn't just some loopy, hippy-dippy kid who was being ridiculous . . . no! Another person like me was taking it seriously. That was very important for me.

BV: *How do you balance the liberation of your personal oppression with animal oppression?*
Kez: I use my own marginalizations as guides for how I want to liberate other people, and I include nonhuman animals in the definition of a person. Even when I was very young, I knew that suffering is suffering—even if that person didn't look like me. My nicknames growing up were "monkey" and "Sasquatch" (white people called me these names), so I knew how it felt to be an animal, and how you could be animalized, and how people would treat you differently because of how you appeared; that they didn't think you had the same capabilities as they did. If I have known those marginalizations, why would I continue to marginalize others?

My marginalizations also make it easier for me personally to understand other marginalizations that I don't share with others. I was a supervisor at a transgender homeless youth shelter that was really close to my heart. It was an experience that made me feel like I was making a difference. I also joined organizations that elevated Black people; I joined my parents at protests, especially when Trayvon Martin was murdered in 2012. That was a huge part of my life.

As a multiply marginalized person, therefore, I try to show up for other marginalized persons. That includes the animals, because that sphere is very white—or the ones that are most visible are white. And, like Pax Ahimsa Gethen, I want other people (whether they are like me or not) to see that when we care about other people—including nonhuman persons—our movement is stronger. Right now, I live with Corrie, who is a liberated chicken from one of the nearby egg farms here. Corrie has been a wonderful light in my life and has taught me a lot. So, I think we have so much to learn from each other; and that's what's really important. How am I going to do for the rest of my life? I don't know. I'm only twenty-six. Hopefully, I have much of my life ahead of me. ✺

8

"GRAB THEM" AND "CULTURAL CO-OPTING"

Poems by Donald Vincent

Grab Them

—A found poem

I moved on her and I failed.
I'll admit it.
I did try and eat her.
She was okay.
She's totally changed her look.
I've got to use some Tic Tacs,
just in case I start kissing her.
You know I'm automatically attracted to beautiful—I just start kissing
them
It's like a magnet. I just kiss.
I don't even wait.
And when you're a human,
they let you do it. You can do anything. Yeah those legs, all I can see is the
legs. Grab them by the beaks.
You can do anything.

Cultural Co-Opting

define blackness: (adj) an expectation,
fabricated histories of hoodoo,
ethnic features (ass shots)
savage barbarians of black magic,
cannibalistic tendencies, backwardness,
waywardness fetishes, social stigmas,
slave traders, day laborers, niggers.

I did not create the meaning, it was
already created. consciousness
committed to experience knows nothing
of determining a being. the creator
enforces inferiority, but he needs
my sauce, my flavor, my swag.
I am a poet of this world

& in tune with its vibrations &
cosmic understandings. the creator
has discovered poetry that has nothing
poetic about it. he is locked in his
whiteness. I am black—living & losing
myself looking for acceptance,

sympathetic to the skipped heartbeats
of my generation while the blackface
man, however educated he may be
can never understand Miles Davis
or Jay-Z (pre-rap-retirement). I am
black, not because of my skin,
but because I embody struggle
defyning expectation every day. ✸

9

CULINARY CLIMATE ACTION

*A Conversation Between A. Breeze Harper, Ph.D.
and Ietef "DJ Cavem" Vita, Ph.D.*

Breeze Harper: I think we first met one another at a Green Festival in San Francisco in the early 2000s. You had asked Queen Afua a question about what foods she ate to not get gestational diabetes. We talked, and I learned you had prepared to be a midwife and did unassisted home birth, which I thought was amazing because that's very rare, especially for a man in the United States. We have this crisis in the United States with Black women's maternal mortality rates, being higher than, I believe, any other racial group. Then I learned about the work you're doing as a vegan and environmental justice activist using hip hop. How do you see your role of engaging with racial justice and Black maternal-health justice? Because you taught yourself to understand reproductive health, plant-based diets, and assisted full births with this holistic vegan diet in mind.

Ietef "DJ Cavem" Vita: I came to the plant-based lifestyle through Rastafarianism, and came to understand a little more about how Black people were eating worldwide. This opened up the opportunity for me to think about equatorial culinary climate—available food, especially from the motherland. Coming from a large family, but at the same time feeling like a black sheep, I developed my own lifestyle as the only plant-based vegan within my family. I did not trust hospitals already for multiple reasons, but during the time I had my first child, which was a learning experiencing in itself, I didn't feel it was necessary to have a baby there, knowing that my grandfather had delivered all of his children pretty much in a bathtub. Through that knowledge and my own studies about the reproductive system, I decided not to give up my power and to take control over what I ate in my home.

As an artist and activist, I was aware that food is medicine, and I needed to take that power within my own hands.

Breeze: You ended up doing home births two more times, right?

Ietef: Yeah, all of them Full Moons: all unassisted; all in water. My two youngest share the same Full Moon cycle—on the corn and harvest moons. My oldest was born on the Spring Equinox. The farming calendar knows how important planting and harvesting are around those moon cycles. To have all three girls born during that time was a cool blessing.

Breeze: You're pretty much the father of eco hip hop. I discovered your music when I listened to your 2007 debut song, "Wheatgrass." The video with the song shows you and two other Black men hanging out on the corner, and one of them says they're going to the convenience store to get some chips. Before that, there's a conversation about the police and implied racial profiling. When you started doing this work, the mainstream vegan world was very much race-neutral and white, and assumed everyone had a white, middle-class, food-secure relationship to food. "Wheatgrass" and especially the video tell a completely different story.

You released the album *The Teacher's Lounge* in 2010 and started doing very intersectional work about the prison-industrial complex, racial profiling, and what it means to be a Black man in this country. When I visited Denver, you showed me the neighborhood where you lived, and I remember you telling me they were going to build a new prison right across the street from where you were working on a garden community. Could you talk about the "Wheatgrass" video and what you were trying to teach your community?

Ietef: Around 2002, I started a holistic health hip hop festival called the Brown Suga Youth Festival. I was in high school at the time, and I was involved with a lot of artists and activists around me. I felt it was important to talk to the hip hop community about how to heal each other. I was asking questions, such as: *What do artists eat when they're on tour and they* *are plant-based? How do you cure yourself using homeopathic remedies? Why are B-boys the yogis of our future? And how can we use hip hop for social change?*

I thought about all these issues and developed the idea and genre called eco hip hop in 2007, and engaged with some of my elders, who helped me with some of the energy. Supanova Slom/Hip Hop Medicine Man really focuses on the eating component, but not the gardening or environmental awareness components. Dead prez have "Be Healthy," and they did one song focused on a social justice revolution. KRS-One composed a song with Boogie Down Productions called "Beef," which talks about meat consumption, but he doesn't make the connection with the environment in his music.

That's where I wanted to continue that conversation. If we can do a whole genre dedicated to gangsta rap—to selling drugs and fashion and car culture—then we can definitely talk about culinary climate action and redefining the image of wealth and hip hop.

I wrote "Wheatgrass" because I was growing wheatgrass at the time at an interactive grow space in Colorado called The GrowHaus. I was reading a curriculum called "Going Green Living Bling." In 2011, I partnered with Van Jones and his organization, Green for All, and became a fellow. This was right before Van was appointed to the Obama administration. My partnership was a good opportunity to talk about sustainability and hip hop, and have a little bit of funding behind me, working with a non-profit focusing on creating green jobs. I thought that was dope, because a lot of people in the hood weren't thinking about solar panel installation, let alone organic gardening to sequester carbon.

With "Wheatgrass" talking about sustainability and hip hop, it felt pretty seamless to do a song on the corner, and easily sprinkle in ideas of how the injustice of police brutality is affecting communities who are also dealing with redlining and lack of access to healthy foods. It felt inclusive to also talk about working in the education system, since at the time I wrote that song I was teaching college prep courses for CU Denver, as well as performing internationally, speaking at different universities as an educator with my own curriculum, and educating educators on how to utilize hip hop for social change and to engage with sustainability.

This was how I felt it possible creatively to take my work to the next level and allow people to see hip hop for what it was. "Wheatgrass" also gave a spark to community development: to provide vegan food on a national level with organizations that were like-minded. I originally started off doing a juice-a-thon called Roots, Beans and Greens. This was a break-dancing jam where we had two different juicers set up with a gang of fresh produce—bring your own produce, bring your own cup. We literally break-danced in the middle of Five Points in Denver, showing films and drinking fresh-pressed juice, including wheatgrass, to promote health and wellness and hip hop culture instead of blunts and 40s. A few years before "Wheatgrass" dropped, the first environmental hip hop album, Felonious' *The Produce Section: Volume One*, helped highlight other artists who were like-minded. *The Produce Section: The Harvest* came out in 2012.

Breeze: My kids and I listened to that album nonstop, and absolutely loved it. I remember the song "Gz Up, Hoes Down," in which you kind of re-appropriate or redefine Snoop Dogg's concept of gangsta rap and create lyrics around eco hip hop. This was a profound song for me, and our family. When I gave talks about your work and showed the video, many people who weren't acquainted with hip hop that was more about environmental justice were surprised both that it existed and by the information you were conveying. Could you talk about the video and the song?

Ietef: The song was birthed out of the fact that I was working in the garden and at a farmers market every Saturday morning, selling greens on the block where I was growing. I had a mentee called G, aged about twelve or thirteen, who was featured in the first verse of that song. His father was *my* mentor in the hip hop community: a well-traveled hip hop artist from a group called Heavyweight Dub Champion, which had more of a conscious reggae influence. It was interesting to pass that torch on, and there was definitely intergenerational dialogue for that specific song.

The song provided the opportunity to talk about our lifestyle of growing up in the inner city, gangbanging, which was what I was exposed to. When I met G originally, he was into gangsta, and I thought, *All right. We're gonna flip this to gardening and we're gonna talk about garden "hoes" instead.* I wanted the song to conjure up positive, feminine Mother Earth energy; we needed to ground it. So I contacted Sa-Roc, and she threw down the most fiery Kali voice to describe where we were coming from: living in a hood, surrounded by genetically modified foods. She laid down a verse that was pretty seamless. My style was to connect with some of the gangstas I grew up around.

I've had the opportunity to go to Pennsylvania Avenue and spit this verse literally in the office of the head of the Environmental Protection Agency, as an example of how to talk about issues facing my community. And they understood it in the form of rhyme. I thought that was important, and the conversation continues.

For example, the first part of the second verse goes:

> Real G's got hoes
> Pocket full of seeds as I'm making my rows
> See me in the sunrise watching it grow,
> Irrigation for the water and I'm watching the flow
> I'm saving money fo sho.

We're teaching people how "growing food is like printing money," as my mentor Ron Finley would say. After I wrote that song, I came up with two different TED talks. The first one was on marketing, environmental hip hop, and culinary wellness. I think it was important for educators to see how they could utilize hip hop for social change.

I'm happy I hear a lot of dope vegan plant-based rappers nowadays. Because there was a time when I was the only one. Supanova and I would laugh about this. When I dropped "Wheatgrass" on *The Teacher's Lounge*, he came to Denver and we did a panel discussion on what we need to do to engage the community. He knew my mother, who was an activist and organizer in Colorado and developed a poetry scene in the arts community around Pan-Africanism. This exposure helped me feel more grounded in activism. Being exposed to poets like Amiri Baraka, Oscar Brown, Jr., and Sonia Sanchez definitely helped craft my mind when it came to using art for social change and when it came to developing the idea of having a space for environmental hip hop. Our first show was with The Last Poets and with dead prez, and this came about because the poetry community had groomed me to understand how to write for the revolution.

Breeze: Talking about your taking the song to the EPA in Washington, there's a visual in "Wheatgrass" of you in front of the Capitol with your fist up. I think about the hundreds of years of enslaved Black people who built the economy through their agricultural labor; but also how a lot of mainstream history in K–12 education teaches that Black people were just slaves. It's as if they didn't bring with them science, math, and art when they were abducted and forced to come here. A lot of Black folk don't realize that wealth and this nation's capital (in both senses of the word) were built because of Black agricultural labor *and* knowledge. I think of your work as decolonizing that history and thinking of what it would look like if we were to go back to our roots of cultivating the land—but in a different context to the colonial one.

When you're speaking to youth with your eco hip hop curriculum, do you bring a lot of that history into it—talking about how wealth has been accumulated, mostly by white men, and that it came not just from enslaved Black people's labor, but their intellectual knowledge of understanding the land?

Ietef: Yes. To free the minds of the people definitely starts with knowledge itself. Our sense of our intellectual history needs to go beyond [eighteenth-century polymath] Benjamin Banneker. We have to acknowledge who we are: that we were building pyramids, as were our cousins: the Olmec, the Quechua, and the people of Turtle Island. They are also a part of us. A lot of the information we hear is a lie. We already know that there were people on this continent who are our distant relatives, who were adopting ideas of land stewardship and understood the ideas of sustainable water harvesting, and that we're not here just to rape and pillage the land.

When I think about how Black farmers in the past were stripped of the land, that's no different than what happened to the Arapaho. When I think about what's happening in Flint, Michigan, I think about what's happening on the Navajo reservation: both situations are horrendous when it comes to water poisoning. A lot of what's happening now is due to fracking; back in the day, it was oil drilling and land-grabbing. As Africans in America, we have a big responsibility to transform our community. We have to stay more in alignment with our friends and our family.

I'm not here to teach fear, but I'm definitely here to teach unity, and I think hip hop has unified the world. There are reparations that have been made in other nations, but when it comes to acknowledging true self-worth, and what to do with the money, or the opportunity, or the land, what is truly needed in our community is to redefine the image of wealth.

Food helps us have clarity and peace of mind. It helps us understand how we can create that carbon and put it right back in the soil. It is a part of our everlasting breath in the ecosystem of life—when we think about consuming for nourishment and not consuming out of greed. In the vegan world we already know food is over-processed; sometimes it's genetically modified. It's cool we're taking plastics out of the ocean to create new products and combating environmental waste. However, at the same time, it's pollution that enables us to do these things. So it's a catch-22. We may like plant-based, processed, genetically modified food; but at the same time, it's pesticide-sprayed, and it's messing up our water.

Talking to people about organic gardening and land stewardship means moving away from the chemical era, being more aware of biomimicry. That's the conversation we need to have, because being plant-based and being vegan are two different things. Coca-Cola is vegan, and a lot of people ain't reaching for kombucha like they should.

Breeze: I'd like to talk about the role that capitalism plays in veganism, and how to create a resistance toward what is labeled "green capitalism," as if the word *green* makes "capitalism" better. In my research, capitalism has never yielded anything positive. It has yet to present an equitable system for all, especially the most marginalized. We have products that are taking off, such as Beyond Meat, the Impossible Burger, and plant-based cheeses. These processed, modified products are marketed to everyone as more sustainable and ethical, but it's still about capitalism and profit. What I'm hearing you're offering is something completely different: plant-based and holistic. It's questioning capitalism itself and the commodification of ingredients and the continued exploitation of certain land resources and the displacement and suffering of certain people to get these "vegan," "cruelty-free" products. Could you talk about your perception of that, and your philosophy around green capitalism and new vegan products from Beyond Meat and Impossible Foods, which are not just processed but packaged in plastics that are obviously not compostable, and add more detritus to the environment?

Ietef: The petroleum industry is behind a lot. They control the way that people think about things being fresh and being new: *If it comes in plastic, that means it's fresh; if there's a nice plastic seal on it, that means I can drink it.* So, in terms of "safety" and all these other things, they've interjected themselves.

There are many different resins available. The hemp industry is contributing to taking harmful pollutants out of the soil and also creates sequestration and takes them out of the air. At the same time, it's full of protein and one of the strongest fibers: industry is turning it into "hempcrete." People are making airplanes and soil out of bio-matter, and taking everything from algae to corn to make gasoline to transform the petroleum industry.

We have to think how influential the petroleum industry is in the food industry, especially in packaging and recycling. There's an eco-classism when it comes to ideas about packaging and freshness. Because, a lot of times, people don't want the bananas that are actually more nutritious with the spots on them. Stores are taking oranges, slicing them, peeling them, and putting them in plastic packaging. It's a throwaway generation now, in which we think we can just toss everything away and it never comes back.

That conversation is great to have with my plant-based friends. When I go to places, I acknowledge that it's beautiful they're involved with sustainable movements, but they gotta be more aware of who they are. Everybody is at a different time in their lives. Some people gotta go to work every day, and they can't make it to the protest. But that doesn't mean we don't *see* them. What's on people's plates is no different than me taking an airplane to talk to somebody about sustainability, when it took tar sands for me to get there. It's a conversation about knowing how to balance it out and give thanks for what we're using to be able to be present.

Breeze: I know no one is a hundred percent perfect in what they do. I do pause, though, around this push for food and technology and plant-based diets. A lot of the leadership is more focused on these things as commodities, and not necessarily the justice and equity aspects of a plant-based diet. I have become concerned about the lack of awareness around that. If you've always been a consumer and not someone who's on a plantation or been displaced from your land to grow these plant-based commodities; if you're someone who's not been affected by waste, because you don't come from communities of color or poor people, who live next to incinerators and landfills; and if you live in white, middle-class areas, you're more apt to buy these products. I ask these questions because, even though people have good intentions, they don't know who's being affected. These plant-based ventures and commodities continue to be funded, and I'm wondering what that means for racial and environmental justice for the most marginalized.

Ietef: Well, you already know where I stand. When it comes to the hood, food deserts are real. But they also are transforming, because people are growing in vacant lots. What's real is the fact that people are growing grass for no reason. Everybody's trying to compete with their neighbor for the perfect lawn because it's what they saw on TV. What they really need to do is compost, put some mulch down, and try to harvest as much water as they can.

But like I said, these conversations are about redefining the image of wealth. Many times, Africans in America are dealing with the cellular memory and the internalized oppression of not wanting to grow food because they relate it to slavery. We need to heal our mind and our body by replacing our value system, as my wife would say. She's been studying the mind and addiction, and how people need to replace the idea of the Supreme and God.

A lot of times, Black people see ourselves with certain ideas about wealth because of how it's been stripped from us. Systematically and visually, there's not enough imagery of a sustaining Black family sustaining Black wealth; or a sitcom that promotes knowledge itself. We'll always have a food desert if people don't think about growing outside in their yard, or about transforming their communities through openness, awareness, and engagement. That is so important. Yes, it starts with family recipes changing, because a lot of times we're stuck on the ideas of "Oh, my great grandma's favorite recipe." But times change. We're not using a dial phone. Come on, we can evolve. We're free now! We ain't gotta eat like that no more.

I'm just having fun on that, because we have to do it with love. We can't go around trying to teach organic gardening out of anger. That ain't gonna work with veganism, or even just understanding what it means to be in solidarity with migrants, with women and children, reproductive rights, and everything that needs to happen. We need to know who is going to provide the food—and have the time and access—to feed the revolution.

This is why I've been going really hard on creating opportunities in organic gardening. We started a label called Plant Based Records. All the beats are made out of beets, conducted with electricity for the next upcoming projects, along with albums that are going to be released on packets of seeds to sequester the carbon, with growing instructions on the inside of the packaging. There'll be a QR code on the back of the seed package that goes directly to the download of the album. At the same time, it shows people that they can grow food and be rewarded for listening to music at the same time.

It's about transforming the mind. There are a lot of songs about drugs; so we gotta make songs about kale and arugula . . . that's how we make them cool. Because we know how to market the drug culture and fashion cultures, and to get people to want to be involved with that; now we need to reprogram and redefine that with hip hop.

And we need to apply that knowledge to the way we spend our money, because a lot of people are investing in the same businesses, and we're kind of running in circles. Many people would love to get solar panels on their houses and drive electric cars, and it's about creating access and availability in our community. But what that starts with is *the awareness*. Everybody still wants a Chevy Impala, but we might have to start thinking about the Tesla or Scion iA.

Breeze: You talk about Tesla. In your album *Biomimicz*, which is an album/seed pack, your song "Model X" redefines why, if you're going to get a car, it's important to think about why Model X is different from other cars, and how it's more sustainable. I really enjoyed that.

Ietef: That song was in my mind originally to pitch to Tesla. For instance, I saw the way Eminem used his work in GM commercials. I saw my young brothers, like Jaden Smith, really pushing hard on Tesla. But I see the culture changing and I'm excited. Alkemia, my wife, and I are going into schools, doing assembly programs to develop ideas of creating gardens in schools, planting with kids, turning up to perform at farmers markets, and doing what we call Culinary Concerts. She's my rock. That's how we've been able to flow in these new concepts of hip hop and sustainability with culinary climate action.

Alkemia is a raw food vegan chef, healer, and energy practitioner; and I'm a chef bringing hip hop appeal. We're hitting these platforms where people can see something different than the dynamic of performance culture—talking about it not just as entertainment but as a platform for education. It's even aligning with STEM education.

We need to be optimistic with young people in a time of anger and climate change. We need to give them something to be inspired by: that plant-based eating and organic gardening might be one of the dopest ways to green the planet, regenerate and sequester the carbon, harvest the water, and find that true sense of peace with our culture. We need to help young people who are serious about the intergenerational tyranny that's happened with the elders not being present; withholding and wanting to think about the narcissistic selfishness that has really turned our world upside down.

These kids are hearing scientists talk about 2030 being the end of the world . . . and the water [level] is rising . . . and Colorado is going to have a beach. So, these kids are hyped up and they're marching or going on strike. To be a part of some of these marches—in Germany, Denver, New York—is inspiring. It's like the start of the civil rights movement, but what they're fighting for is different. A lot of these young people are adopting a plant-based mentality, not because of holistic health, but because of the call to action to address climate change. These kids are not thinking about Llaila Afrika and Queen Afua. They may like my music because it touches on the ideas of what it's all about, but they would have been doing this regardless. It's almost as if they have no other choice. ✾

10

FROM STIC.MAN TO A HOLISTIC MAN

Khnum "Stic" Ibomu of dead prez

As a hip hop artist, producer, and long-distance running coach, I do a lot, but I'm most passionate about bringing music—hip hop in particular—together with health and wellness into people's lives. I call it Fit Hop—using hip hop to inspire healthy living.

My lifestyle is based on the movement that I founded with my wife of twenty-six years, Afya Ibomu. It's called RBG FIT CLUB (www.RBGFITCLUB.com), and it grew out of our passions: mine for hip hop, hers for health. Afya is a bestselling author of plant-based cookbooks; she has a degree in nutrition, and she's a certified holistic health counselor. I think of her as the Harriet Tubman of healthy living. She was a vegetarian when we met—she had "already escaped the plantation," so to speak—and she has been the leader in developing our consistency over time. Since she's a chef, she invents ways to enjoy the kinds of food we grew up with, whether it's Soul Food or Mexican and different cultural foods, but she'll make them plant-based and non-allergenic, to suit the occasion.

Afya and I looked at what it has taken to really transform our lives, and came up with a holistic platform based on five principles: knowledge, nutrition, exercise, restoration, and consistency. Those principles shape how I approach healthy living.

THE FIVE PRINCIPLES

I'm always studying and, to use a martial arts reference, in the "white belt" mind-state. I believe you have to learn through experimentation, and not just become stuck and dogmatic. That's why it's important to always seek and be open to new **knowledge**.

As far as **nutrition**, I became interested in plant-based eating because I was sick. I was in my early twenties—smoking, drinking, and self-medicating—and woke up with gout in my leg. My wife saw I was suffering and introduced me to veganism as a way to heal. Some people come to veganism because of the ethical concerns around the treatment of animals; some through how it helps the planet in different ways. For me, with gout as a lesson in disguise, it was how veganism could transform how the body could heal itself, if you give it the proper tools. For about ten years after, I cleared up the gout (it only took a couple of weeks to heal, which just blew my mind), and I dived deep into the plant-based lifestyle. This was a complete 180 from the street-life mentality I had before being sick. I learned the foundation of nutrition—eating well, especially whole foods—and how this truly strengthens your health.

In terms of **exercise**, I started practicing martial arts, such as Wu Shu Kwan Kung Fu and Jeet Kune Do, and African Montu (martial) arts Ile Ijala and Egbe Ogun—as well as yoga, meditation, and boxing. Soon, I was bitten by the running bug: 5Ks, 10Ks, all the way up to marathons. From there, I became certified as a long-distance running coach. I started learning archery and became certified with USA Archery. In a nutshell, fitness was about attaining strength, flexibility, endurance, and vitality. Having regular practices such as these helped me cultivate those qualities.

Because of the knowledge, nutrition, and exercise, **restoration** was necessary. I learned that if you go hard and push and don't rest, your immune system and your physical body will break down, and your thinking won't be clear. As an entrepreneur with multiple businesses—creating music, traveling, touring, not to mention fatherhood and being a husband—I need to keep healthy and focused. So, I make sure to meditate, take breaks, schedule spa days, and go to the steam room, as well as rest and schedule my life so it is more sustainable and realistic, and I can maintain my vitality.

Finally, there's **consistency**: the "thumb" on the fist of the four "fingers" of these principles; the thumb allows the other fingers to work together. We can have a little bit of knowledge, adopt a more nutritious diet, take a new exercise class, and meditate for a couple of days, but if we're not consistent, then we're not transforming our lifestyle. Because you're not always going to be motivated, you have to learn to be *disciplined*. The way I maintain my discipline is to stay inspired. I think of my wife, my purpose, and the example I'm setting for my family. I remember where I come from, and what I used to go through when I didn't have healthy habits, and I remain committed to being an inspiration for other folks who are hungry to grow.

This is how the five principles of RBG FIT CLUB shape my lifestyle. Every day I'm learning more and unlocking new aspects of how I can apply these principles in life. As a dad, I instill these principles with my children, too. I have a self-defense standard: that you have to take two years of martial arts. You can take more if you want, and my kids have done this, but two is our minimum. We have all kinds of standards around health throughout the year. We fast at different times. We do vision boards for the winter solstice to prepare for the New Year. My kids undertake rites of passage every seven years to learn different skills based around the seven stages of manhood. All that being said, what my kids are learning most from me—more than what I'm telling them—is what they *see*. I think they understand that family is a priority, that health is wealth, and that entrepreneurship is powerful.

RBG means a lot of things, and it grows with us:

> **R**ed, **B**lack, **G**reen
> **R**eal **B**lack **G**irl
> **R**elax, **B**reathe, **G**row
> **R**ice, **B**eans, **G**reens
> **R**eaching **B**igger **G**oals

RBG is the tofu that you season according to your consciousness and creativity. It's hip hop, fundamentally. We're about **R**eaching **B**igger **G**oals and **R**eturning **B**ack to that **G**reen.

The whole development of RBG FIT CLUB has been humbling, because I've seen so many examples of people who have found something that resonates with them. There are people who listened to my first Fit Hop album, called *The Workout*, who lost sixty pounds. Some folks talk about gaining the weight they always wanted to, utilizing the plan from my book *EAT PLANTS, LIFT IRON*. My wife's mother had MS and through changing her diet she was able to manage the symptoms, have less pain, and not be in a wheelchair. My own mom was in the hospital with diabetic complications. We kidnapped her from the hospital, moved her to Atlanta, and changed her diet. Now she is insulin-free. She's painting, acting, singing—just enjoying her life in her seventies.

I'm humbled by people who listened to my song "Sober Soldier" and gave up cigarettes, alcohol, or hard drugs. My mom always used to say, "I can hear a sermon, but I'd rather see one." I understand this now: I receive letters all the time. It allows me to see the impact in real life, in real time, and it keeps me inspired.

TAPPING INTO OUR AUTHENTIC SELVES

For the follow-up album, *Workout II*, we partnered with the yoga brand Lululemon for creating a series of promotional "Fit Hop" content. With *Experience Fit Hop*, a seven-minute mini doc, we tell the story of a young lady I met five years ago when she was nine years old. She had wanted to be a boxer; it was in her blood: her granddads and uncles and others had been boxers. Her dad, who is a friend of mine and who I trained in distance running from zero to thirteen miles so that he lost about sixty pounds, was an old-school chauvinist: "Nah, my daughter's not gonna box," he said. "That's for my sons." So his daughter snuck in to gyms, trained, and created an opportunity for herself. Fast forward: For five years straight she's been the National Female Boxing Champion in Georgia, a nine-time titleholder in the whole United States, and she just qualified for the Olympics. And she's so sweet; you'd never feel like she's got that kind of badassery! But she's completely breaking the stereotypes.

Experience Fit Hop tells this young lady's story with music from my album *Workout II* as the theme music. The piece is just one example that shows how the mission we have with Fit Hop is impacting people. It's a blessing—because I've been so impacted by hip hop and healthy living, the least we could do is try to share the wealth.

This young lady also reminds us that we need to tap into our own authentic selves. That's what I encourage people to do. Men like Bruce Lee, Muhammad Ali, and Malcolm X are great examples for me because they all, in their own way, were original beings who were able to say: *I found my path, my calling, my purpose.* Bruce Lee did his through revolutionizing martial arts, although he was so much bigger than martial arts. Ali was a boxer, but he was so much bigger than boxing. Malcolm X went from the street life to becoming a radical activist, and he continued to evolve as an activist into a globally conscious humanitarian. I'm a hip hop artist, but what I've always been about is bigger than hip hop.

You have to find what you are authentically called to do (what the old folks describe as "what you would do for free"), and then do that to the best of your ability—but putting your family first, of course. A lot of times we chase after what we think our family wants, whether it be resources or material opportunities, and we put so much into trying to be good providers that we actually don't give our family our *presence*.

That's been a conscious action for me—to make choices where I can be present for them. Yes, I sacrifice certain things to be present in their lives, but making these choices gives me strength. I don't feel like I'm missing my children's lives or not prioritizing my relationship—and everything else benefits from that presence, because I can bring all of it to my work. I try to live my priorities: first, family and health; then, everything else.

ORIGINS AND GROWTH

I live in Atlanta, Georgia. We were in Brooklyn for ten years prior, but we wanted more space, more green, and a better quality of life. We also needed to move for our longer-term plans as a family—to own land, and to be able to use that land for a new creative vision that promotes health and wellness. In addition, Itwela, my oldest son, has been able to grow up with more outdoor activities. He's camped over a hundred times and gotten all these skills and awards for his outdoorsmanship over the years. My youngest son, Nkosua, is currently five years old. Both of their names are of African origin. *Itwela* means "to defend yourself or your community" in Setswana, a language of southern Africa. *Nkosua* comes from the Akan language of West Africa. Although the translation is more complicated, the name in essence means "value your culture."

Names and language are very important in our culture and as a means of telling a story. Our name, dead prez, summed up where we were coming from when we formed in New York City in 1996. We chose our name because, first, "dead presidents" was slang for money. We definitely were trying to get money on the street, and were at the bottom of the economic ladder. We knew that if you live in an ocean of capitalism, you've got to know how to swim—that's the hustle.

But we also knew that capitalism was rotten to the core and was founded on the exploitation of African labor, as well as the resources and cultures of many other people around the world. When voting advocates would show up every four years, saying, "Rock the Vote! You gonna vote for this politician or that one?" We'd reply, "That's dead. That's dead for us. Whoever the president is, that don't matter. He might as well be dead, 'cuz nothing don't change for the community."

This was another dimension of our name: The president was dead to us. Our sentiment was: All that is beating a dead horse. We also wanted to remind people that if you looked at the African traditions before slavery (the pharaohs, warriors, artisans, healers, kings, and queens—our ancestors) they are *our* dead presidents. That was when *we* ruled, when we *presided* over own lives.

So the name "dead presidents" spoke to our ancestral kinship, to capitalism being dead, and to the pragmatic reality that "we still gotta get this money." However, when we were signed to a label, a copyright search showed there was some punk band from another era called Dead Presidents. The lawyers thought there might an issue, so we suggested dead prez as an alternative. And once the searches cleared, we officially became dead prez.

That was a long time ago, though, in terms of our mentality. A lot of growth and change have happened since then, especially when I think about politics and voting. When I look at my political ideology today, I'm mindful about not letting a viewpoint crystallize into rigid dogmatism. For instance, Malcolm at one point said that his "politics" was Black Nationalism; at another point, I believe it became more international. Tupac died when he was twenty-seven; what would he have thought at forty-seven? Bruce Lee died at thirty-three; what would he have been teaching at seventy-three? I'm forty-six today, gratefully, and if you'd have asked me what my politics was at sixteen, I would have told you, "Tear this shit down. That's my politics." If you would have asked me that again at age thirty, I might have said, "African Internationalist." At forty-six, I've learned that all of those perspectives were largely influenced by politics that were already in place . . . not fully my own perspective.

The real challenge is to find what your perspectives/perceptions/contributions are *outside of the boxes that have already been set up for you to choose.* On the census form or job application and so forth it'll ask you "Who are you?" and give you boxes to check. What if you don't feel like you fit into one of those boxes? Do you conform to *Well, this is how they see me, so this is who I am?* Or do you develop and cultivate your own authentic self and perspective, and let your life be shaped by them? I believe the latter is the most liberating thing to do. So, as I continue to evolve, I would characterize myself as being a student of life, being open to different perspectives, and putting in the real work where I feel I can best utilize my wheelhouse of skills, resources, and interests to impact our communities constructively and positively.

At the end of the day, I believe in justice, I believe in wellbeing, and I believe in empowerment for people in general, and especially people who are systematically exploited, marginalized, and oppressed. That said, the whole world—even those who benefit from oppression—also have to be impacted, or they will keep perpetuating it. So I would say my politics today lean to a more Taoist outlook—Tao: *the way things work in nature.* I try to follow the Tao in my perspectives, activism, health, and in my daily schedule, and it's been working well. I feel like I've made quantum leaps since I let go of focusing on everything I'm against—*I'm against this, I'm against that*—and started focusing on optimism and putting in the work on everything I'm *FOR.*

To that extent, therefore, my vote is my lifestyle. I always say that if people feel like they want to test the electoral process and whether or how it can make a difference, they should do it. It's not gonna hurt you to vote. You should test whatever theory or candidate you believe might be strategic. You should be informed, get out there, and exercise the rights you have to participate in that system—*if* that is what you want to do.

As far as I'm concerned, though, marking a ballot and putting it in a box does not absolve you of the greater responsibility in a democracy. Your actions and your choices every day are votes too, not just at election time. The places you patronize and do business with are your vote. The products you consume and how they impact your health, environment, and community are your vote. I encourage us to ask ourselves: How can we vote with our lifestyle more? How can we get that kind of activated awareness popping and trending?

And more than trends, how can we commit to engaged holistic activism—personal and communal—as a sustainable way of life?

I try to live a lifestyle of voting for what I'm for, and that's what I'm going to be voting for come the next election and whatever is beyond that. I'm going be waking up, training. I'm going to be trying to be more green and act more sustainably when I bring any products into my household. I'm going to be supporting independent schools. I'm going to be using my platform to inspire and encourage other people to be healthier and to not get caught up in addiction. I'm going to be encouraging people to own their talents—and so forth and so on. That's what I'm voting for.

BROTHERHOOD

Another very important aspect of my life and work is brotherhood, which includes women *and* men. Brotherhood involves connections between people that honor each other, and is about cultivating respect for the fact that we go through the same shit in different ways. It's about understanding that teamwork makes the dream work.

Now, men definitely have a special kind of relationship and bond as they relate to issues that may be biological or social. However, I recently had an experience called The Huddle, created by Lululemon. The Huddle involved thirty or so other people—mostly men, but some women—who are all nationally recognized wellness influencers in their areas of expertise. We went through three days of sweating, personal development, and life-changing experiences with strangers. One thing I learned, as it relates to brotherhood, is that there are no strangers. When you choose to connect with people, you instantly learn, for instance, that he's not "the old white man," but a writer, who has two kids, and one of them is smoking weed. You discover that people are whole beings.

After I was on my way home after The Huddle, where I had just built a connection with all these different types of folks, I walked through the airport and found myself observing the other travelers and thinking of all the potential connections I would have ignored before this experience. I realize there are no strangers, just beautiful people you can choose to connect with or not. I think that's what Malcolm saw when he traveled to Mecca and had that awakening about the brotherhood of humanity. It's what Bruce Lee always talked about when he said, "Under the heavens, there is but one family." Brotherhood is about recognizing that we don't need permission to be a part of the community of life.

Finally, in terms of brotherhood, I want to acknowledge how big an inspiration Omowale, the editor of this book, has been to me—from the early days, when we organized the Uhuru Movement together, and I met him as a fellow brother activist. Years later, I glanced at an article and thought to myself, *There's a guy that's boxing, and he's a vegan!* I put the article in a file, thinking that he might be great story to share for our RBG FIT CLUB newsletter, and it was only later when I read the article that I realized it was Omowale. I had known he was an activist and organizer, but I hadn't known he'd been boxing as a vegan. I had a file of clippings on him, and when we finally ran into each other at a vegfest in Atlanta, we connected again.

I'm very thankful that Omowale is not only telling his story, but giving others a platform so that our collective experience and trajectory toward healthier living is echoed in all the various brothers' contributions. I salute him for his leadership qualities: He's a very humble, quiet-spoken person in my observation, but the things he's doing are big, badass, and bold. I want to give him some love for being an awesome inspiration. ✺

11

THE HEART HAS ITS REASONS

Anteneh Roba, M.D.

"The heart has its reasons that reason cannot understand."—*Blaise Pascal*

It began with Nikita, a six-month-old Maltese whom I adopted after my cousin Seble found out that the building where she lived in New York City didn't allow dogs. Seble, who'd been given Nikita by an office colleague, called me up and asked me whether I'd take Nikita until she found another home for him.

I was relatively young and had just moved from Florida to Houston, Texas. It was 1999, and I was partying, as Prince sang, to suit the year! At first, I wasn't enthusiastic: I didn't feel a particular affinity for dogs, or animals in general. When I was a child, my grandfather had bought me a German shepherd, which scared me, and my mother's brother had acquired a monkey in Ethiopia, which is where my family is from. When I was offered the monkey as a pet, I wasn't interested. I had no opinions about animals, except that I enjoyed eating them.

Nikita was, therefore, neither wanted nor expected—I was looking after Number One, and didn't have time to babysit a dog full-time. Initially, I asked a friend to periodically look after Nikita on weekends and when I traveled. However, I'm close to Seble, and I knew how much she loved animals, and so I reluctantly agreed to look after Nikita until she could take him back. He and I warily circled one another for several days, but a couple of months into my fostering experiment, it became clear to me how powerful I was in relation to this bundle of fur, how much Nikita depended on me, and therefore how responsible I was. Over the course of a couple of months, much to my surprise, I fell in love with the little guy, and I told Seble that I wasn't returning him.

Nikita wasn't obviously lovable. He was stubborn, wasn't impressed by hoopla and noise, and didn't suffer fools gladly—especially when they annoyed him. Perhaps he resembled me a little too much! In any event, he and I became the closest of companions—traveling together all over the United States. In fact, it's not an exaggeration to say that Nikita completely changed my life.

One day, deep into our relationship, I was carrying Nikita in the crook of my arm. There was nothing unusual in this; sometimes it was easier to get around this way. However, at this particular moment, as if for the first time, I felt Nikita's heart pounding steadily in the palm of my hand. The sensation struck me like a thunderbolt: *This is a living being with a beating heart,* I remember thinking to myself. *All animals have this—including human ones. What is the fundamental difference between us?* As you might imagine, I thought of the cognitive abilities, language function, and the other determinants that we humans have constructed to separate ourselves from the other animals, and that allow us to justify our domination of them. Yet I kept returning to the central fact of Nikita's heart pumping blood around his body at the same time as mine was doing the same around mine. And that led me to the next question: *What is the fundamental difference between Nikita and the other animals I eat or wear?*

Over the course of the next few months I read a number of books—*Animal Liberation* by Peter Singer, *Eternal Treblinka* by Charles Patterson, and *An Unnatural Order* by Jim Mason, among others—that reinforced, deepened, and expanded that physical connection I'd had with Nikita. They reminded me that we are all animals, and they demonstrated that the animal-industrial complex is responsible for multiple ills that have at their root the essential separation of one group of beings into undesirable, exploitable, and killable—by another group of beings that manufactures reasons to consider them disposable, "Other," and unworthy of life.

This was how I became an animal advocate. However, it was not the only gift that Nikita gave me. As it turned out, Nikita was also responsible for my discovering the essence of my profession as a medical doctor.

A career in medicine had been expected of me from an early age. My mother died when I was three or four years of age. She'd taken me from Washington, DC, where my father was attached to the Ethiopian embassy, back to her homeland after my parents' marriage had begun to unravel. When she passed away, suddenly and from an unknown disease, my father flew over to Addis Ababa and took me back to the United States.

My father encouraged me to become a physician. "You can find out about what happened to your mother," he would say, "and take care of people." He bought a toy stethoscope and would lie down and let me listen to his heartbeat. In this way, he instilled a desire in me to study medicine. I went to medical school in Europe, and after I graduated, I returned to the United States to take up a residency. It was a rotational internship unattached to any one particular field, which allowed me to develop a broad perspective on the various specializations. I found out that I enjoyed the challenges, variety, and hours that emergency medicine supplied. This is what I was practicing when I moved to Houston and Nikita came into my life.

The natural corollary of recognizing Nikita's and other animals' right to life was that, within a few years, I decided to stop eating them. Like many others who take such a step, I began removing certain meats from my diet and then stopped consuming dairy products and fish. Unlike many people, my initial reasons for no longer eating animals were ethical rather than worries about the environment or concerns over my own health. Yet here, too, Nikita's influence opened up a whole new world for me.

As many people aware of diet's impact on human health have discovered when they visit their primary care physician, very few doctors have more than a cursory knowledge of nutrition. Until relatively recently, we received virtually no education on it in medical school, and the tendency then—and unfortunately it remains so today—was to prescribe pills rather than dietary change to deal with chronic disease.

I saw the failures of our medical model all the time in the emergency rooms of the hospitals I worked at in the United States. Patients would arrive suffering from conditions that either directly stemmed from, or were exacerbated by, obesity, stroke, Type 2 diabetes, and certain cancers. These conditions, I was to discover, were either preventable, treatable, or even reversible in patients if they changed what they ate, incorporated more exercise into their lifestyle, and reduced their stress. As with my ethical awakening, these medical revelations were buttressed by my reading books from a number of doctors—such as those by T. Colin Campbell of the China Study and Neal Barnard of Physicians Committee for Responsible Medicine—who had compiled compelling evidence of the efficacy of a whole-foods, plant-based diet.

My increased sense of responsibility toward Nikita and my newfound ethical focus intensified my wish to give something back to my parents' homeland. In 2006, Seble, whose care for animals was long established and whose ethical diet pre-dated mine, joined me in this mission. We cofounded the International Fund for Africa (IFA), a non-profit that combines our passion for human health with education on animal issues in Ethiopia and beyond.

It was during IFA's second trip to rural parts of Ethiopia in 2011–12 that I came to realize how profoundly diet impacted both personal and public health. Over the course of twelve days, IFA's team of thirty physicians and nurses from Ethiopia and the United States treated nearly five thousand people, many of whom lived in the sparest of accommodations with very few amenities, medical or otherwise. Yet, of the roughly three thousand adults we saw, fewer than ten had medical conditions that could be associated with hypertension, heart disease, or diabetes. Indeed, of those patients in their forties, fifties, and sixties, many had sugar levels that were so low that the Americans among us were performing sugar tests to ensure these individuals weren't hypoglycemic. The glucose readings we were getting—55 to 60 milligrams per deciliter—were far below what we were used to in America. In the United States, it is common to treat patients who are hypoglycemic, with glucose levels below 70, with a sugary substance to bring their levels back to "normal."

I vividly recall one lady on our trip who'd come to see us for cataracts, which we were able to treat. To reach our clinic, this woman, who was in her eighties, had been obliged to walk twenty kilometers barefoot at an elevation of up to five thousand feet above sea level. For food, she had brought with her a little bag containing nuts, and there was very little body fat on her. Yet her vital signs—including her endurance and resting heart rate—were those of an average person in their thirties in the United States. A combination of living at altitude, strenuous daily exercise over mountainous terrain often carrying heavy objects, and consuming an essentially plant-based diet had kept her remarkably healthy, physically fit, and mentally alert.

Now, it should be pointed out that life for many such women and men in the global South is hard. They suffer from communicable diseases, such as tuberculosis, and waterborne illnesses, as well as cataracts. In lower-lying areas, malaria may be a killer. Such people aren't necessarily vegan by choice; meat may be too expensive and the farmed animals they come in contact with may be more valuable to them alive than dead. But the Ethiopian calendar has many days of fasting, during which it is expected you will not eat meat, and this has led to a culture blessed with a rich plant-based cuisine. This woman may have had few material possessions, but she was not deprived, and her underlying health enabled her to live life to the full.

In Ethiopia, as in many countries in the global South, as folks become wealthier in terms of cash and possessions, and as many move to the urban areas in search of more work and greater opportunity, lifestyles are changing. Instead of walking, people in the capital, Addis Ababa, take cars or taxis; they ride in elevators rather than climb the stairs; they work in offices rather than labor in the fields; and they eat many more animal products and do it more often. Across Ethiopia as elsewhere, diabetes, hypertension, heart disease—and the complications stemming from them (including erectile dysfunction)—have reached epidemic proportions. In our clinic in Addis, administered by Seble, are three doctors and a U.S.-trained nurse. The clinic now treats more and more individuals—including young men and women—with the same non-communicable diseases (NCDs) as my patients in the United States. Thankfully, the situation is nowhere near as dire as it is in America, but the trends are worrying.

They are especially troublesome because medical services and public health funding throughout the global South are already stretched. NCDs are much more costly than preventive medicine (vaccinations, regular and nutritious meals, appropriate hygiene). Mass migration to the cities has led to informal settlements, poor housing, and many people (including large numbers of children) living on the streets. Sewage systems and sources of potable water cannot keep up with the increase in their utilization, and infectious disease outbreaks are common. If the health service budgets are taken up with treating NCDs, then efforts to improve public health as a whole suffer.

In addition to founding the IFA, Seble, a number of dedicated Ethiopians, and I established the Ethiopian Vegan Society, which has over ten thousand followers around the globe. As a medical doctor and an Ethiopian-American, I'm well aware that I have a platform in that country to talk about NCDs, which are skyrocketing, even in rural areas. I'm able to share with other Ethiopian professionals as well as citizens about how, in our clinic in Addis, we've been able in a matter of months to halt the progress and even reverse diabetes and hypertension in some patients by putting them on a plant-based diet, which has allowed them to come off pills and take back their lives. I emphasize the removal of meat from the diet and the incorporation of exercise, and I insist on supplementation. Unfortunately, because of the modern industrial food system, with its emphasis on pesticides, herbicides, and artificial fertilizers, the soil in which food is grown has been denuded of the necessary minerals and nutrients to stay healthy. In combining all three, we are able to obtain phenomenal results—whether it is Ethiopians visiting my clinic in Addis or Americans visiting my practice in the United States.

Through IFA, Seble and I have also been able to develop a vegan lunch program, which feeds many hundreds of schoolchildren in several schools in Addis. These kids are from some of the poorest families in Ethiopia, many of them functionally homeless. Through our efforts, for the last five years, these pupils have received at least two nutritious meals a day throughout the school year, with the side benefit of removing the stigma they may experience from not being able to eat when their classmates can. We're very grateful to our partners at A Well-Fed World for making this possible.

Finally, to complete the circle, in 2009 IFA worked with Humane Society International and Best Friends to persuade the Ethiopian government to stop killing homeless dogs on the streets of Addis and to allow us to conduct a pilot spay-and-neuter program, which proved to be more humane and practical. We became involved with two veterinary universities and brought in independent vets funded by the Humane Society of the United States to conduct a ten-day training on spaying and neutering dogs and how to treat small animals. In Ethiopia, the vet schools are geared toward treating large animals for production, so we were filling a need. This is difficult work, because dogs are often seen mainly as protection for property, which means that from dawn to dusk the animals are chained, and then let loose in the evening.

As for promoting broader concerns about animals and veganism as an ethical practice, it remains as hard in Ethiopia as it is elsewhere in the world. Ethiopians generally associate a meat-free diet with religious practice rather than any particular obligation to nonhuman animals. Seble and I have learned the hard way the necessity of emphasizing the value of a plant-based diet for personal and public health. That said, people around the planet are beginning to recognize that the preservation of the natural world and the other animals who share it with us is key to our survival, as well as theirs. It is this recognition that I hoped both to reflect and to stimulate in my book *Africa and Her Animals: Philosophical and Practical Applications*, a collection of twenty essays about the continent that I co-edited with Rainer Ebert, and which was published in 2018.

I've been very fortunate in my life to have been allowed to pursue my passion for medicine, and to do so without being hindered because of where I came from or what I look like. I recognize that this is unusual, and these inequities compel me to move forward. My commitment to social, racial, and gender justice is discussed at length in my chapter "Injustice Everywhere" in the book *Circles of Compassion*, edited by Will Tuttle. These issues of equity combine with my passion for animal rights in the tenets that all animals, including humans, should be allowed to spend time with their families and communities, be respected for who they are independent of their perceived utility to others, and be allowed to pursue their interests. These have propelled my mission to use my skills to help the vulnerable and the sick—of many different species—in whatever way I can.

My education has certainly helped in this effort, and my daily experience as a physician in Ethiopia and the United States has proven essential. However, beneath the intellectual knowledge and the practical experience, there lies the beating heart: whether it's my father's heard through the stethoscope when I was a child or Nikita's felt through my hand.

I lived with Nikita for a little over twelve years until his death, which occurred at 6:04 a.m. on November 28, 2012. Yes, I remember the moment of his passing to the minute. I'm not embarrassed to say that I loved that dog like a son, and not a day goes by that I don't think about him.

Nikita did more than remind me that we all have a heart. Simply put, he opened mine wide open: to the suffering of so many sentient beings at our hands; to our capricious decision to care for one species while mutilating and killing another; to the violence and injustice that we mete out to people who don't look like us; to the indifference we may have to the homeless, the poor, and the needy.

I'd like to hope that compassion was always there, awaiting someone to bring it forth. But I won't know, because Nikita was in my life when I started my advocacy for animals. He was my companion as I promoted plant-based diets, and then established neonatal units in two hospitals in Addis, helping over three thousand kids make it through their first few weeks. And he was my inspiration as I began our food services for schoolkids, our veterinary clinics, and so much more. And Nikita remains in my heart now, as I find ways to give back to the country of my heritage *and* the country where I now live. ❀

12

THERE IS BEAUTY IN THE DARKNESS

An Interview with Stewart Devon Mitchell

Brotha Vegan: *Tell us about your childhood and family.*

Stewart Mitchell: I had a decent childhood growing up. I don't think it was much different from that of any other child growing up in Brooklyn in the eighties and nineties. I lost both of my parents to AIDS before I turned nine years old. I was raised by my father's sister, who was, at times, verbally abusive. In retrospect, I think it was because she had raised two teenage daughters (nineteen and twenty) who had just moved out, and now she had to raise me and my younger brother; it might have been a little too much for her. Besides that, we had a pretty fair childhood. We had all the necessary provisions, but we lacked nurturing and emotional support.

BV: *Are your children vegan? How are you educating your children about veganism?*

SM: Yes, my children are vegan. I teach them that it is important to adhere to a vegan way of life because of the atrocities humans commit against the environment and animals every day. They understand the negative impact that humanity has on animals and why animal consumption is unnecessary. I taught them compassion for animals and each other at a very young age, and about the quality of each individual's life, regardless of their species. I showed them how to make their own smoothies, and I try to highlight the importance of eating nutritious and natural food that's provided by our planet.

BV: *What was your introduction to veganism?*

SM: I was introduced to veganism through my job in food service. I used to question why we had access to so much poultry, because my limited understanding at the time was that animals lived on farms in the open air and on green grass. I started to research about factory farming and realized that everything I thought I knew about farming was absolutely false. Animals were just being bred to die for nothing, simply because they "taste good." I saw the fear in the animals' eyes, and hearing their screams for help resonated with me. Another introduction to veganism was through hip hop music, believe it or not. I would hear some prominent MCs talk about eating healthy, plant-based foods, and that made me curious as well. It was inspiring to hear young Black men taking accountability for their health and wellness without sounding wack!

There has always been a link between veganism and hip hop, which is about social and conscious change. At its core, it's about positivity and uplifting our people. Certain artists have come along and left a mark on the hip hop genre, always advocating for clean eating and peace with our fellow sentient beings. I took note of these artists early on and incorporated what I've learned into my lifestyle.

BV: *Can you describe your approach to animal activism?*

SM: Animals, like humans, need political advocacy. Changing laws that benefit the welfare of animals is a major priority in this day and age, regarding animal rights activism. We need lawmakers who are just as concerned for animals as they are for the constituents of their neighborhoods and the communities they serve. I try to get people to see animals as the sentient beings they are. We must understand that they are deserving of rights and a life of fulfillment—without human interference or corruption. Protests and outreach are important forms of activism as well, because so many people are still in the dark about how their simple, everyday choices affect animals. Education is important, and having open conversations with people about animal welfare might change their perspective.

BV: *You have written three books about veganism. Please tell us about them.*

SM: I wrote *Kayla the Vegan* to help kids understand the choices they make and how they affect innocent animals. It was also written to teach kids why bullying is wrong, how to accept people and embrace their differences, and how to effect positive change. I also wrote *Liberation Summer* to show people of color why animal advocacy in poor communities is crucial. These animals become cheap fast food products, like fried chicken, Big Macs, cheese in our pizza, and other harmful, cheap products. These products are directly targeted to cater to low-income communities, and that's why there is an abundance of them across America, where there is also a lack of fresh, affordable produce. *#GreatestWrapperAlive: A Memoir Recipe Book Inspired Through the Power of Conscious Hip Hop Lyrics* was a fun recipe book to share what influenced me to go vegan. The book offers a bit of hip hop history, my personal story, cool and fun recipes, and dope lyrics from MCs past and present.

BV: *You seem to be someone who is sensitive to mental illness, particularly depression. Are you able to share struggles to educate more men?*

SM: I think there are more people suffering with mental illness, depression in particular, than we know about, and it's mainly because mental illness is treated as a contagious disease. Most people are afraid to talk about depression, anxiety, and other mental disorders because they do not want to feel ostracized from their family and community. Many people are uneducated about depression, how it affects millions of people in the United States alone, and why it is the leading cause of suicide for young men between the ages of fifteen and twenty-five.

Men and boys have a hard time dealing with depression because they feel obligated to be "strong." There is a huge misconception of what a man or boy should be. We're not allowing boys to be human—we are teaching them to shut out their emotions, and this is what causes most young boys to grow into men with mental health issues. Most men never get a chance to sort out their problems, because they were taught to hold everything inside for the sake of being "tough."

BV: *What are your coping methods?*

SM: My coping methods include writing and exercise. The more you are able to express your creativity, in whatever way that may be, the more productive you are and the more fulfilling your life is. People need a sense of fulfillment and purpose. The more you follow your passion—whether it is writing, dancing, or just anything creative—the more you feel a sense of self-worth. These are just some of the ways I cope with depression. I must stress that these are not cures. Some of us battling depression have dealt with traumatic experiences that are tough to let go of, so healing requires more than just "thinking positive" or "being happy." Being depressed is the ultimate feeling of vulnerability and self-loathing, and it's hard to be positive in this frame of mind. I cope by trying to be productive and providing a sense of relief for others.

BV: *What are some ways you've been educating more Black men about depression?*

SM: I wrote a book called *There Is Beauty in the Darkness.* It speaks to people, especially men. My book tells them that it's OK to be open and honest about their mental health, that having depression or any mental health condition doesn't make them any less of a man or a human being. I've also been very vocal in interviews and on social media about the topic, to spread awareness. Most men who are dealing with depression can't or won't admit to it because they fear being vulnerable. We have to break the stigma and teach them that there is nothing weak about battling depression.

BV: *How has depression impacted your activism?*

SM: I think the key to coping with depression is doing things you are most passionate about. Activism involves a level of passion because I'm fighting for what I believe in. If anything, it helps me deal with depression because I'm doing something productive. It keeps my mind focused on the task ahead.

BV: *As a New York City animal activist, how do you feel about the bills banning foie gras, as well as other legislation passed in 2019?*

SM: I think it's incredible, especially that it's happening in New York. It's a progressive step in the right direction, as we are setting a standard in animal rights and setting a good example for our children to follow. We are showing future generations that animals are not items but, rather, deserving of protection and not to be commodified as food, clothing, entertainment, or otherwise. The passing of these bills shows the rest of the world that we, New Yorkers, care about *all* species and that we are doing the best we can to offer these animals some relief.

BV: *How should we approach masculinity in the Black community in 2020 and beyond?*

SM: We have to break the misconception that masculinity is somehow rooted in being rugged and hard, and being oblivious to our emotions. Masculinity should be rooted in responsibility. Men have a moral responsibility to be a provider and protector of women and children. This doesn't mean that men should act in a brutish manner. Not every man is aggressive and competitive, and that should be respected. Many of us are intellectuals.

It is an overlooked quality when we talk about masculinity. Just because a man is more in touch with his emotions, it doesn't disqualify him from being masculine. All Black men should learn the art of self-defense and discipline as a means of self-preservation. Every man must have a skill so he can be productive in society and provide a service to others. We must learn to let our young, Black boys be open about their emotions and give them the necessary support they need to deal with their inner feelings. That means letting them express their hurt, letting them cry, and letting them be expressive of their love through hugs and kisses; because, one day, these boys will be men with their own families, and we don't want to pass down a tradition of making boys into men before their time. Let boys express their emotions so that it's easier for them to identify when someone is hurting, and allows them to be a source of love and support. This is not teaching boys to be soft or weak—it's teaching them to be self-aware.

BV: *Thank you very much for your time. Do you have anything else to share?*

SM: I would like to thank G.A.ME and Black VegFest for being a positive presence in our community, for giving people of color a positive perspective on health and wellness, and for advocating for our people and for animals. Thank you for the opportunity to talk about these topics that are of great importance to me. I believe this will help more people moving forward. ❀

13

I'M FREE.

A Poem by Malc

At birth, our bodies and minds
are claimed by traditions and systems
put in place before us.

Most accept what was before them.

Since veganism, my mind is mine.
My body is mine.

I'm free. ☀

14

A SACRED OBLIGATION

Milton Mills, M.D.

My journey to veganism began in 1972, when I joined the Seventh Day Adventist Church, at the age of fourteen. The Church recommends that its members become plant-based because the Bible teaches us that this was the original diet that God designed us to eat (Genesis 1:29). In fact, this mandate was one of the elements that attracted me to the Church. It made sense to me that if God designed us, He would be concerned about what we ate, and that what we eat would have an impact on the quality of our interaction with Him. (Throughout this essay I will use the terms *vegan* or *veganism* and *plant-based* interchangeably to essentially mean the same thing, which is a diet composed entirely of plant foods.)

YOU WILL KNOW THE TRUTH, AND THE TRUTH WILL SET YOU FREE.—JOHN 8:32 (NIV)

Up until that point in my life, I had been a big meat eater. While the SDA Church recommends that members become plant-based, it does not require it. It does, however, require that we stop eating animals the Bible considers "unclean." When I joined the Church, I complied with these stipulations, which meant I changed my diet substantially and no longer ate pork, shellfish, and the other "unclean" meats. Although I was trying to be more health conscious, I didn't become plant-based, because I simply didn't think I could live without eating hamburgers and steaks.

In September 1974, about eighteen months after I'd joined the Church, I found myself struggling with some personal issues. I was talking to God about it one night, when He said to me very clearly, "If you want a closer relationship with Me, you need to have a clearer mind. For that, you need a better diet. You have to stop eating meat." I remember the frisson of panic I felt at that moment, when I realized what He was asking me to do: to never eat meat again! I didn't think I could do it. I replied, "If You want me to stop, You've got to take away the desire to eat it." And He did. And I stopped!

I became a lacto-ovo vegetarian, which meant I continued to include eggs and dairy products in my diet along with plant foods, but I completely eliminated all animal flesh, including fish and other sea animals. Because I'm profoundly lactose intolerant, I never drank milk or ate yogurt. I was also never particularly fond of ice cream, so I didn't eat a lot of animal products even then. My limited animal-product intake during this period of my life mainly took the form of dairy and eggs in "invisible" forms, such as in baked goods, or cheese on pizza, or in a burrito. I transitioned to veganism around the year 2000.

When I initially turned plant-based, the benefits were clear and undeniable—not only physically but also spiritually. Within a matter of days, I had more energy, my mind was clearer, my acne cleared up, and I needed less sleep. More significantly, I felt that many of the barriers that had interfered with my ability to communicate and get closer to God were lowered or removed. And because of the great health benefits I had experienced, I felt compelled to share this good news with those around me. I began to give talks and share posters and literature about the plant-based diet with friends, relatives, and other Church members, and also with a variety of civic groups in the community. It was this passion that would eventually help lead me to study and practice medicine.

I went to California State University at Hayward (now Cal State East Bay) for my undergraduate degree, and Stanford University's School of Medicine for medical school. I completed my residency in internal medicine at Georgetown University in Washington, DC. I currently practice as a physician working in the ICU, taking care of critically ill patients, but I also work as an internal medicine doctor in several outpatient clinics in the DC metro area. Throughout my education, in my work, and as someone actively involved in the plant-based movement for well over three decades, I see on a daily basis how important it is to change our diet to reduce the risks for developing chronic conditions and to try to reverse those diseases we may be struggling with.

IN ALL YOUR GETTING, GET UNDERSTANDING.—PROVERBS 4:7 (NKJV)

My approach to advocacy is to use different arguments to appeal to different people, depending on where they are in their lives, and to avoid a one-size-fits-all approach. For me, a subject has always had to make sense in order for me to believe in and embrace it— and I have approached the issue of adopting a plant-based diet through that same lens. I want people to understand that human beings are neither omnivores nor carnivores, but rather are designed anatomically and physiologically to be *strict plant eaters*. That conclusion is based on considerable data I have collected through extensive research that shows that the closer humans get to a *purely* plant-based diet, the lower are our risks for a variety of diseases, the longer we live, and the more functional (including mentally) we remain throughout our lives. Moreover, there are abundant data that show that when humans consume a plant-based diet, it is much better for the environment and we leave a much smaller carbon footprint. This makes sense when you understand that being a plant-based species is our true ecological niche.

Once people have wrapped their minds around the reality that we are *meant* to be plant-based, it becomes possible to help them understand that it's possible to receive all the macro- and micro-nutrients we need on a purely plant-based diet. Indeed, my conclusion based on the scientific evidence is that plants provide a broader range and are *healthier* sources of the compounds and nutrients that are so important for the proper functioning of our bodies. In fact, many nutrients such as fibers and a variety of essential phytonutrients can only be found in plant foods. When people eat a Western-style diet centered on animal foods and containing limited amounts of plants, they often lack many of these key phytonutrients and cellular cofactors, and this may help explain the increasing prevalence of disorders like chronic fatigue syndrome, fibromyalgia, depression, anxiety, and other ailments.

The health benefits of a plant-based diet and lifestyle are clear-cut and incontrovertible. We now have well over a hundred years of accumulated medical and scientific research showing the benefits of plant-based diets for preventing and curing chronic diseases, decreasing risk for autoimmune diseases and infections, increasing longevity, and decreasing the risk of developing dementias as we age. Moreover, the latest research is also showing that plant-based diets enhance and optimize human physical and mental conditioning and performance. Documentary films such as *Game Changers*, *What the Health*, *Forks Over Knives*, and *Eating You Alive*, among others, also document the tremendous health benefits that come from adopting a fully whole-foods, plant-based diet.

Although I have dedicated my professional life to encouraging people to change their diet to improve their health and decrease their risk of disease, I recognize that dietary habits can be hard to change—particularly when it comes to one's family and friends. My grandmother was from the South, and a very good cook. She was used to putting pork, ham hocks, and other animal-based flavorings into her vegetable dishes, but she changed and learned to use liquid smoke, herbs, and seasonings. Nonetheless, she continued to eat meat (although less than she formerly did). I tried to convince her of the benefits of a fully plant-based diet, and that being "half in, half out" didn't work as well, because the moment you start eating those foods that encourage inflammation you negate much of the benefit you've obtained from eating plants.

Likewise, one of my friends was having issues with his prostate, and I explained that he should stop consuming dairy products. He did cut down, and that has helped. He changed to drinking almond milk and cut out most cheese, and he eats veggie burgers instead of regular burgers now. But I'm frustrated that many of my loved ones have not benefitted as much as I think they could if they'd become completely plant-based. I think most people who are plant-based experience very similar resistance with their families. Even Jesus noted, "A prophet is not without honor except in his own town, among his relatives and in his own home" (Mark 6:4 NIV).

CAGES

From the moment he enters the world in the country that is the United States, the Black male child is maligned, abused, and socially handicapped. We're told in thousands of different ways that we're somehow defective and not quite good enough. We're taught through images and words that we're not as smart or as capable; that we don't function well as heads of households; and that we don't take care of our own. This relentless barrage of disapproval and disparagement is designed to bring us down, destroy our self-esteem, circumscribe our worldview, and make us see ourselves and each other negatively. Whether we realize it or not, we consciously and unconsciously ingest these destructive images and messages of having less value and ability. If we don't learn to step back and take a critical examination of what is happening to us, that negativity can affect how we view ourselves and each other, and how we relate to our children.

Many years ago, I realized that America only likes and feels comfortable with Black men when we're confined in cages. Those cages can be either literal cages, such as a prison cell, or virtual—such as on a football field, in a baseball diamond, on a basketball court, in a boxing ring, or on an entertainment stage. As long as we remain in that real or virtual cage, society considers us a defined and "known" entity. Essentially, America only feels "safe" and comfortable with us as long as we're confined and limited to that circumscribed place and space.

The phenomenon of "driving while Black" (which is the American version of "Show me your papers!") is one way of letting us know we are out of our assigned area, place, or space, and that we don't "belong." And if we step out of that prescribed space either figuratively or literally, then God help us! We will have become what American society fears, abhors, and does not understand: an independent, free-thinking, free-ranging—and therefore "threatening"—Black man.

This was never better illustrated than in 2018 when LeBron James spoke out in support of the Black Lives Matter movement and against ongoing police murders of unarmed Black men and women. In response to his comments, Fox Network host Laura Ingraham uttered her infamous comment that LeBron should just "shut up and dribble." When Black men step outside the cages this society has created or imagined for us, and thereby create discomfort for white America, we're likely to have the actual police or some other entity representing the "policing power" of our state, school, or employer called or in some other way brought to bear on us. All we have to do is dare to engage in the kinds of ordinary, innocuous activities all white Americans take for granted, such as going for a drive, walking into a Starbucks, visiting the library, or bird-watching in a park.

BLACKNESS, FATHERHOOD, AND THE AMERICAN EXPERIENCE

The first cage America tries to force us into is the one it seeks to place around our minds. Our society attempts to limit what we believe we can be as Black men and to make us think there is only a truncated list of things we're capable of doing and achieving. Most of those "society-approved" activities involve us using our bodies in lieu of our minds. America has always coveted the bodies of Black men as slaves, laborers, athletes, warriors, entertainment icons, or sexual objects. But it has rarely if ever wanted our minds or thoughts.

Our job as Black men, Black fathers, and Black male vegans, therefore, is to refuse to allow ourselves to be confined to those mental, virtual, or physical cages. That includes the cultural cage that defines a man as an emotionally limited, violence-prone, meat-eating, randy automaton. Our challenge is to ensure that when we step outside these artificial and imposed confines, we are strong enough, self-aware enough, and fit enough in *every* capacity. It's imperative that we be prepared so that when society confronts us—as it surely will—we will be able to resist them mentally, spiritually, and physically, and be able to maintain our hold on who we really are. Having and retaining that strength has to start with reclaiming our health.

Historically, the first step in the subjugation and control of any population or people has been to gain control of their bodies and their health. In the history of Africans in America, the influence and effects of the shackles and chains of slavery are obvious on our bodies and health. What are less obvious but even more pernicious have been the influence and effects of what enslaved prisoners were fed and, unfortunately, then learned to eat during their years in bondage. Africans imprisoned on the slave labor camps known as plantations were force-fed the literal garbage of those facilities and did their best to turn that refuse into acceptable food. They were given the rotten and rotting cast-offs of the slave owners, which is why they got the feet, tails, ears, entrails, and neckbones of the animals.

This is one of the reasons African-Americans traditionally use a lot of seasoning in our cooking. Originally, it was to mask the flavor of rotting body parts. These "plantation food" diets were very different from the traditional West African cuisines, which are rich in green leafy plants, legumes, whole grains, root vegetables, and fruits, etc. Over time, this plantation food led to increased illness and chronic disease in the enslaved individuals, and although illness decreased productivity somewhat, it also made the inmates more docile and easier to control. Sick people are less apt and less able to foment insurrection or try to run away, and they are less likely to run off and leave a sick parent or family member.

Unfortunately, after the *institution* of slavery ended, we kept the *culture* of slavery with us by continuing to eat a diet that is essentially a vestige of the plantation and oppression. The real tragedy of the Black experience in America when it comes to food is that a plant-based diet *is our true heritage* as people of color, not so-called Soul Food. Plantation food is not Soul Food and is not our true cultural heritage. Study after study has shown this food leads to excess disease and premature death in Black populations.

"IF YOU WANT TO BE STRONG AS AN OX, YOU SHOULD EAT LIKE ONE."—UNKNOWN

To improve our health, we have to rethink and redefine what it means to be male and masculine. Too often, "being a man" is associated with meat eating and carnivorousness, which are cultural values and practices largely originating in northern European cultures, where plant foods weren't available year round, and people learned to depend heavily on animals for sustenance, particularly during winter months.

Unfortunately, either by direct observation or through cultural transmission, humans have become mesmerized by the drama of the "hunt." We're transfixed by the sight of lions and wolves chasing down and killing other animals. But what people don't realize is that those carnivores almost always live on the edge of starvation, because hunting is inherently inefficient. These animals are actually rather limited in their exercise ability and endurance and usually only make a kill every seven to ten days. Carnivores as a group have little stamina and somewhat modest strength, which is why they typically prey on the sick, the old, the lame, or the very young. This is what they are *supposed* to do, because in so doing, they keep their prey species strong by removing the defective individuals and less viable genes.

But the biggest, strongest terrestrial animals are now and always have been the plant eaters! No carnivore in its right mind would attack a healthy adult elephant, rhino, hippo, or giraffe (or, for that matter, a large adult Sauropod)! This is because those animals are so large and immensely strong and robust that they'd easily kill or severely injure even the largest carnivores (including a T-Rex). When humans built our civilizations, we didn't hitch our plows, wagons, and stagecoaches to lions, tigers, or bears; we used horses, oxen, and mules because only those plant-eating animals had the strength, stamina, and endurance to get the work done. So we need to reimagine what it means to be "strong" and healthy, because as research and time have shown, meat-based diets result in excess disease and premature death in humans.

What else does accruing, having, and exercising that kind of strength entail? It means that a Black father is present in his family, involved in the lives of his children, and is supportive to his spouse or significant other. A huge part of that role is to make sure not only that you are providing for your family, but also that you are proffering the right things for the family.

The food we feed our children is vital because research shows it will have profound, life-long effects on their health and longevity. Studies have shown that animal food–centered diets consumed by children can increase their risk of developing heart disease, dementia, and breast, prostate, or colon cancer as many as sixty years later! In addition, the food we eat as children and young adults will also impact *future generations* through the epigenetically mediated changes to our DNA that science shows can be passed down to our descendants over three or four generations. With the food choices we make, we're teaching our children dietary habits and practices that will either benefit or hurt them throughout their lifetimes. As has been famously observed, "the reason diseases run in families is because dietary habits run in families!"

I know it can be difficult not to feed your kids unhealthy, disease-causing foods, and fast food junk and other garbage. When I was raising teenagers, we used to get into a running battle about what was acceptable to eat. I admit I can be glib and flippant at times, and I'd tell my kids that they needed me around because they didn't have a mind mature enough to make the right decisions. I jokingly told them I thought all teenagers should be lobotomized at age thirteen and then have the procedure reversed when they turned twenty-five and were mature enough to make better decisions. When they complained about the food I provided, I told them I refused to buy and feed them poison, and since they didn't have jobs, they had no say in the matter. I explained that my job as a loving parent was to do what was best for them, not try to win a popularity contest. I admitted to them that when I was a young teenager I would have liked nothing more than to sit at home watching TV all day eating french fries and hamburgers. Thankfully, I said, my parents didn't let me do that. They forced me to get off my butt, go to school, make my education a priority, and eat more balanced meals. In a like manner, I was going to bring my children up in a way I knew was best for them—and that I didn't negotiate with terrorists, especially unemployed ones.

When I think of my parents now, I can see that they worked incredibly hard as they raised my brothers and me! I still marvel at how my mother every day would go into the kitchen at about two o'clock in the afternoon, pull out a host of things from the cabinet that didn't look anything like food, and by the time my father was pulling into the driveway, she'd placed a multi-course meal on the table: salad, vegetables, main course, the works. My parents didn't know what I know in terms of how important a plant-based diet is, but they had a relatively sophisticated understanding of nutrition as it relates to being healthy, particularly regarding food. This is why I believe passionately that the center of any father's guidance and instruction for his children must be to give them the best options for health and longevity, and to help them reach their peak performance, mentally as well as physically. And that is best achieved through a plant-based diet.

WHAT ARE YOU DOING HERE. . . ?—1 KINGS 19:9 (NIV)

We now have a choice to reject the dietary vestiges of slavery and European patriarchy, to no longer eat "Soul Food," and to embrace our true cultural and dietary heritage. Doing so will give us back the dignity of our true heritage and will restore and affirm our collective health. Changing our diets in this way will help deliver us from the chronic health problems that plague our community.

I realize that many in the Black community don't have easy access to fresh fruits and vegetables due to the lack of supermarkets in their neighborhoods. This is often a function and result of decades of discrimination, and discriminatory housing and zoning policies and practices. Additionally, due to socioeconomic factors, many people might not be able to afford perishable foods if they are available, or they might not have any place to store them due to homelessness or unstable living conditions. This is frustrating, infuriating, and an ongoing tragedy. The correlation between food and poverty is profound, complex, and multi-layered, and needs to be better understood. But it's essential we understand it, for three reasons.

First, it is almost impossible to pull yourself out of poverty if you're sick—particularly if an individual has a major chronic disease. All the family's resources and time are going to be spent trying to treat the disease and to get the individual to and from doctor's visits. And it is often the case that these diseases affect the primary wage earner, which greatly impacts the family's income and limits socioeconomic mobility. What money the family has goes to buying medicine, paying for doctors' visits, and so forth, with little left over for improving housing circumstances or providing better educational opportunities for children.

Second, those chronic diseases often lead to permanent disabilities. Type 2 diabetes, for instance, is at epidemic proportions within our community. According to the U.S. Department of Health and Human Services Office of Minority Health, African-American adults are 60 percent more likely than non-Hispanic white adults to be diagnosed with diabetes, and twice as likely to die from diabetes as non-Hispanic whites. We are also 3.5 times more likely to experience end-stage renal diseases than non-Hispanic whites.[*] About one in four Black women over fifty-five years old have diabetes,[†] and Black women have a 63 percent higher risk for diabetes than non-Hispanic white women.[‡] These devastating health profiles are decimating our community and keep many hundreds of thousands of us mired in intractable poverty.

Third, we should be clear that the enormous health disparities that exist between the African-American community and other ethnic groups in the United States are no accident.

---

[*] U.S. Department of Health and Human Services Office of Minority Health, "Diabetes and African-Americans", n.d., https://minorityhealth.hhs.gov/omh/browse.aspx?lvl=4&lvlid=18.

[†] Walnut Hill Obstetrics & Gynecology Associates, "Diabetes and African-American Women," n.d., https://walnuthillobgyn.com/blog/diabetes-and-african-american-women/.

[‡] Julie K. Bower, et al. "Racial/Ethnic Differences in Diabetes Screening and Hyperglycemia Among US Women After Gestational Diabetes," *Preventing Chronic Disease* 2019 16, http://dx.doi.org/10.5888/pcd16.190144.

Throughout the history of this country, people of color have been removed from areas where they are self-sufficient and able to grow and eat their own plant foods, and been placed in circumstances where they are forced to become dependent on the government for food handouts.

This happened to Africans when they were kidnapped from their ancestral lands and brought to the New World to be enslaved on sugar, rice, tobacco, and cotton-growing plantations owned by Europeans. It happened to Native Americans when they had their lands stolen from them to create these lucrative plantations and they were either slaughtered or brutally force-marched onto and confined to marginal, non-arable tracts of land designated as "reservations." It happened to New World Hispanic populations who'd lived for thousands of years in western and southwestern parts of North America when their lands were wrested from Mexico and these peoples were suddenly deemed "illegal" or "undocumented." These individuals were then forced into a tenuous, semi-nomadic existence that placed them and their families at the mercy of unscrupulous, exploitative American agricultural employers. The government, in turn, sells the people in such vulnerable, at-risk communities unhealthy, processed commodity products to enable farmers and agribusiness to make billions of dollars at the expense of the health of these communities.

On top of all of this, fast food chains deliberately target low-income communities of color in which to place their establishments, and from them they purvey their subsidized poison as cheaply as possible. People in these communities think they're eating an affordable meal, but what they're really getting is toxic garbage that is causing men and women to come down with colon cancer in their thirties and forties and breast and prostate cancer in their forties and fifties! This is in addition to the astronomical rates of heart disease, hypertension, stroke, diabetes, and autoimmune diseases we see in our communities.

This unhealthy food is killing us—across the board. Most recently we have seen in the COVID pandemic that people of color are at increased risk of contracting and succumbing to this disease because of the high prevalence of people suffering from multiple comorbidities and reduced immunity due to chronically ingesting nutritionally bankrupt unhealthy animal and fast foods. COVID has inadvertently highlighted the ways in which systemic racism intersects with poor-quality food and limited food availability to create and exacerbate health disparities and increased disease risk in the Black community.

A SACRED RESPONSIBILITY

We live in a profoundly important time in American history: the issues that have held African-Americans down—policing, poverty, poor health, injustice, systemic racism, and lack of opportunity—are coming to the fore. Many of these problems have existed since the inception of this country because of its "original sin," which was codified racism in the form of the legal enslavement of human beings based on their "race." America and its founding elites had to invent, embellish, and embrace *their theory of racial inferiority* to justify their abuses and mistreatment of Black people.

Through DNA studies of the human genome, we now know that the entire concept of race is an illusion that has no basis in actual science. Race is an apparition conjured by Europeans to explain and justify the brutality and legal cruelties visited on Black people and other people of color. This shape-shifting apparition is propped up and maintained by institutional and systemic racism through its various forms and surrogates. These include continuing to teach a sanitized, white-washed version of American history that celebrates and promulgates the myth of white exceptionalism, while glossing over or minimizing the evils, cruelty, brutality, and hypocrisy of Black enslavement and Native American genocide. These fictionalized accounts of American history also downplay or completely ignore the contributions, accomplishments, and actions of people of color and women in helping to establish and advance this nation.

In my own way, I have tried to address and redress these pernicious lies, distortions, and myths as a doctor, a citizen, and a plant-based advocate. For instance, I have voted in every single election since I turned eighteen. It's not just personally an act of civic responsibility; I consider it a sacred responsibility. As the 1989 movie *Glory* starring Denzel Washington recounts, Black men who had been slaves fought for the Union Army in the Civil War, and gave their lives, so that I—and every Black man and woman who came after—could enjoy benefits and rights that were denied to them. One of those rights was the right to vote. We owe it to them to honor their sacrifice and courage, and likewise to recognize the struggles of Black men and women who fought for our rights through Reconstruction, Jim Crow, World War II, and the civil rights era, and broke the back of the regressive, discriminatory, racist legislation, and lynching and redlining so we could run for office and fill in our ballot. It really is the very least we can do.

I cannot forget that some of this work took place in my lifetime. I remember watching tapes of Fannie Lou Hamer at the 1968 Democratic Convention. She is famous for saying in 1964, "I am sick and tired of being sick and tired." She was not well educated by conventional standards, but she was nevertheless a brilliantly intelligent sharecropper from Mississippi who had to deal with the Ku Klux Klan on a regular basis. Like many such folk, including Medgar Evers, who was shot by a white supremacist in Jackson, Mississippi, in 1963 for trying to register Black people to vote, they knew and dealt with real *personal* danger from violent domestic terrorist organizations and individuals like KKK members and Southern white supremacists every day of their lives.

I carry all of these lives and deaths with me when I enter that voting booth. I may not be thrilled by the candidates; I may be disenchanted by the democratic process; I may feel alienated from the politicians, but I can't *not* vote! Too many lives have been taken and too much blood has been spilled for me not to vote. All of us have to realize democracies are always coalitions and collections of cobbled-together compromises. Nobody ever gets everything they want: if you expect that, you'll end up "holding out" your whole life! The entire history of Black people in America has been a series of "hold-your-nose" compromises with less-than-perfect candidates, many of whom were frankly racist. But we've had to vote for them because they were "less" racist than their opponents. That is what has gotten us closer to where we needed to be.

Black Americans have always had to take a strategic approach to voting and in our political outlook. Sadly, our progress in this nation has always been incremental—painfully and frustratingly so. I find the demand for and/or expectation of absolute perfection in a candidate to be immature and offensive, an attitude that is the province of privilege, which is a luxury that people of color don't have in America. The bottom line is: I may not get the *exact* result I want in a given election, but then you don't always land a date when you go looking for one! That doesn't mean you stop looking.

Furthermore, only by running for office and voting for candidates will we begin to shift the policy emphases of this country away from the destructive practices that have kept our community down. We need to restructure tax laws so that a good education won't bankrupt you or keep you from pursuing your dreams because you have to repay punishingly high student loans for tuition. We need affordable housing so people aren't living on the streets, and we need fair taxation so that the income disparity between the one percent and everyone else is closed. Right now, the middle class has been squeezed into the working poor.

We need to stop worshiping wealthy tycoons and pay people a living wage. It is unconscionable that a huge percentage of Walmart's workforce has to depend on food stamps and other government support programs just to feed their families and make ends meet, while the corporation and its owners make billions of dollars in profit every year. The American taxpayer is effectively subsidizing Walmart's profit margin every year. The company could afford to take a few billion dollars less in profit in order to pay its workforce a decent, living wage and get off the public dole.

A political and professional class that is more representative of the racial make-up of the United States is also essential. Black folks need to grasp their own power and recognize that although we may be marginalized and not in the majority, we have, according to our Constitution, inalienable rights that are no less valuable or important than anyone else's.

We're finally, subsequent to the murder of George Floyd, beginning to see movement on policing. We need police departments to be forced to institute screening for racist ideologies. We need them to acknowledge what the FBI has found out: that white nationalists have infiltrated them. And we need them ejected. We also need gender- and ethnicity-sensitivity training for those who have the ability to use deadly force. And we need swift justice for those who are killing unarmed civilians who are people of color.

Now, I understand that police officers do a dangerous job, but that doesn't give them a right to kill people, simply because they're scared. Their job is to protect and serve others, and doing so involves risk. I know this because I too took a similar oath when I became a doctor. I vividly remember when I was an intern during the AIDS crisis. A patient came in to the hospital who clearly was in the advanced stages of AIDS. One of the other interns refused to draw blood because he was afraid of accidentally sticking himself with a needle. The attending physician pulled that intern aside and read him the riot act. He told him, "Either you go into the room and draw the patient's blood, or you will be kicked out of this program. You took an oath of responsibility to care for sick people when you took this job. You don't get to choose who you're going to serve based on what diseases they have. Being a doctor comes with some risk, and if you don't want to take that risk, then you need to do something else."

I've never forgotten that incident, and it is why I take my responsibilities very seriously as a citizen, a doctor, and an advocate. Given the sacrifices of my parents and grandparents to ensure that I had educational opportunities they never had, I could not imagine the kind of shame I would have to bear if I didn't take advantage of those opportunities to help others and to engage productively with the rest of society. This is why I am infuriated when some people simply want to sit around, indulge in mind-altering substances, listen to ignorant people on the radio, and then watch so-called entertainers act like bug-eyed minstrels in commercials pouring champagne on a cellphone and then stupidly give their political support to a vile racist and hate-monger.

My father is unfortunately suffering from dementia now, but I remember him as a highly intelligent man who, if he'd grown up in a different time than the 1950s, would have been a college graduate, and perhaps gone on to study law or engineering. He worked every hour he could. Indeed, the only time I remember him staying at home from work was when his arm literally got caught in a machine, and the company where he worked, called General Cable, told him he had to go to the doctor to be stitched up. He did, and he was back at work the next day. That's the man he was. I take inspiration from him for his perseverance and belief in what he was doing. I take courage from him and our ancestors and pioneers. It is my motivation and sustenance, and I try to instill that in others. By realizing what I owe these people, I gain strength in my commitments to generations after me. When I get to the end of my life, I want to be able to look back and say I did my part, and that I fulfilled my sacred obligation.

[Y]OUR BODIES ARE TEMPLES OF THE HOLY SPIRIT...—1 CORINTHIANS 6:19 (NIV)

The Bible teaches that our body is "God's temple." Though this passage is well known and often repeated, I don't think most people really understand the true import and deeper meaning of these words. In the Book of Genesis, we are told that prior to the entrance of sin into the world, humans enjoyed the wonder, happiness, and privilege of face-to-face communication with God. Once we became sinful, however, we could no longer physically be in God's presence, because He is holy, sinless, and perfect, and His "essence" would destroy us as naturally as light destroys darkness. To get around that problem (until we are made perfect again) God promised He would put His Spirit within us to show us the way to salvation, and to counsel us on the right paths to take in life (Ezekiel 36:27; Isaiah 30:21; 50:4). What that means practically is that God must now communicate with us through our *minds*. Thus, the *strength* and *quality* of that communication will depend on the health and vitality of our minds. As God told me over forty years ago, if we want a closer relationship with Him, we will need clearer minds. That clearer mind will arise out of the healthier, stronger *body* (tissue) and more robust and finely tuned *physiology* (cellular functioning) brought about by eating an entirely plant-based diet.

I have discussed the physical benefits of a plant-based diet. Another important but often underappreciated aspect of plant-based diets is the effect they have on the human psyche. Multiple studies have shown that healthy vegan diets markedly decrease risk for depression and anxiety disorders. Furthermore, research conducted and experience gained in adult and juvenile correctional facilities that provide entirely plant-based meals for their inmates have shown a significant decrease in overall aggression, inter-inmate conflicts, and violent and aggressive behaviors toward staff.

In addition to the foregoing clinical observations, many people self-report that after changing to a vegan diet, their mental outlook and thought process changed to become more kind, thoughtful, and compassionate toward other people and other beings. Although these personal reports are anecdotal and therefore non-scientific, they are nonetheless consistent and typical in nature across many individuals, which implies that this change in psychology is a real and reliable phenomenon. Hence, adopting a vegan/plant-based diet will not only heal your body, but evidence and experience suggest it will likely also help heal your mind and soul.

Health is our ultimate wealth; without it, we have nothing. I remember reading a poignant post on social media from a woman who was a very successful author. In effect, she said: "My money, possessions, and big house—all that I have accumulated throughout my life—don't mean anything now, because they cannot save my life or restore my health." I took her to mean, of course, that material possessions won't help you in the final analysis if your life is ebbing away because of poor life decisions. It's also a lesson all of us need to make sure we don't squander our most valuable resource: our health.

> "Of all the words of tongue or pen, none are sadder than these, 'It might have been'."—from "Maud Muller," by John Greenleaf Whittier

I want to remind every reader that all of us were born without any dietary preferences. All of the foods we feel we like in life, someone *taught* us to like. And just as we learned to like things that may not be good for us, we can unlearn those bad habits and learn new ones that improve and preserve our health, and don't injure the planet or other sentient beings. No piece of dead flesh, cheese, or strangled, suffocated sea creature is worth the price of our health or that of our families. Our happiness and health need not be predicated on the suffering and death of other creatures nor the destruction of Earth. Let us learn to let go of traditional ways of doing things and free ourselves from the cultural cages that confine us and step into and embrace the freedom and improved health that a plant-based diet and lifestyle brings. ☀

15

PLANTHERO

An Interview with Charles McCoy

Brotha Vegan: *Tell us about yourself and how you became interested in plants?*
Charles McCoy: My name is Charles McCoy, and I'm affectionately known as the PlantHero. I'm a certified plant-based nutritionist and vegan chef, and I have been a consultant and spokesman for a range of organizations and products.

I have a college degree in horticulture and landscape design, which is what my true background is. I was doing landscaping, initially, and people would ask me whether I could help out with their garden. Because of my passion for horticulture and dealing with plants, I gravitated toward gardening. However, at that stage I was not paying attention to permaculture, the health of the soil, but rather was concerned with just getting things growing. I didn't care what I used: the herbicide Roundup, anything! As long as it killed the weeds and helped me to make things grow, I used it.

About ten years ago, I visited a school for Career Day. I'd brought along a bunch of gargantuan vegetables for the kids to try and to take home. When I went to give one of the tomatoes to a little kid, he said, "My dad told me that anything that's big like that is a GMO." Now, I'd heard the term, but I didn't know what it meant, and I just said, "Oh." I was kind of ashamed. In fact, this kid was adamant about not taking the tomato, and the other kids didn't either, because of him. This little kid sent me back to school and taught me an important lesson: you can learn a lot from people if you just pay attention.

I had to relearn about permaculture and GMOs and became more concerned about what I was planting and putting into the soil. I went online to the College of Herbal Medicine, which was easier for me than sitting in a classroom, especially since I was very busy. A schoolroom was also difficult for me because I think I have a form of ADHD. Labels are problematic, because it's sad to stigmatize someone—especially when they're a child. There's no telling what they could do when they grow older, if their mind is allowed to flow and they can be active and creative.

I chose the College of Herbal Medicine because I was interested in what herbs could do, and felt they offered solutions to a lot of health concerns. What I then discovered was that what you eat can be your medicine; and if you don't eat properly, then you can end up eating medicine for food. I received a nutritional health certificate from Cornell University in 2013 and was certified as a nutritionist with the College of Herbal Medicine that same year.

BV: *When did you go vegan?*

CM: I went vegan four years ago, at the age of 62. I'm not really comfortable with the word *vegan*, because for me veganism is not an issue of food; it's a way of life. I always had a concern for animals, the environment, and human rights.

BV: *How did you get your nickname, PlantHero?*

CM: I was the green roof engineer for the Hyatt Hotel in Connecticut. The management sent me down to The Big Show, which is what they called the Grand Hyatt in Manhattan, where they were going to institute a green roof program. It was during the recession, just after Obama was elected, and so the company had cut back a lot on expenditures and had put the green roof program on hold. Every year, they promised to bring it back and didn't. Finally, they laid me off, and I was miserable. I'm a doer; I wanted to be out doing stuff, even if it wasn't work I wanted to do.

Since I was out of work, I began to spend more time with my children, including my youngest daughter, who was in first or second grade at the time. One day, she was stung in the eye by a bee and became incredibly scared of anything that flies. I felt it was my job to let her know why bees are valuable. I began to read all kinds of books to her while she was at home, with her eye swollen. For a week to ten days, I read and talked to her, and we went on nature walks. I tried to teach her to stay calm around insects, to recognize that when we humans go outside and in nature, we're in *their* world. I told her that if they were in the house, I could understand if she wanted to get rid of them, but that she could open a window and let them go, because they were probably trapped. They didn't want to be inside, any more than she wanted them to be inside.

Finally, my daughter went back to school. Three or four days later, I was dropping her off at school, and the teacher came running up behind me. Now, my daughter is feisty; she don't take mess from nobody; and I started thinking that somebody had bothered my daughter about her eye and she'd socked them. So, with the teacher yelling "Mr. McCoy! Mr. McCoy!" at me as I'm walking away from the school, I'm thinking, *What did my daughter do?!*

Finally, she caught up with me, and said, "Would you mind coming to the school to read some of the books you've been reading to your daughter?" (I did not see *that* coming!)

And I said, "How did you know that I'm reading to my daughter? And what made you want to track me down and ask me to come to the school?"

The teacher said, "Well, she's been explaining how you've been telling her about the birds and the bees." The look on my face must have been something, because she explained what she meant, and we had a good laugh over that.

"You know," I replied, "I'm not working right now, and I'll be more than glad to do that. How soon?"

"As soon as you can," she said. "Because everybody's really excited." She raised her arm. "The class is really up to here with what you've got to say and what you know."

The next day, I took some of the books I'd been reading and sat on the floor and talked to the kids. I'm a very expressive, dramatic reader, and the kids listened and laughed and had fun. I even did a little improv, and they *loved* that.

The next thing I know is that the school asked me to come to some other classes. And so I thought, *OK, now I've gotta up my game.* And because I'm creative, I created this character called PlantHero.

That's how the name came about: because I wanted the kids to know about the pollinators and how the plants need them. That bee sting changed my daughter's and my life.

BV: *And how did you get the costume?*
CM: I went to one of the caricaturists on 42nd Street in Manhattan and told him that I wanted a picture of me happy, standing on top of a building like a superhero. Then I

created a superhero costume: green bodysuit and a yellow cape, with a marijuana plant
headdress and goggles. And the kids loved it!

As fate would have it, a week later I was called back to work. And I wasn't happy at all: I
had no tolerance for anybody, and I just wasn't *there*. Then a friend of mind in the healthcare
industry told me there was money available for companies to start a horticultural therapy
program, and thought I'd be a great fit for it and that I should interview for a position.

I was unsure, but I put on my suit and tie, and went for an interview at a well-known
healthcare company. There were about twenty or thirty others there to be interviewed also,
who looked way more qualified to be horticultural therapists than I did.

BV: *How so?*

CM: Well, I felt that I didn't have what it takes. I was sitting, waiting for the interviewers
to call my name, and I saw these guys coming in and out and they looked really sharp:

younger, better dressed. I thought to myself, *I've gotta do something to surprise these people when I go in there.* I returned to my car, where I had my PlantHero costume. I put it on and walked back in. The woman at the front desk thought I was in the wrong part of the building, and said, "You're supposed to be down the hall." (I didn't even know what she was saying—or what was going on down that hall!)

"No, I'm here to interview," I said, and told her my name.

She gave me a look. "And you're going to go to an interview like *that*, sir?" (All the other people waiting to be interviewed were looking at me like, *Look at this cat! What is wrong with this guy?*)

I was meant to be third on the list, but the woman said, "Look, I'm going to have you go in right now." I think she wanted to get rid of me because she thought I was a knucklehead or something was wrong with me.

Anyway, I walked into the interviewing room, and they went berserk. I think they were shocked I'd had the nerve to do it. But they told me I'd been the highlight, because everyone else looked the same. They wanted to know what I could offer, and I told them. And you know what? They asked me how much I wanted per hour and hired me on the spot.

BV: *How much did you ask for?*

CM: $200 an hour. Honestly, I was getting so much money with them at one time that I used to feel legitimately bad. I worked four or five hours a day, four or five days a week. We moved, I bought a new car—all because of that costume.

BV: *Tell us about your career as a chef.*

CM: I actually started cooking when I was seven or eight years old. I was a troublesome kid coming up—getting punished all the time and made to stay in my room. So I gravitated to my grandmother, who did most of the cooking. And she let me be in the kitchen with her, and I would learn through touching and preparing the food with her. You see, my grandmother was a live-in maid, and sometimes we wouldn't see her for a couple of months. In her absence, I found myself in the kitchen, which (along with the bathroom) were the only places I was allowed to go when I was being punished.

I went to New York Restaurant School purely because I happened to be on 34th Street in Manhattan. (The school subsequently moved to the Village.) I was walking on 34th Street when someone stopped me. The school was trying to get people to fill out forms so the school could get funding via enrollment, and I went in—without any intention of actually signing up for a class, especially as it was clear I would be the only Black person there. Nonetheless, I filled out the forms, and was denied funding. However, the administration liked how I handled myself in the test kitchen and that I came out of Harlem. They wanted a little bit more color in the classroom, I guess [*laughing*], and I didn't mind being the token Black guy. So they gave me a shot, and I did well enough. I ended up taking up an internship at Sylvia's [the legendary Harlem restaurant], but I was fired because they had a thing for char. You know what char is?

BV: *It's like the goop that's been cooked for a long time on the grill.*
CM: Exactly. I was scraping and cleaning the grill all the time, and they were upset with me. "What are you doing?" they would say. "You can't take the seasoning off." That's what they called it: "the seasoning"! But it was unsanitary. So they gave me menial work, and I left.

I'd befriended a man who ate at Sylvia's who owned a building, and we made a deal to open a restaurant I called Chewy's. "Chewy" was the nickname I gave my son Charles Jr. because he ate everything. Charles Jr. was interesting because he used to eat all his vegetables, and the meat would be the last; and when he wanted seconds, it would always be more vegetables. Whatever the vegetable, he wanted more of it! Chewy's was a lot of work. Unfortunately, I got sidetracked and neglected the business—staying out late and calling other people in to open it up. I eventually turned the restaurant over to my brother Jimmy, a.k.a. "Pop."

BV: *You're a vegan chef. What's the difference between a cook and a chef?*
CM: The difference is that you can be taught to be a cook, but you can't be taught to be a chef. A cook will know the basics for different things: the herbs, the seasonings, and the temperature and so forth. But when you're a chef, you're not out to satisfy everybody. In fact, you're gonna dissatisfy a lot of people before you get the dish right. The chef is

the creative side of the cook—an artist with the stove as his easel. You're using different thicknesses of brush to paint on the canvas: a little red or blue, and you see the shapes forming. You use saffron or green onions or shallots, instead of scallions.

And sometimes you fail in your experiment: you'll give a dish to ten people, and eight people will hate it, and two will offer suggestions—things to add, or ways to prepare it. And you'll go back to the lab and try again. For instance, the first person who thought to take an artichoke, take the guts out, and stuff it with breadcrumbs and herbs was a chef. It takes creativity. You have to take what's normal to people, and put a whole new spin on it.

A chef is also an explorer. People shouldn't limit themselves to the supermarket or even the green market; they need to go to other cultural places—such as a Chinese supermarket. You ask questions there: "How did you fix it? What do you do with it?" And then you think to yourself, "My culture might not like it like that, but how about if I did *this* to it?" So, you adapt it and you present it, always risking the fact that people might say, "What the heck is this?" and not eat it.

That's what qualifies me to be a chef: because all chefs are self-taught at that point of creativity. The more you teach yourself and learn from experience, the higher up the scale you go. Now, being a cook can be very boring, and some people don't want to be a chef, because it's intimidating to be thrown a bunch of stuff and have to create a dish.

BV: *Tell us about the time you appeared on* Shark Tank.
CM: Well, as you know, I'm a horticulturist, and I've had a couple of horticultural businesses. I used to live in Connecticut, where I was the head horticulturist and a designer for a landscape company that handled the estates of Luther Vandross, Donna Summer, Keith Richards, Michael Bolton, and Diana Ross. One of my biggest contracts was for Martha Stewart's property.

I grew up on the Harlem streets, and I was a hustler. I always made money, but I found out that when you chase the money, you'll end up out of breath. I never had a problem making money, and I made a lot of it with this horticultural business. I'm always looking for the home run and either avoiding the difficult stuff or hoping it goes away, and I stay away from the haters. Because all that stuff is a distraction, and you have to get rid of it or reduce it—or at least not worry about it. Because of this background, I bought cars—Range Rovers—and neglected what I should have been doing, such as paying taxes. And I ended up owing a lot in back taxes.

I had been in communication for a number of years with Duncan Burns, the inventor of VeggiDome, who used to work for ABC and on a number of feature films. He'd always respected what I was trying to do with PlantHero, and was very concerned about health and trying to make sure that people eat whole foods and cut down on waste. Duncan presented me with his idea, and I helped him tweak the concept.

I told Duncan that his idea was so good that he should think about going on *Shark Tank* with it. He told me that he had connections with folks on the set and that he'd reached out to them. The producers were impressed with the idea and they wanted Duncan to come out to California for the three auditions. Well, Duncan wanted me to be the promoter of it because I'm gregarious and he's not. He was the numbers guy, but I own thirty-two different costumes, and I can make a sale! I turned myself into a big carrot for *Shark Tank*.

So I went for the first audition, and passed. For the second one, I had to fill out a lot of forms to say I wasn't a pedophile or an axe murderer. I skipped the question about the tax issues, not because I was trying to be nefarious but because I didn't think that was their business. Now, this was the winter of 2017, and Southern California was experiencing mudslides because they'd had a lot of fires in the summer, and then winter had been very rainy. As it turned out, they ended up giving us the seed money but not taping us, because the mudslides slowed up production.

BV: *Tell us about VeggiDome.*

CM: The VeggiDome is a glass container that minimizes waste. When people buy vegetables they often put them in the crisper, which is the container at the bottom of the fridge, and forget about them, because "Out of sight, out of mind," right? The VeggiDome keeps vegetables fresh and, because it is in front of you, it makes you remember to eat fresh vegetables.

The dome itself is made of glass and not plastic, which is fine, but it can mean they break in the shipping and they're heavy. I told my partners that I thought we needed to find something lighter, and make a bigger version as well. The problems with plastic were

Bisphenol A (or BPA), which is a proven carcinogen, and Bisphenol S and F (BPS and BPF), which replaced BPA, but are also unsafe. So, there is no safe plastic, and it is everywhere. This is especially true for those still eating fish, because there's so much plastic in the water. So, the VeggiDome is made of glass.

BV: *What are you working on now?*

CM: I'm currently a community nutritionist at a few adult day care and senior centers, and I'm the senior culinary specialist at PS 150. I continue as the founding director and CEO of Plant Harmony Health Center, which I started in 2014, and really helped me with my prostate cancer and shingles. I still do events. For instance, I did a big, three-hour event in Williamsburg, Brooklyn, in 2019 on making your own milk. I did a blind taste test: dairy milk, cashew, walnut, and soy. It was framed as a competition, with prizes—but the event was really educating about health, comparing dairy milk versus nut milk. I hope to do more shows like this in the future.

Health is very important to me, for my family and for others. All I want to do is educate others to start making better choices about what they eat, and then encourage them to share all that they have learned with everyone they care about. Sort of like: Each one, teach one! ☀

16

THE BEST THAT I CAN BE

Ra-Leek Born

My name is Ra-Leek Born, and I'm fourteen years old. I'm an amateur boxer and have many titles. I visit different countries as well as my hometown, New York City, fighting my titles. I also enjoy playing basketball as my hobby.

The first title I ever had was my first belt, which I won in Brooklyn, New York; one of my most valued titles was at a national tournament in Independence, Missouri. It took about twenty-four hours for us to get there, and I had to fight three people before I reached the finals, going through different rings. Once I reached the finals, I had to fight one other person. In the end, I was victorious and got to meet a lot of famous people. By the time I turned twelve, I was rated seventh in the United States for boxing in my age group, and had gained six belts and many trophies, and had fought forty-three matches.

Boxing is organized by age and weight divisions. In all tournaments, you're drawn in brackets. Everyone competes with one another until there are the finalists. Competitions take place all year round, and you can find them in many ways—on the Internet, Instagram, and even through friends and flyers posted in the neighborhood. In larger tournaments, you have to pay and apply online, and fit into the categories.

Boxing has allowed me to travel internationally. I won an international tournament in Canada, which was the first time I'd left the United States. It was fascinating to see not only the different landscapes and communities, but also how people operated in the ring was entirely different. Between every round, the referee let us know who won that round, which was not my experience in the U.S. I fought there three times, and the feeling of winning was amazing.

I first got into boxing when I was turning ten years old, and my dad and I went to an Ultimate Fighting Championship gym for a few weeks. I was really interested in the boxing classes, so I kept attending them. I soon learned that I was a natural, and the coach training me at the time gave my dad a list of other gyms that had boxing programs. We chose the Eastern Queens Boxing Club, which is where I currently train.

Boxing has given me better conditioning and focus, and helps me to do good things in my life, such as be a leader and pursue my interests. It also means that I remain disciplined and work hard, stay in the gym and don't go off track. In about twenty years I want to be the best professional boxer there is. I also want to own a bunch of vegan restaurants.

I was a fighter before I became a vegan; in fact, I only found out about veganism as part of my routine and training. I've been a vegan for about four-and-a-half years. I first became aware of it when I discovered that fighters during training often change their diet so they can go twelve hard rounds. I found out that the boxer Timothy Bradley was vegan (although he isn't one anymore). I discovered that heavyweight boxer Bryant Jennings was also a vegan. Bryant appears in the documentary *Game Changers*, directed by James Cameron, which demonstrates how vegan athletes can excel in their sports.

At that point, I really wanted to go vegan for my health and to improve my performances when I fought. I kept asking my dad about transitioning. At first, we became pescetarians and then quickly transitioned to vegetarianism. Within six months, my dad and I were already vegan. At the time, my dad was suffering from Type 2 diabetes and high blood pressure; he was on four different types of medication. Veganism changed his life and reversed those illnesses. Only after going on the journey did I learn about animal cruelty, which only made me want to continue to be vegan.

To see my dad's life improving before my eyes, and to see how our entire family could change, was inspirational. When I was younger, I had no idea what veganism was. I knew my sister was vegetarian, and I remember asking my mom when I was about six years old if I could become one. She said no, because she thought I was too young. It's too bad, because all the things that medicine does, veganism can do it better, and there are no side effects. And you lose weight. In fact, my five-year-old brother has been a vegan since he started eating solid foods at three. My stepbrother is in boxing, too. My whole family—my dad, my mom, and cousins—keep me guided and focused on training and health, and they motivate me.

In terms of my daily routine: it's school, boxing, homework, and sleep. For breakfast, I may eat homemade pancakes out of spelt flour or a chickpea omelet, to which you can add vegan cheese, basil, or arugula. I will also prepare a smoothie: coconut milk, sea moss, bladderwrack, banana, dates, and blueberries each morning. For lunch, I might have quinoa and veggies, like asparagus, kale, sweet potato, or broccoli. I also have favorite fruits, such as pears, green apples, oranges, and bananas. Other meals are chickpea salad. Meals that I make myself include pasta dishes or quinoa. I might also make a chickpea meatloaf, by smashing the beans and onions together, baking it, and putting sauce on top. My favorite dish is fried oyster mushrooms. After training, which often ends at night, I have smaller meals, so I don't upset my digestive system. We also make sure that our final meal is no later than eight o'clock so we're not having our digestive system overtaxed when we're sleeping at night. When I'm training I prepare a special drink: coconut water (for hydration), sour oranges and limes (for an energy boost), and ginger.

Training and becoming a boxer has improved my performance in my schoolwork as well. It has given me focus and some discipline.

Several of my peers are interested in talking to me about veganism. I bring my own lunches to school, and my friends and associates ask a lot of questions about what I eat, and some want to know about animal cruelty. Two of them have become vegetarians, and I hope many more will follow suit. On social media I talk about how I'm a vegan and a boxer, and my aim is to incorporate a cooking aspect to the platforms. My hope is to create another site, Young Vegan Boxer, in which I showcase my life as a young vegan.

Veganism has helped my boxing: my stamina is higher, and my soreness and aches go away more quickly. This means that there's less break time between my fights, and during that time my body is in better condition. Veganism also helps me lose the weight I need to get into a particular weight class or maintain the weight for that class. I usually will go on a ten-day diet of only fruits and vegetables—eating raw foods. During that time, I will work out seven days a week.

I take off the day before a fight to relax and get my mind into a positive and focused space. This means thinking about how I *have* to win, how I can win a lot of money, and how this particular contest could offer a huge opportunity for me and my family. I will also have done some research to figure out who I'm fighting and what their technique is, so I have a game plan in my mind on how to beat him.

Whether I win or lose the fight, I always learn something from the experience. I will find out if I need to throw more punches or practice more of the techniques that I developed in training. I will learn if I need to train more, increase my stamina, get my strength up, or even go up or down in a weight class. ☀

17

THE BRIDGE

An Interview with Fred "Doc" Beasley II of Hip Hop Is Green

Brotha Vegan: *Tell us about yourself.*

Doc: I've had an opportunity to live all over New York City: from the Bronx to Brooklyn to Queens to Harlem in Manhattan, and I currently reside on Roosevelt Island with my wife and our four children. Growing up, I was always creative, an athlete, and a very inquisitive person. As an adult, a father, a son, and an uncle, I am an entrepreneur. I was able to kind of combine all my passions into one thing. I feel like I'm in a really good space and hitting my stride, trying to find new ways to reinvent myself and to use my creativity to be a platform socially, as well as economically, to take care of my family as well. So it's been a very interesting journey, and I feel that it's just getting to the good part.

I'm forty-eight years old. One of my friends asked me the other day, "How come you don't dye your beard?" I was like, "For what? I earned all those gray hairs!" Especially in mainstream society, the onus is put on "being young," whereas when we look at traditional cultures or indigenous populations, it was the elders who held a lot of weight and were considered of benefit. I am happy I've kind of transcended into being that elder in many circles. I relish that opportunity to share the information I've learned, to share my experiences, and to be an elder that's a stand-up person. Too many times we have elders—older people among us—who try to play to a position they shouldn't play. Does that make sense?

BV: *Absolutely. When we become older, we have a sense of responsibility: to ourselves, our community, and the people we love—because we've been here longer and, therefore, our job is to guide. Sometimes older people can act young and won't necessarily use that wisdom to guide younger people and almost turn a blind eye to what young people are going through.*

Doc: Exactly. I think that we survive what we've been through for a reason. One of my favorite quotes from Muhammad Ali is: "Service to others is the rent you pay for your room here on Earth." So what better way to serve people than by sharing your experience and your expertise! My sons are teenagers, and it's funny, navigating the space with young men. They think they know what they know; and they do know a lot of great things. But I tell my sons all the time: "Your parents are like street signs, like stoplights. We're here to tell you you're going in the right direction: to guide you." A lot of times with young people, it can be a really contentious relationship, because they're trying to establish their independence. At the same time, as a parent, you want to let them know that there are still some things you have to be aware of and look out for.

So, I've learned to balance becoming more of a listener than just speaking *to* my children. I want to speak *with* them more. To be able to guide them, but let them live their life and have their journey as well.

BV: *How do we build love and trust in our families?*

Doc: I'm at the point where I am the bridge between the older generation and the younger generation. My great aunt, who was my grandmother's oldest sister, recently passed away, and we had a memorial service for her. In the anime cartoon *Avatar: The Last Airbender*, the power of Aang, the main character, comes from his being able to tap into his ancestral line. When he does so, all the other avatars before him appear. I feel that when my great aunt, who came from a family of nine sisters and one brother, made her transition, she allowed me to tap into my entire ancestral line. I felt that power at her memorial service, because I had the opportunity to be the host.

So, family—not only the one in the household, but also the ancestral family—gives us the ability to use love as an adhesive that binds us together. Yes, it's easier said than done; yes, we will have ups and downs. But at the end of the day, it's that love that combines us and unites us and that pushes us. That is the foundation, or one of the building blocks, of family.

My wife is a very important person in my life: the foundation piece in our family. She's an acupuncturist, a healer, and an empath by nature. Our relationship sets the tone for our immediate family. My younger sister has three children, and the youngest son said to her recently that he wants to be married like my wife and me, because he felt that power.

My nephew lives in the South and he got a chance over one summer to come to New York. His arrival gave us a great opportunity to connect the children and help me build that foundational bridge of family. Family is so, so important. Better people build better families; better families create better communities; better communities create better worlds.

Now, I feel like we have different layers of family. For instance, Omowale Adewale, Black VegFest, and I are family; we've connected, and we've become family. It's the energetic tie that connects you to like-minded people.

BV: *Tell us about your vegan journey.*
Doc: I've been plant-based for four years now. For me, the change was about being a better person; growing. It was like my body kind of told me what I needed to do. I first stopped eating pork when I was fourteen years old. I slowly stopped eating beef; then I went to chicken. For a long time I was a pescetarian, and would go back and forth. But then, finally, I decided that I wanted to be just plant-based.

I don't use the word *vegan* because when some people talk about it, they say, "Veganism is for the animals." I'm well aware of the definition of veganism. As a Black person, I feel our food has been very connected to us. Once you realize that a lot of the food we've been eating has been counterproductive, and that we are taking back our health, that realization spills over into everything else. My journey has been about a love for self that has opened me up to a love for the animals and, of course, the planet. But it's centered on love for myself, for the Black man, and my family members.

As we speak, it's the holiday season, and there are going to be people eating a lot of chicken and turkey. A nurse recently told me, "Don't you know that during the holiday season, we have the greatest number of heart attacks in the country?" Many of us thought, and continue to think, that heart attacks and diabetes are passed down through the generations. They're not. It's the eating habits, the thinking habits, and the behavior patterns that are passed down. I want to be the one in my family who "upgrades" our bloodline, in a manner of speaking.

This is the work with Hip Hop Is Green. I try to meet people where they are. I tell them, "I don't want to be the vegan police or the plant-based Gestapo. I want to provide you with more options or opportunities to look at food from a different perspective." A pastor recently told me, referring to the Last Supper, that "the dinner table itself was the first church," and food was the sacrament. And that struck me, because the dinner table is where people would sit and discuss their worldviews and a greater power; and it was over food that these conversations happened.

So, I feel that the work we're doing is very powerful. It's uniting people. Once you give people a full belly, it gets their minds to open up a whole other level of thinking. It gives you a lot of different opportunities to speak very clearly.

These projects—*Brotha Vegan* and the Black VegFest—are great opportunities. With Black VegFest we get so much pushback. People say, "What do you mean, Black VegFest? What do you mean, Black? You're being racist." What we're doing is taking back our responsibility for our health and wellness. We're saying we are unapologetically Black and we are planting our flag in this vegan world. We are the engines of culture, so when we say "we are planting our flag in this vegan world" and saying that Black people need to have access to the best foods, and the best experiences around food, it's a very powerful statement—a revolutionary declaration, in fact.

The entire experience is referencing hip hop, because hip hop at its core is revolutionary. Young people from the Bronx started something out of nothing. They had no instruments in school; they had no after-school programs. But they still had this creativity . . . and their creativity manifested itself through the music. So, now we manifest the creativity in different ways: Black VegFest, Hip Hop Is Green. These things are by-products of our creativity, and combining that creativity with culture.

BV: *How did you get into hip hop?*
Doc: I've been part of hip hop since as long as I can remember. I was about five years old when I first heard hip hop music. Actually, I had a recording contract with Columbia

Records in the so-called golden era of hip hop. So, I've had a chance to perform with people like Tupac, Biggie Smalls, Wu Tang, LL Cool J—any of the greats that you can name. But when I moved us to New York in the early '90s, because the music now was becoming more economically valuable, corporate entities started to put a mandate on how to create the music.

They began to tell us how to make the music: "This is what we're looking for; this is what people want to hear." (Only a few short years before, hip hop hadn't existed in their corporate structure, and they had no idea what people wanted to hear.) What I'm saying is that the corporate entities purposely pushed an agenda of so-called gangsta rap on us. I was part of that transition from music that was more celebratory, more an information grapevine, to an overly "gangsta" type of vibe.

BV: *You mean like with Queen Latifah: when it was uplifting?*
Doc: Yes. You could say Queen Latifah, Poor Righteous Teachers, Brand Nubian, Public Enemy. You could say that about the first documented rap songs: the Sugar Hill Gang talked about social issues; for instance, in "Rapper's Delight": "Have you ever went over to a friend's house to eat/And the food just ain't no good?/The macaroni soggy, the peas are mushed,/And the chicken tastes like wood?"

So people were talking about values, morals, and principles—us coming together—even when hip hop was created in the Bronx by Kool Herc. It was him playing records for his sister's birthday party. Once the music became openly gangsta, it became about separating us, pitting us one against the other. As a chapter leader of Hip Hop Is Green, I can still be hip hop, but I can provide some type of healing or balance.

And it's good for me to do that from an elder's position: that I can say I had a record deal; that I did shows with the greats, like LL Cool J and Wu Tang Clan. I'm watching shows about Wu Tang Clan and how they started, and seeing LL Cool J host the Emmys. It's great to see how that's evolved. But we have to know that what was done was completely against the grain. The people who are now being saluted and given respect are the same as those who were told they were doing things that couldn't and shouldn't be done.

BV: *Do you consider yourself on the forefront of changing hip hip's diet?*

Doc: In the future, people like Omowale, Keith Tucker, Supanova Slom, and (hopefully) myself will be looked on as reshaping hip hop culture—because we are absolutely going against the grain to create a new standard of culture. Through Hip Hop Is Green and because of my prior experiences, I'm able to speak authentically to today's youth, and, as I said, provide that bridge that connects past and present, while at the same time sharing information that will hopefully provide today's youth with the ability to navigate successfully the potholes that are purposely placed in front of them.

What do I mean by that? We have a situation right now where children are taught that drinking and taking pills and doing things of this nature are cool. But we can take back and change or control that narrative. I tell kids all the time, "I know you wanna be lit, that's cool. But if you light a candle, a candle can't be lit 24/7. What happens to that candle?" They'll say, "It'll burn out." And I reply, "Yes, and so will you. You will burn out and you will short-circuit your nervous system." I talk to them about having some type of balance. They may not be ready or need to be plant-based or vegan, but, guess what, they could drink a little bit more water; they could try to eat this chopped cheese vegan sandwich and see whether they like it. It's about providing those options.

So, yes, I see myself as a leader, and in that role, I'm having more impact on current artists, not just in New York City but across the planet. They're asking me, "Hey Doc: What do you think I should eat today?" or "Hey Doc: Do you know a good vegan drink?" And I'm able to tell them about my wife and acupuncture, and so on. I stand with people such as Stic.man from dead prez; Supanova Slom, who's Queen Afua's son; Keith Tucker, who is the actual founder of Hip Hop Is Green: all these people form this superhero alliance of people who are once more saying that hip hop is not just a turn-up thing. It's something that informs us; it's something that is part of what we do; it's something that you live.

In that respect, hip hop is a code for culture. To me, hip hop is the blues of this millennium. The blues is hip hop; jazz is hip hop; gospel music is hip hop. Why? Because they have that call and response, and call and response is the basis of Black creativity. Even in Black VegFest, you get the call: "Hey we're doing Black VegFest." The response has been overwhelmingly great, and interest is growing. That's call and response; that's the basis of hip hop.

BV: *Can you talk about veganizing hip hop?*

Doc: Veganizing hip hop, in my opinion, is not done by preaching to the choir. It's done by having conversations with hip hop artists. You're not trying to beat them over the head and say, "Hey, this is what you do." It's that consistent contact, so that they say, "Man, Doc: I've noticed I haven't seen you eat a steak? How come you don't eat steak? How come you not eating any fish?" It's that concept and that conversation that start to have an impact.

My brother is a manager for a group called The Shoreline Mafia. They're one of the biggest groups on the West Coast right now. He also manages another guy, called 1TakeJay, and they're actually reshaping the sound of LA. In 2019, we did an event at the Paradigm Talent Agency, where the food was catered by Urban Vegan Kitchen and a brother by the name of Chef Don, who's actually from Brooklyn and who's an alkaline vegan chef. I tell you, he can make mushrooms taste like fried chicken. He had the artists in the event saying, "If I knew vegan food tasted like this, I'd go vegan right now."

So it's about putting artists in situations where they can have food that is culturally rooted in what they know, but done with a twist: to me that's veganizing hip hop; or that's making hip hop more plant-based. Those are the things that I'm excited about. At that Paradigm Talent Agency event, the vibration was so high and the food was so good. Our agency said, "We gotta do this again—not just for the young people, but for people in our office. They both need this conversation." So for me, my main focus is the children, because I feel like once we teach the children, the children will go back and teach their parents.

We have even advanced to taking students to Urban Vegan Kitchen, where we did something called The First Supper. The First Supper is us basically engaging inner-city youth who live in what used to be called "food deserts," and what they're now calling "food apartheid." These are areas where generations of people have not been eating nutritionally dense food. So we take them to Urban Vegan Kitchen, and we feed them, for free. A nutritionist, Samantha Bailey, speaks to kids directly about plant-based nutrition. So, again, it's just repackaging or repurposing the conversation—meeting them where they are, and then gently raising them to another level: raising the vibration.

BV: *How do you help Black children go vegan?*

Doc: A thirteen-year-old girl once wisely said to me, "Dr. G., I don't care what you know, until I know that you care." My wife asks me all the time, "Are you listening?" Because listening to someone equates exactly to showing how much you care. I've found that when I listen to young people, it makes them more open to having a conversation with me. This gives me the opportunity to share my experiences, which gives me the opportunity to introduce veganism and plant-based living. My father used to say, "You have two eyes, two ears, and one mouth. You should be doing twice as much listening and watching as speaking. Stop using your head as just a hat rack—open your mind, open your ears, open your eyes." And that's what I try to do with students, my family, and my children.

This is proving to be a successful formula. Because most young people, if you are listening, start to ask you questions. When they ask you questions, then you can provide insight, and it's received better. As opposed to me going to someone, "Hey, you gotta do this. You can't eat that, it's bad for you." Just listen, first. When they say, "What do you think, Dr. G?" I reply, "Thank you for asking . . . here are my thoughts." That becomes a much better vibe; a much cleaner, easier conversation. I tell everybody that the main ingredient I use with young people is *love*. So I try to be open-minded and open-hearted. I try to come from a loving perspective, and that's the way I introduce it.

Of course, hip hop and popular culture become entry points to speak to them. So, for instance, I might say, "Hey, I see you got a new pair of Yeezys. Oh, they're nice! Guess what? Yeezy makes those in America. You know why he makes those here? Because of how much it costs to put in the dye. You know how much it costs to have cow farms? You know how much it costs to produce beef? How much it costs to make blue jeans?"

And the kids are amazed. The entire back end of the product is engaged: the food, the responsibility to health and to family. All are entry points. The conversation gives me a lot of leeway, but that's done by listening first. So in this case, as I listen, I say to myself, *Okay, this person likes fashion, so I can go the Yeezy route with them.* Or, *This person likes music; I can go the Lil Baby route with them.* Or, *This person likes Popeye's chicken sandwich, so I can go, "Have you ever had plant-based chicken before?"*

BV: *Tell us about your role in Black VegFest.*

Doc: Black VegFest is like Wakanda: not only a celebration of us as a people, but a showcase for economic empowerment, entrepreneurship, and family life, including the extended family. Being the host of Black VegFest provides me with a platform to utilize all my skill sets at one time. The second Black VegFest in 2019 was held in Weeksville, one of the first free Black settlements, in Bedford-Stuyvesant in Brooklyn, and in the middle of so-called housing projects. Nor was it a coincidence that New York City tried to cover up Weeksville with housing projects, and nor was it a coincidence that Black VegFest could tap into the sacred ancestral energy that was there, and made it a hundred times more powerful. Being the host of Black VegFest was for me an honor and a blessing. It gave me the opportunity to connect with people on many levels.

Now, people should know that Black VegFest is open to everyone of any race. We call it "Black VegFest" because our main focus is on our community. And it is also Black people opening the door and saying, "Welcome to our home." It's also something where we are in control and not being controlled. People came from as far away as Philadelphia, Detroit, and even London, and had never seen anything like it. It's legacy-building in its purest form.

BV: *What attracted you to education?*

Doc: The root word of *education* is from the Latin: *educare*, meaning "to lead out." And I think that the more you know, the more you grow. My mother was a teacher, who passed when I was six years old. Her death when I was so young made me want to study the body to learn how to increase our longevity and maximize our experience in the physical form. Education gives me the opportunity to share; that sharing is at the root of us growing as a people.

Teaching is all about relationships. The first relationship is the one you have with the higher power, however you choose to name it. That connection gives you more power to have better relationships with others—other humans and other sentient beings and the world as a whole. The other relationships are with the young people you teach. I love working with them and seeing that flash of insight and curiosity; I love seeing that connection being restored and filled with hope.

BV: *What would you say are the main issues our communities need to get over to succeed? And what are your goals?*

Doc: The main thing for us to get over and succeed as a people, is love. Once we embrace the love of self, individually and collectively, that will spill over into how we conduct ourselves economically, how we conduct our businesses. Some people might say, "Well, love is a very abstract thing." I would say that love is a concept and an adhesive. Some people love to hate, and this will exclude them from certain things. When you have love for yourself, that love will force you not to accept a lower standard of living, housing conditions, education, politics, food, and so on. You won't accept those standards, because you have a love for yourself that trumps them and forces you to step onto a higher ground.

My immediate goal for New York City's Hip Hop Is Green chapter is to have one in every school in New York City. What do I mean by that? Every school has a glee club and a track club. I want each school to have a Hip Hop Is Green club where they teach that health and wellness are part of their responsibility. By having these clubs, children in the individual school become the engines that run the club. And I want to put the children in power. I want to have them say, "Hey, Doc: Can we get a Hip Hop Is Green club in my school? *My* particular school is in need." So a school in the Bronx would be different from a school in Harlem, and very different from a school in Brooklyn. Again, it's opening up lines of communication, listening, and then asking, "What do you need at your school? What do you need here?"

That creates a pipeline of resources that you can help move children into the Hip Hop Is Green club with. Black people don't know this, but Ivy League schools are looking to give full scholarships to Black and Brown children who have A averages. I want to provide that pipeline from the inner cities for these educational and corporate opportunities for children who aren't boxed in to a particular mindset.

In 2019, Omowale and I spoke at an animal rights bill signing at New York City's City Hall. This is how we get on the radar and combine grassroots activism, politics, and the corporate and educational fields to open up opportunities for change. Bringing these together is where the power really rocks. Allowing children to find their avenues of excellence is part of that.

Personally, I'm working on a series of Young Adult books where the main characters are plant-based. One is about a young man who lives in the inner city, and the story is about how he navigates the hood as someone who's plant-based. Another series is for plant-based younger children. I'd like to do more public speaking: at schools, colleges, and with businesses. Hip Hop Is Green conducts workshops on building professionalism and creativity. I want Generation Z to understand that they don't have to be drunk or high to tap into their creative side.

I'm looking forward to doing more work in music, learning more, and then tying those things together. I'd like to build a family business and legacy. I'd like my children to travel with me as I take my business around the world and have them see firsthand how important it is to be able to look someone in the eye and be responsible for your word. I'd like them to enter new relationships and to use their creativity to make a way for themselves as entrepreneurs, as opposed to being someone else's employee.

BV: *Any final pieces of advice?*

Doc: I just want to tell people: Be patient with yourself. We're all growing. Nobody's perfect, but enjoy the process of growing into your best self. Try to find ways to reconnect and recalibrate yourself. I tell my wife, *Sometimes I have to log out so I can tap in.* Take deep breaths, drink your water, eat your fruits and vegetables. Find ways to be your best self and to love yourself, and then use that love to become a force field that pushes you and helps you as you go out into the world. And use your smile to light up the world. ☀

18

A JOURNEY TO CONNECTEDNESS

Anthony Carr

Veganism to me is a journey to connectedness: connections to myself, my Blackness, and Earth. It is a revolutionary rejection of violence and the violence that continues to happen to Black and Brown bodies. It is a glimpse into a world without violence.

As I look at my own journey, I struggle with media representation of male Blackness: overly violent, overly sexed, and separated from Black women and children through incarceration or physical or emotional disconnect. Coming into early adolescence during the advent of the hip hop and rap movements, I saw that African-Americans continued to find their own voices as they did through jazz, R&B, gospel, and the blues.

In many ways, hip hop was a cry of people in the inner city to tell their own stories. It started out by providing a lens for Black artists to express themselves and their own experience. Those artists spoke of violence in the inner cities. Grandmaster Flash and Furious Five's song "The Message" provided an important social commentary on what was happening in the inner cities. Rick James' album *Street Songs* provided an eighties funk response to these rising voices. Being a Black middle schooler from the Maryland suburbs singing along to Rick's "Ghetto Life" or reciting Flash's "It's like a jungle sometimes. It makes me wonder how I keep from going under," seems ridiculous now, but I could relate.

As a Black suburban kid who lived with both parents in a house and did fairly well in school, I always felt that other Black kids either didn't think I was Black enough or thought I was trying to be white. Through the music my parents listened to—Smokey Robinson, Nina Simone, Nancy Wilson, Nat "King" Cole, Ella Fitzgerald, and others—I knew there was not one way to be Black. I felt that our struggles may have been different but we all shared a common experience, and that my social status or my parents' marital status did not shield me from the pain of racism or exclusion. As a result, I was placed in the awkward position of not being Black enough for Black folk and not being white to white folks. I grew up feeling rejected by both communities for not being enough and I struggled with fitting in.

My parents were very concerned that my brother and I find our own paths, and wanted us to know that those before us sacrificed and died so we could have the freedom to be who we wanted to be. We watched *Roots* on television; we read biographies of Dick Gregory and Malcolm X, James Baldwin and Martin Luther King, Jr., Mahalia Jackson and Jackie Robinson. My parents would tell and retell different ways of being Black, and ensure that I had a deep connection to my extended family. When we visited my grandmother in North Carolina, she would tell me stories of being raised on the farm and eating from the land. My brother and I would spend summers visiting her, snapping green beans and listening to her stories. Part of my experience is the Soul Food we grew up on: black-eyed peas to usher in the New Year; sweet corn and potato salad on the Fourth of July; collards and yams for Thanksgiving dinner; my mother's sweet potato pie at Christmas.

I learned that my parents gave me a gift that some Black people don't possess: to be able to navigate both Black and white spaces. Sometimes the code switching that Black and Brown communities have to do is perceived to be negative, but in my opinion it makes us strong and teaches us how to survive. By the time I got to college, I learned more about the Black and women's liberation movements, and I saw budding movements in response to the AIDS crisis. Filmmakers like Spike Lee and John Singleton were providing a vision and critique of Black communities; Public Enemy brought us back to the Black Pride messages of the seventies.

It was in this context that I was first exposed to veganism. It was the first time I'd even considered that eating meat might be wrong or could be causing harm to other beings. Many of the changes in my points of view over the years had been to do with shifting my intellectual perspective; this was the first time I was being required to make changes in the ways I ate. Yet most of the time at the outset of my journey toward veganism, I appreciated it from afar, and used deflection. I thought that as a Black man I had to worry first about the liberation of my people.

Years went by. Two careers and a failed marriage later, I took a look at veganism again. By this stage in my life, I was far removed from the stories I remembered from my time on the farm; the music era was now not so much about revolution as about materialism. I was struggling to live an authentic life in line with my values.

So, in 2008, I made the decision to become vegan, and began to look at people who were vegan. I received lots of support from Black vegans in Chicago and learned how to veganize the foods I loved as a child. I listened to songs such as dead prez's "Be Healthy." This song spoke of how veganism was Black and revolutionary; that it could be a struggle, and reminded me of how I felt like an outsider.

Some Black people don't understand veganism or think it is for white people; some Black people struggle with loving the richness of Soul Food too much. When I talk about my veganism, I speak first about the healthfulness of the diet. However, no message of veganism is complete without addressing the violence of factory farms and how corporations continue to hurt and exploit the most vulnerable. Veganism is about living a life of peace and nonviolence with all creatures on Earth, of reconnecting to the earth. I believe that part of my Blackness and my maleness involves living with compassion in this world. I hope I can provide an alternative vision of how we as inhabitants of Earth can relate to each other.

I am currently studying for a Ph.D. in counseling. One of my focuses is Black people and mental health, and how organic gardening can be a tool to get us reconnected to the earth and to ourselves.

As I write this chapter, I learn that the New York City police officer Daniel Pantaleo won't face civil rights charges for the illegal chokehold death of Eric Garner. This case reminds me that some Black bodies are not worth the cost of loose cigarettes (cigarettes never found). It recalls to me the senseless slaughter of animals whom we don't need to live or have to use for food. Veganism is a glimpse that another world is possible: that all inhabitants of Earth can live in peace with one another and, through creativity and vision, build a nonviolent world. ☀

19

LIVING LIFE IN FREEDOM EVERY DAY

Torre Washington

My name is Torre Washington, and I hate to put myself in a box or label myself, because I do many different things. I coach, train, compete, speak, spread compassionate awareness, and live to the fullest I can, in freedom, every day, as much as possible. But I am known as a bodybuilder.

I became a spectator and fan of bodybuilding when I was about sixteen years old, although I didn't start it as a career until 2009. I've been vegan since 1998, but when it comes to food, I find the questions that follow when I mention the fact to be very interesting, because I'm not sure what the person asking me is looking for. One thing I realize and recognize when it comes to dealing with human beings and individuals is that everybody's different. We have different metabolisms, and our bodies react to food differently.

So, for instance, I am sometimes asked about whether I have a specific meal or what I eat for breakfast before I go to the gym. However, I don't sit down and say to myself, *OK. I'm going to have this, for this purpose, because it's going to do this for me.* I usually just eat what's in the fridge or what's around me that I want to eat. Training for me in the gym is *mental*, and not necessarily a function of needing some outside physical process to give me the energy and desire to go to the gym. To put it another way, when I go to the gym or work out, my goal is mentally stimulated, because I have an idea of what I want to accomplish. Whether or what food I have in my stomach, I'm still going to go ahead and accomplish that goal, so there is no "typical" meal for me. However, if I were to imagine such a thing, I would say it's tofu, Japanese sweet potato, and some other vegetables.

I used to have the same attitude regarding monitoring my calorie intake. From my start as a competitor in 2009 to about 2016, I didn't track anything specific that I ate based on what I want to accomplish. What people need to realize is that when it comes to the presentation of your physique on stage, judges aren't asking you what your body fat percentage is or how much you weigh. They're looking to see if you have the total package when it comes to definition: mass, muscularity, symmetry, and proportion. Therefore, in and of itself, the amount of calories in versus calories out is essentially the catalyst for fat loss or fat gain—and no more. Because I was able to eat food intuitively, I felt that I didn't need to track anything. I was able to lower my caloric intake mentally—eating five chips instead of twenty—and not by looking at a number on a scale, etc.

Then, around 2016, I recognized the fact that every coach has a coach, and every *great* coach has a coach, and that applied even to me. So, I hired someone to help me get to that next level, specifically by taking me off a process of dealing with clients and dealing with myself. I recognized I needed to be in a space where someone could examine me from the outside, because like many people, I tend to be more critical of myself than other people. This person wanted me to start collecting data and tracking my intake, and so I did.

Even so, I don't obsess about my intake. My caloric intake can go anywhere from two thousand to five thousand calories or even ten thousand calories, depending on where I am in the training sessions or the country. If I'm in Los Angeles, where there are myriad places I can go and have food that's based off plants, I'm at about five different places in one day. So intake could change, based on my location. Overall, my weight remains relatively constant. If I'm in competition, I will weigh between 160 and 163 pounds. When I'm not competing, that will increase by five to ten pounds. I don't like to get too heavy, because I don't like to look puffy. I like to look pretty much in shape year-round. I've always wanted to stay in a good condition, and not to have this way-off look, where I'm shocking my metabolism just to get a certain look in sixteen weeks.

ITAL

Ital means that you live off the land for food and life. It is one of the principles of Rastafarianism, and it influenced my decision to switch to veganism. I was raised a vegetarian because my mother is a Seventh Day Adventist and I grew up in a Seventh Day

Adventist household. My mother is very devout, but even as a young child, I found that Adventism didn't line up with my ideals, and I questioned it a lot—particularly events in the Bible that didn't make sense to me. Of course, when you're raised in such a household, people respond to what you ask by saying, "Don't question things from the Bible. Who are you to lean on your own understanding?" However, I wasn't satisfied with such a response, and I started to seek out ideas that seemed more in line with who I was as a being.

Rasta came around because I started to grow locks out of a desire to appear fashionable. I also had grandparents who were Jamaican. However, they didn't know anything about vegetarianism, and so I was given non-vegetarian foods when I lived with them for a time. I moved to South Florida and started to take on a Rasta identity—first because of the fashion, and then because I began to study it. That said, Rasta was only the start of my journey. I realized that Rasta was, like Seventh Day Adventism, based on Biblical standards, although watered down and altered. However, although I am certainly Rasta in that I appreciate the plant-based lifestyle, I cannot say I am a full-fledged Rasta. I certainly don't believe that Haile Selassie was God. Nonetheless, I can appreciate the ideals of "I and I. Love inside; love everyone" and "You are connected with the universe." In fact, I've studied many things, including our Egyptian heritage.

The way I feel about Rastafarianism is also the way I think about veganism. To label oneself *vegan* is, for me, constricting. It puts you in a box and forces you to stay there, because you are assumed to be someone who is, for instance, compassionate only toward animals and not human beings, or you adopt a certain set of practices. For instance, if vegans are not supposed to wear leather, then am I really expected to throw away clothes that I may have had for years, only for them to end up in a landfill? We all carry our past with us. It's how we learn from our past that makes us a kinder and more compassionate human being, a better person.

Yet I can say that Rasta led me to veganism, because my lifestyle started changing and when people asked me why I ate the way I did, and I explained it, they said to me, "Oh, you sound like a vegan!" At first, I didn't know what *vegan* was, at least partly because if those around me knew of the term, they associated it as something that was for and by white people. When I finally learned about it, I thought, *I guess I am.* I began to embrace the idea when I started competing and mentioned it in my biography. However, I had been practicing a vegan diet since 1998.

COMPETING

My entire philosophy of bodybuilding is to be a better version of myself in each competition. I am aware that I am considered a "vegan ambassador," and that pushes me on to show that you don't need animal secretions or flesh in order to build muscle. My wish to compete is my wanting not only to redefine what it takes to create a muscular physique, but also to recognize that it is possible to continue to grow and maintain mass over many years. There are individuals who have been vegan bodybuilders for three, four, and five years; there are others who have been competing and maintaining peak fitness as vegans for fifteen, twenty, even twenty-seven years. They may not be as social-media savvy as the younger, newer guys, but they deserve respect. They have demonstrated longevity, and they show that you can eat no meat for decades and still maintain, let alone build, muscle.

A further reason to compete is to show that not only have I been a vegan and a bodybuilder for a long time, but I have done it without taking any type of steroid or enhancement drug to increase my protein synthesis. I have achieved this by training consistently and eating enough food—and enough of the *right kind* of food—for my body to put on muscle. A plant-based diet has also enabled me to recover faster, with less inflammation and joint pain. Nor, for that matter, do I suffer from constipation. From what I hear, most competitors are unable to go to the bathroom days or even weeks before a show. This is because their bodies are so depleted of carbohydrates and so full of animal protein that their intestines are clogged.

L.I.F.E. LESSONS

My background and my profession have taught me the importance of L.I.F.E.: Living in Freedom Every Day. What I mean by this is that we should not be reliant on other people's money or any other such situation to dictate how we live our lives. This is true freedom, and it means owning your own thoughts and decisions, and not relying on another to make them for you. When we live in freedom every day with our health, our finances, and our attitude, we become stewards of humanity.

I especially think this attitude applies to our health. It's very sad to see, especially among people in the Black community, that we don't change our lifestyle until there is a crisis. We are very reactive, instead of proactive. It's sad to see us chasing down Popeye's chicken and other animal-based foods that we have grown up and been raised with, because of their texture, taste, and tradition—and for us not to recognize that in the end these foods are poisoning us. By the time we reach sixty years of age, we finally realize we have to change our lifestyle. But we have oftentimes left it too late—the effects have been compounded over sixty years—and the results of cleaning your lifestyle up may not work as you would wish. A friend of mine recently passed away from cancer. She had just started to go vegan and improve her life. Before I knew it, however, she was gone.

Now, I don't believe it's ever too late to improve your health and eating habits, but we need to live in freedom every day by making the change when there is plenty of time left to enjoy the results. That means recognizing that, although something may be tasty and you're enjoying it in the moment, you are only risking negative outcomes later on. An attitude of, "Well, you've got to die of something," is not helpful, because while this statement is literally true, it ignores the fact that you don't have to die of self-inflicted conditions or to do so prematurely. ☀

20

IN SERVICE OF OUR OWN PEOPLE

Baba Brother-D B. Aammaa Nubyahn

Greetings everyone.

I'm Baba Brother-D B. Aammaa Nubyahn, and having read and appreciated *Sistah Vegan*, i feel highly gratified to have been asked to contribute to its brother-written counterpart.*

Let me state upfront that i follow a viewpoint some of Us call Scientific African Nationalism: the systematic acquisition and application of knowledge and skills for the Best Interest of African People. Our Best Interest means that which is conducive to the survival and development of African People worldwide. Some of my personal history follows.

As a fifteen-year-old in 1971, my mounting militant motivations moved me in June to join Our neighborhood gang, the Black Spades, and then that September the countrywide college-based Student Organization for Black Unity. As part of SOBU's high school cadre, i eagerly embraced Revolutionary Pan-African Nationalism, and have continued to do so. As much as i would like to convince large numbers of African People to also accept and act on this viewpoint, i realize that i was predisposed to running with it prior to being more formally introduced.

Not eating pork was one of the things i picked up from interacting with folks who were into some form of pro-Black thing. The older young people i was around in YOBU (the word *student* was changed to *youth*), the Black Muslims in my Bronx housing project, Five

---

* Editorial note: The non-capitalization of the word *i*, except at the beginning of a sentence, and the capitalization of the first letter of the first person plural pronouns (We, Our, Us), are intentional. Baba Brother-D writes that these typographic choices come "from a strong identification with a growing motion away from the highly individualistic orientation of our currently dominant society, toward a more collective/communal/cooperative outlook. Of course, this takes some getting used to."

Percenters, Orthodox Muslims, Hebrew Israelites, Rastafarians, and others who seemed to be into something politically, spiritually, and/or culturally "conscious," often said they did not eat pork. Since not eating swine seemed to me to be the thing to do, in December '72 i decided to stop eating pork. Writing this has me laughing as i remember picking small pieces of pork from my bowl of what was presumably pork and beans. Among other things, that gave me a big push to do more food shopping for myself.

In the spring of 1975, as an organizer in the National Black Science Students Organization, i became infatuated with a sister who was an officer in a different college chapter. She said she was a vegetarian, and that just seemed so-o-o cool to me. A few weeks later, while eating the lunch provided at a student conference, a mentor of mine in Black Science began to talk matter-of-factly about what had been done to the meat We were eating. He was eating it, too, and i don't recall any of Us acting disgusted. However, after finishing, i told myself that i would not eat meat again. That was May '75. i was not yet nineteen, and i have not knowingly eaten any land-based flesh since.

During the following three years, i went back and forth around eating fish, and i also became skinny. Although i had a growing circle of folks with whom to be "vegetarian," these dietary changes of mine were not accompanied by any specific source of instruction. i heard this from that one, and that from this one. As of the fall of 1977, i became and remain part of a small group, earlier called the Alkebu-lan Youth Collective, and currently known as African National Science. Refraining from smoking, alcohol, and other intoxicants has remained part of Our code of behavior. Since the early days, with few exceptions, almost every member has been some form of vegetarian, even though this has never been one of Our rules. So i've enjoyed much social support in my dietary restrictions.

In June of 1978, circumstances culminating in the killing of Our pet cat caused me to become extremely disgusted with my mother and myself in particular, and people in general. That was the first time i recall really feeling that my personal behavior was in conflict with my politics. Here i am seeing myself as fighting for African People's independence from imperialist domination, yet i callously collude in the often deadly domination of other animals. i denounced the ease with which people disregard nonhuman animals, as We say things like, "it's only a dog" or "it's just a mouse." People have readily said the same things regarding other groups of people, and consistently act that way when it's not seen as acceptable to say so. Feeling infuriation for the f—ed-upness of humans in general and myself in particular, i wanted to do some kind of penance, something more than my simply taking a position against people owning pets.

So i decided that for seven years, in addition to the land-based flesh, i would not eat egg and milk products and sea-based flesh. Nor would i buy clothing made from animal products. Conveniently, i told myself that i could continue to wear the wool and leather items i already had. Also, my continued consumption of honey didn't bother me. In those days, the word *vegan* was not yet in my vocabulary, but i was living it or close to it depending on what description of vegan you go by.

Seven years later, pretty much to the date, i resumed eating milk and egg products. That night, i greedily gobbled down a dinner of cookies and ice cream. However, i've never gone back to seafood nor wearing wool, silk, or leather.

From 1985 to 1992, without using the term (not sure if i even knew the term), i was an ovo-lacto-vegetarian who did not wear animal products. By May of '92, a mounting motivation moved me to give up the milk and egg products, as well as the honey. (Maybe if there was a Black vegan gang close by i might have wanted to join.) Also, around this time i stopped buying rodent glue traps, having long since refrained from using the snapping kind. i began seeking ways of removing a mouse from one's house without killing it, and several years later i started applying this consideration to insects as well.

Talk about extremism. Perhaps many of you reading this are thinking, *This m-f is weird.* Maybe some of you feel reinforced in a consistent tendency to not get too close or organizationally connected to any movement, "cause some people be carrying stuff too far." Well, for the record, nobody else in my immediate circle lives by the same restrictions. To my knowledge neither has any other of my close comrades during this half century of Black Nationalist involvement and intersecting radical activism.

Even among vegans and other vegetarians, i'm "out there." i've found few who are in synch with abstaining from intoxicants; fewer who zealously avoid eating and wearing any animal products; and hardly anyone who views pets as slaves, or who goes to great lengths to avoid killing mice and roaches. i'm sure there are others like me—or even more extreme—and i just don't know them, or perhaps i'm unaware of the behavioral restrictions of some sisters and brothers with whom i'm already acquainted. And perhaps Our numbers are on the rise. However, it should be kept in mind that the distribution of any given characteristics within a population will include folks at each extreme, with most people being somewhere in between. i'm not looking to move you to behave as i do. NO! I'M LOOKING FOR MORE OF US TO WORK AT SHIFTING THE STATISTICAL MIDPOINT MORE AND MORE IN THIS DIRECTION!

Like the overwhelming majority of vegetarians to my knowledge, i cite personal health as a central motivation. i also include political and economic considerations in that far too much of Our food supply goes to raising animals for slaughter, such that a whole lot more humans could be decently fed otherwise. However, i am vegan for mainly philosophical/ spiritual reasons. i'm repulsed by the preponderance of anthropocentric beliefs and behaviors, or as i prefer to say it, "human-all-that-ness." i'm convinced that this mentality plays a major part in Our present predicament on this planet. Beyond healthy diet, being behaviorally vegan helps me combat those tendencies in myself.

Now, writing this essay has pulled me to pause and compare and contrast my convictions to African People's wellbeing, including Our extrication from non-African control and the overturning of human-centrism, so dangerous to humanity and life.

Wow—i just imagined myself as primarily being a vegan activist for the wellbeing of nonhuman animals who in my immediately personal behavior live in a nationalistically African manner—n-n-n-NOT!!! (Just had such a laugh writing that.)

While a combination of causes compels me to live in a vegan manner, my first and foremost allegiance is Our Best Interest: that which is conducive to the survival and development of African People worldwide (as stated earlier). Our existence is threatened beyond the impending ecological calamity that endangers everyone. Humans might miraculously get through this, while Our people's fate continues to hang in the balance, or more likely gets worse. Making a better world means little to me if my people are not around to partake.

This does not mean that i can't see any connection to non-African activists engaged in ecological and/or anti-speciesist work. i'm about being supportive of these and other socially beneficial efforts. But We must be careful in not allowing Ourselves to be distracted from more pressing work. Our central task at this time has to do with drastically increasing Our people's capacity to coordinate Our spiritual, mental, and physical energy in the service of "Ourself," Our collective wellbeing. Working toward other socially positive goals is great as long as We can use that endeavor in increasing Our people's "coordability."

Since that reminds me of efforts to get Our people more involved in animal rights activism, let me comment on the portion of Black folks who feel insulted at the comparison of animals raised for slaughter and the circumstances of African captives in this hemisphere over the past few hundred years. Some of that insult indicates a taking for granted that the former is basically okay, while the latter is not. Maybe you think the latter occurred and continues to occur due to some kind of misunderstanding in which the people in charge are mistakenly treating Our people differently from how they treat each other. Perhaps you're holding out hope that they will see the error of their ways, and you think that comparing Our historical situation to that of animals for slaughter interferes with getting people in positions of power to see Us as they see themselves.

Well, i'm neither White nor an animal rights activist. But bear with me as i assert that the animals-for-slaughter comparison is much more accurate than most of Us care to acknowledge. So allow me to share a brief piece i wrote a while back.

More or Less Happy Meals

The idea of one group of people "feeding off" another, or as a colleague recently said, "eating Our flesh," can be heard as fairly figurative expressions of an extremely exploitative relationship. But few realize that phrases like these are far more than metaphorical.

Let's review some biological basics. Unlike plants that make their own food from air, water, and sunlight, animal life forms live off the consumption of plants and/or other animals. Once this food is acquired and perhaps put into a necessary or desirable form, it must be ingested in manageable quantities. Solid sustenance is often cut, torn, or otherwise broken into pieces small enough to fit in one's mouth. Generally, chewing makes pieces of food ready to be swallowed and further digested. Digestion is the process by which food is broken down so that fuel and other potentially valuable materials can be extracted. What's left is then usually excreted.

To put it bluntly, the subjugated Black Nation in North America is food for the subjugating White Nation. We are continuously beat down, chopped up, torn apart, cut, chewed up, swallowed, broken down, defecated out, as well as defecated on. We continue to react to the last clause of the previous sentence, and generally have little response to the rest. At times when We're not reminded of being defecated on, We are by and large a group of HAPPY MEALS. We are not paying attention to this overall digestive process.

Don't-Worry-Be-Happy-Meal-Negroes show so much more concern with being mistreated by those who are dining on Us than We do for Our own collective long-term wellbeing. But regardless of how humanely the livestock is treated, the end result is still slaughter.

It's been clearly documented that the fantastic wealth of not only this country, but the whole of the Western World, was derived from stolen African labor on stolen Native American land. The trade in and forced labor of captive Africans provided the accumulation of capital needed for the Industrial Revolution in Western Europe and North America.

New Africans (a term some of Us prefer over African-Americans) continue to provide huge sums of wealth for the dominant population, especially the economic elite who feed off of everybody else. And while it's true that their human food supply has expanded to include most of the world, in many other countries those leaders who are really loyal to their own people are preoccupied with breaking free of this feeding frenzy.

Meanwhile, We seem to gripe over too small of a cut in America's feasting over the planet. Picture a protest by pigs for prettier pens, benign butchery, and the choice of chicken or steak dinners. Our key focus for change should not be treatment, but rather Our own Collective Self-Control. Otherwise We not only sell out the rest of the current world, but Our unborn generations as well. 7/27/2015

It's not unusual for people to verbally accept appeals to rationality regarding the correctness of doing something that seems so completely contrary to their comfort zone. For instance, a smoker with no intention of stopping might admit to the correctness of an anti-smoking message. Think of all the health professionals who have taught others one thing while continuing to do another. And maybe it's most of Us who from time to time dabble in doing things in better ways, but only briefly. However, while it is possible, it is highly improbable that a person will make a major change in how one lives simply based on logical explanation. As i was alluding to near the beginning of this chapter, i'm not expecting to talk anyone into a different viewpoint and lifestyle. i was predisposed to embracing a Black Nationalist outlook and involvement. That involvement along with other factors, conscious and not conscious, combined to predispose me to a chain of dietary changes. These and other changes have predisposed me to further developments in thought and action.

So while it might happen, i do not expect to sway you to the service of Our own people. i don't expect to persuade you to improve your diet. And i don't expect to convince you to be more compassionate of other animals, human and nonhuman. (Oh lawd, i just thought about all of y'all who react to the idea of being considered as animals. But that's a different essay.) However, if you are already so inclined in any or all of these ways, i urge you to connect with other sisters and brothers of similar inclinations in seeking to improve Our practice. While We are unlikely to trigger major change in those who are not already so inclined, We can, however, set the stage upon which many others acquire the required predisposition.

Lastly, let me say to those of you who currently act on your pro-Black sentiments, and currently practice and improve upon healthy eating and other habits, you are manifesting a greater than average attitude and discipline level from which more effective leadership is more likely to be developed. Get with a few others and form something tight-knit within which and out of which greater skill and coordination can grow immensely. ☀

21

MY PLANT-BASED JOURNEY

Richard W. Rogers Jr.

My dad's parents and grandparents arrived in Norristown, Pennsylvania, four generations ago as part of Black migration from the Saluda and Dillon areas of South Carolina. Folks were in search of opportunity, which Norristown offered through the steel industry and other possibilities. My father and his seven siblings were raised by my firm-handed, forward-thinking grandfather, Lemuel Arsea Rogers, and his wife, Jesse Lee Mason. My mother, Loretta Fisher Rogers, hails from the rich family-farming tradition of Vienna, Maryland. The generation above her consisted of her mother, Mildred, and thirteen siblings raised by the wise and savvy Maggie Chester Pinder (my great-grandmother) and her too-soon-deceased husband, James L. Pinder.

My father, Richard, and mother raised my two older siblings (Bruce and Tracey) and me in Blue Bell, a suburb of Philadelphia, to which we moved when I was three years old. My father maintained a legal practice in Norristown, a short drive away from Blue Bell. Although his practice had great breadth and scope, I love that he was also committed to service in his community. He was a dynamic attorney, known as "the lawyer of the people" and "the community lawyer." My mother served the community as an educator in the Norristown Area School District and was active in several business and civic organizations.

I still live in the Blue Bell area and maintain strong connections to my youth. I grew up in the 1970s with a large extended family and with ties to my father's Norristown church community. In school, however, I would usually be one of the only Black kids in class; we were one of the only Black families in Blue Bell at the time. In fact, we were the first to move there. Luckily, my first grade teacher, Mrs. Davidson, was a Black woman (you don't realize how much of a blessing that is until you get older; she's still alive today and still asks about me when she sees my mom).

It was a weird time. I was born in 1968, one week after Martin Luther King Jr. was killed. I think back to that timeline and am amazed to realize that I came into the world when the civil rights movement wasn't ancient history but actually happening. A few years prior, my father had left the first law firm at which he was employed to responsibly create Norristown's first Black-owned firm with his buddy Charles "Charlie" Wharton Smith III. In retrospect, I also realize my siblings and I were well insulated by our parents—perhaps so we'd not have to deal with the societal/racial struggles from their past and present experiences. It was a beautiful way to maintain the innocence of childhood; at the same time, it allowed me to discover issues on my own, later. We talked about many things in memorable and important conversations, but I guess one wonders as a parent: *Do I need to tell my child everything, or do I let him discover certain things as he grows older?* Perhaps, there was the hope that some things would no longer exist to be discovered.

My family was very food/nutrition conscious, or at least I was as a result of being encouraged to eat the right things. I remember hearing my mother saying over and over again: "Eat your green vegetables." Back in the 1970s, there was an emphasis on eating a "well-balanced" meal, which at that time meant you had meat, starch, and your vegetable with some kind of dairy involved. Fruit was encouraged somewhere in the mix. (Obviously, we now know these requirements aren't true.) My early appreciation for whole foods, fruits, and vegetables came from spending time on an uncle's farm. During two weeks of every summer, my mother, Bruce, Tracey, and I would visit "the country" and stay for a week on Uncle Granville's farm in Vienna, Maryland, and then visit my favorite Aunt Corinda's house in the nearby town of Salisbury, only thirty miles from Ocean City. While there, we'd spend time going back and forth to the beach. These were beloved times.

Although Uncle Granville farmed hundreds of acres, he kept a family plot, too. I still carry the memory of walking that garden with Uncle Granville. He would reach down, pick a tomato, pull a little salt shaker out of his pocket, sprinkle a little on the tomato, and bite into it. He would grab another tomato or sometimes a cucumber, and give me that next ripe fruit. Uncle Granville's was one of my favorite places to go during the summer. I remember the big meals we had. There was meat on the table (usually fried chicken and some fish), but we always had about five different kinds of vegetables/fruits, and they were always fresh—pulled straight out of the garden. We'd all help to prepare them: plucking the ends off string beans, shucking corn, popping lima beans out of their pods, slicing cucumbers, helping make the salad. I remember sitting around with cousins, aunts, and my grandmother with our hands working the food. It was partly a chore, but I think we knew even then that it was also part of a tradition.

Corinda Pinder was my favorite aunt, and I shared her sense of humor. She always knew what to say and how to keep me intrigued. I remember the heartiest entire-family laughs happening at her house. What a great family blessing! The Pinders simply had a mix of what was right and what needed to be done for the family, and an undercurrent of joy and perseverance. Out of all the Pinder women, Aunt Corinda also most reminded me of my mother.

RUNNING AND THE MOVE TO VEGANISM

I've been a runner since I was eleven. (I remain so and always will be, so long as God provides.) My dad shared his joy for running and the runner's mindset with me early in life, casually running in our favorite part of Philadelphia's Fairmount Park System known as Valley Green. In middle school I began to run competitively. By high school, it stuck, and I became a three-season runner. As a runner, I had concerns about my well being and what I was eating; although in those days, one assumed you could eat everything and anything and simply burn up the calories to get rid of the bad stuff. I recall consciously giving up soda in high school. I was never a big fan of milk, so I didn't drink much, and if I did, I drank skim milk. I was already past my days as a candy freak. I didn't want a lot of sugar on my teeth, because I didn't want to deal with a dentist.

The other conscious decision I made then was to give up eating hot dogs. I felt I had eaten my share of hot dogs by the time I'd hit sixth grade and I knew they were a terrible food. I remember thinking: *This has got to be the worst kind of food that's being made.* I considered lunch meat and hot dogs the same things, so I stayed away from both.

The next couple of decades were a slow movement away from meat and dairy. Even though I still loved rare steaks and burgers, moist chicken and delicate salmon, I remembered my mother's reminder to eat my green vegetables, and as a home cook, loved to experiment with all foods. During my college years, I would declare some summers an "official vegetarian summer" because it was hot in the kitchen and I was often near broke. My palate and cooking habits adjusted accordingly. Even before going a hundred-percent plant-based/vegan, I considered myself to be plant-based, although I did allow a little bit of meat and cheese in my diet.

I started reducing meat and dairy in the early 1990s, when I began making many different discoveries about health and food. Because I wasn't ever ill, it wasn't poor health that set me on my journey. At every stage of life, I've tried to eat the best way I know how, drawing upon whatever understanding and knowledge were available at the time.

In graduate school, I became conscious of fresh juices. I worked in a restaurant at the time, and one of my close colleagues was "doing a juice fast." One day, she invited me over to her house, and I drank fresh juice for the first time. It was a no-brainer after that. My colleague eventually gifted that juicer to me, and I dabbled in juicing from time-to time.

In the late 1990s, then a teacher of third graders in my local school district, I remember going through different phases with my lunches. Sometimes I would make sandwiches, stacked high like those at Jewish delis; other times, I would make tasty salads; and other times, I'd be on a cereal kick. I wanted cow's milk on the cereal at that time, so I ventured into a Whole Foods (back then it was called Fresh Fields) and found their dairy fresh skim milk. I regularly purchased it and used it for my cereal until I started to notice a particular rumbling in my stomach and other digestive problems. I thought about it, rationally, and said to myself, *I can't continue to blame these kids for this mysterious gas in our classroom! What's new in my diet and world? What am I doing differently?* Putting it all together, I decided it was probably the dairy milk, and I bought rice milk for the very first time. I instantly got my stomach back. That was when I realized that although I didn't eat much of it, dairy was causing me the grief. If it was a "dry" product like cheese, it didn't affect me as much; but my reaction to dairy milk made things obvious! The visits to Whole Foods/Fresh Fields allowed me to see other options and learn about new foods. Best of all, I became very curious.

After my episode with dairy, I had the consciousness that I was going to keep dairy out of my life as much as I possibly could. Still, though, the mentality that I assumed then was one of moderation. I know it is very different now.

THE CLEANSE

Things really started to shift for me about 2003. I learned something pivotal on, of all things, *The Howard Stern Show.* Howard's fellow broadcaster, Robin Quivers, was drinking some kind of concoction on air. The team teased her about it all the time. She would never talk about it, but one day she said, "Okay, I'll give you guys four minutes to ask me anything you want about this drink." I heard enough to Google search and learned that she was doing something called the Master Cleanse. It's a specific drink recipe for detoxing. The drink was like a spicy lemonade, and you had to consume a certain minimum amount per day according to your weight. Water was allowed, too, in any desired quantity. I decided to try it out.

The first day was easy: I fasted for half a day before starting the cleanse. On day two, the cleanse directions advised taking it easy. I read that I might feel tired or sick, as if I had the flu, or even see parasites coming out of the body! I didn't see any parasites, but I spent my second day sleeping. I couldn't stay awake and barely opened my eyes. I remember lying in bed feeling drained.

The third day, however, I woke up at six in the morning with my eyes wide open. This was when the greatest seed was planted. Throughout the day, I thought to myself, *I want to know how I can feel like this ALL THE TIME!* Of course, like any dietary change, there were rough patches. In this case, I was going to the bathroom very frequently. That's why I recommend that if anyone wants to undertake the Master Cleanse, you do so when the time is your own and you're less than twenty minutes away from the nearest bathroom!

The cleanse was life-changing. Throughout that week, I remember feeling very introspective; there was some emotional cleansing happening, too, and I was fascinated by the way my body/skin smelled . . . it smelled great! My body was just cleaning out. It was an empowering feeling to know I was in control of this machine; that I was doing something really great for my body and was experiencing positive results. I didn't know exactly what I was doing, but I did the cleanse for fourteen days. In fact, the fast only lasted eleven days, but the other three were spent slowly introducing food back into my system in liquid form.

One positive discovery I had from that first cleanse was that I realized I had previously been putting some ingredients in my body that didn't agree with me. I know now that one ingredient was gluten. All I knew at that time was that there were certain doughs, breads, and other foods that were clouding my mind and messing with my digestion. Another important realization was that for the first time I discovered that my stomach could be calm. There were many gifts in the early stages of this food journey, and they have continued to this day. Like salvation, it's an ongoing journey.

Cleansing didn't permanently change my eating habits right away, but it served as an important stage of my awareness and growth. After a cleanse, I'd eventually drift back to the foods I knew I shouldn't have been consuming. It was a strange pattern of cleansing, slowly going back to the old ways, and cleansing again. I remember thinking, *Okay, so maybe I'll do a cleanse every quarter.* I attempted this, but I also saw I was losing a lot of weight when I did, so I found myself trying to rationalize how the cleanse was going to work with my lifestyle. I understood this pattern was ridiculous: to cleanse and then return to eating terrible foods. But I did have the sense that eventually I would learn some things, fill these voids in knowledge, and bring better foods into my life. From then, it was a very slow, steady progression to learning more and realizing I didn't want any animal products or processed foods in my body.

Another great contribution to my changes at that time was *The China Study*, the landmark study and book by Dr. T. Colin Campbell. The China Study was the most comprehensive human health study conducted in the world at the time. It compared our standard American diet to that of people in nations around the world, particularly in East Asian countries not experiencing the level and type of disease we experience in the United

States. The researchers concluded that people who consumed large amounts of animal-based protein were more likely to suffer death from cancer, heart disease, and diabetes than people who ate mostly plant-based foods. This information helped me understand the reasons I didn't want animal products inside my body and accelerated the process of what I was trying to accomplish in my diet.

I never put negative pressure on myself as I reduced my intake of animal-based foods. In fact, I thought it was fun. I like to cook, so I was always discovering news ways to create meals. The biggest change in my understanding was in the concept of meals—breakfast, lunch, and dinner—and how marketing had determined what we ate and when we ate it; that every dish was meat-centric with "secondary" foods accompanying the meat on our plates. Once I threw that old model out the window, all plant-based whole foods on my plate had equal footing and value. The old understanding of moderation and balance didn't matter anymore. I started to learn a new balance based on different goals and a new understanding of nutrition. The journey is on-going.

The Philly VegFest

I've been an active part of the Philadelphia vegan, whole-foods, plant-based community for the past several years. In addition to the dietary changes I was making for myself, I began to share the knowledge I was gaining with others. In 2016, I was blessed to meet a man named Bill Kraftsow. At the time I met Bill, I was hosting a screening of the documentary *Forks Over Knives*. My brother, who was friends with Bill, suggested I contact Bill to let him know about the screening. Bill was the founder of an active Facebook forum called "Let Food Be Thy Medicine." The forum was a dietary whole-foods, plant-based support group for the prevention and reversal of disease. My brother thought Bill or members of the forum might want to attend the screening.

To my surprise, Bill showed up just fifteen minutes before the screening, and we met and spoke briefly before the start. In that little bit of time, Bill told me of his fascinating and difficult journey. Bill's father had died of a heart attack when Bill was only two years old. Bill grew up with no understanding of proper diet, living on junk food for most of his life. At age forty-two he was diagnosed with congestive heart failure and was advised to undergo quadruple bypass heart surgery. His doctor only gave him minimal information about options. Just before he was scheduled for surgery, Bill's doctor mentioned the word *vegan*. Not knowing what it meant, Bill asked his doctor if that was a viable option. The doctor frowned and dismissively stated, "You can do that if you want and eat carrots and celery for the rest of your life!" Bill looked at the doctor's face and asked him to schedule the surgery.

The surgery was completed and, unfortunately, one of the bypasses immediately failed. During the operation, the surgeon also severed Bill's right phrenic nerve, affecting the diaphragm, and Bill lost the use of one of his lungs. His body didn't react well to the surgery, and he ended up getting severe infection.

I met Bill ten years after that surgery. Subsequent to it, he'd changed his life. He'd watched a video called *Eating*, in which he discovered the work of Dr. Caldwell Esselstyn, the author of *Prevent and Reverse Heart Disease*, among other books. Dr. Esselstyn's protocol is all about whole-foods, plant-based, no-oil eating, and he works with patients with cardiovascular disease in a very strict manner. On this diet, Esselstyn has been able literally to reverse his patients' heart disease. Bill adopted this healthy-eating protocol and started writing about it. People then began following Bill's story, and that led him to the Facebook forum.

After hearing Bill's story, I immediately told him that he had to be on the panel I was organizing following the showing of *Forks Over Knives*. After his appearance on the panel, I joined his Facebook group, and before long Bill asked me to be an administrator for it. "I like what you're sharing," he said. "You have an immense amount of knowledge and seem to really be connecting with people."

"I would love to do it," I replied, "as long as I can contribute what you need. I don't want to take on something and disappoint you."

"Don't worry," he said, "you'll see how it works. Everyone chips in."

What I didn't know about the Facebook forum is that there is a backend channel for administrators. I had only met Bill once in person, but through the backend you can communicate with people all the time and you start to build relationships. Some of the other admins I've never met in person, but we're friends because of the stuff we do together on the forum.

At some point, Bill mentioned the Philadelphia VegFest, and I told him I knew of it but had never attended. He told me that the last ones had been in 2013 and 2015 and it had been run by the Philadelphia branch of the Humane League, an animal advocacy organization. Bill wanted to know why it had ended. In June of 2016, Bill wrote me to let me know he'd organized a meeting with the grassroots coordinator at the Humane League, and I had a seat at the table. Rachel Black, Bill, and I met at a local coffee shop. Rachel arrived with a huge folder, and we learned all about the ins and outs of the Philly VegFest. During that discussion, I really knew that this was something we could do. At one point, Rachel stepped away from the table, and I turned to Bill and said, "We should do this!" I already had experience running an art festival in Norristown, which was three times the size of the Philly VegFest, and I knew I was capable of handling all of the logistics. Bill had the daytime hours to be on the phone contacting people, plus the connections with influencers because of what we do on the forum. We left excited, with a goal of launching the next Philly VegFest for June of 2017. For the next few months, we visited other vegfests, meeting vendors, writing, and planning.

Tragically, Bill passed away in September 2016. I had to take a big pause after that, and even considered calling the VegFest off. That's when I realized how close we had become, because I didn't expect the mourning period that came after. I was able to go with Bill's family to bury him and spent the day with them. I deliberated and debated for a while to see if I really wanted to move forward. I thought to myself: *Bill was a man who was able to handpick people for his forum and lead them to places where they could work on their passions. There is no possible way I can let go of all that Bill worked for and sacrificed.*

Another reason I kept moving forward was because I knew there was *no way* Philadelphia could *not* have its own vegfest! The community was hungry for it. I didn't even have to do much marketing, because when vegans talk, it echoes. This festival is a star and had to come back to Philadelphia. It's a lot of fun producing festivals, and I hadn't previously worked for one that was quite like this.

On a weekend in June 2018, I put on the first revived VegFest, and it was a roaring success. The weather was wonderful, and we had a lot of support from forty great vendors and three to five thousand attendees. The event was free, in a beautiful location called Bainbridge Green in the Queen Village section of Philadelphia. The following year, 2019, we doubled in size. We had more people, and the number of vendors increased, too. After the COVID pandemic ends, I will continue to do Philadelphia VegFest because I love working with the community we have. It's very supportive: from restaurants, to vendors, to people, with stores and different shops developing. I also want to add features to the VegFest, such as highlighting different artists that represent vegan talent, including modern dance.

I visited my first Black VegFest in 2019 and was impressed. Some people, who happen not to be Black, sometimes ask me whether they have to be Black to attend. I respond that of course they don't. "However," I say, "although everyone is welcomed, it's important that you understand the perspective from which it comes." There's so much—human lives along with the lives of animals —that needs to be protected.

Some in the Black community are working on different events, and I follow a few different podcasts and blogs. Some take the same perspective I do about inclusion but express it in a more militant fashion that might turn some people away. I want to do things where both communities have the strength we need. We need everyone involved. We don't want to be on one side of things, not including people because they aren't Black. That would be silly. I understand it's a sensitive subject; there's a lot of tension in some parts of Philly. The influence of our large, vibrant Black community is strong throughout the vegan community, yet there *is* a division that I hope I'm able to bridge. Even within just the vegan community, I want to bridge the gap.

What I love so much about having gotten involved in the Philly VegFest and in the way I eat, is being part of the community, including learning about and meeting other people. There are so many things I would have never thought of fifteen years ago that I'm conscious of now—people and ideas that I'm supporting and making sure I protect. I'm beginning to engage with economic and social empowerment, which I think are the most important vectors for progress.

In the long term, vegans need to focus on ownership. It's a waste of time for us to sit begging those that don't care about animals or taking care of health to make changes for us in their restaurants, in their chains, and with their products. Even if they do make *some* changes, like restaurants adding Beyond Meat and the Impossible Burger, or dairy manufacturers now producing plant-based milks, money is still going to them and it's still fueling their machines to produce dairy and meat products. Dairy and fast food have whatever agreement they do with the government because of surpluses, and this is the money that's going to feed the lobbying to help produce these items. These people are *not* our friends. *We need to produce our own.* We need to replace what they're doing with our power. That's how we can make a difference. Let's get the money moving a certain way: that is so important.

To that end, I am opening a whole-foods, plant-based café in the Philly suburbs. I've always dreamed of the idea, and we're starved for options outside of the city. It will be semi-raw, with some bowls, salads, breads, burgers, and smoothies and juices. I've been cooking since I was little, and through my experiences with many different restaurants and foods, I realize there's not much that they're doing that I haven't either done in some way or can't figure out.

Another area where I feel I can make a contribution is that, as the director of the Philly VegFest, I am able to provide opportunities to people who often get passed over. There may be some in the world of vegfests who have the attitude, "We created this and you had nothing to do with it." I couldn't be more opposed to that idea. We live in a rich, green, fertile continent where, as my family showed me when I was young, there was abundant food. The system we have now is a distraction, and we need to give opportunities to everyone who should be seen. We need to recognize the major contributions made by Black people, which I think are misunderstood and underappreciated. So, I consciously call on specific people for my stages because they need to be heard. In turn, I'm inspired by them.

Another way I hope I can make a difference is over the meaning of veganism. There is currently a controversy within vegan forums on whether veganism should be promoted for those concerned with their health, versus those who want to center animals, versus those who want to talk about lifestyle. One group will argue, "These people are only worried about themselves and their health. Why aren't they thinking about the animals?" Another group will argue, "People are animals also, so why can't we understand that health is just as important as protecting the animals?" I want to find common ground. Let's bridge those gaps to truly understand that everything we're doing is beneficial. Let's recognize what the true purpose of veganism is.

Anytime I'm on social media, I emphasize that veganism is a lifestyle. You may be a vegan who eats plants, but it troubles me when people say, ever-so-casually, "I'm going vegan," and they're talking only about food. There's no such thing as going vegan: you're becoming conscious. Just talking about food is diluting the word *vegan*. For instance, I call myself a "whole-foods, plant-based, no-oil lifestyler with increasing vegan sensibilities and sensitivities."

I believe that understanding will come, and I hope to write and talk about this a great deal—so we get past squabbling internally and really start looking at what we need to do.

When I was little, I used to think that as I grew older, things would get better. I now realize it's the complete opposite: as you get older, you wake up to the reality more and more. We have work to do. There are so many little things that distract our communities that we don't get to the real issues; there are so many thoughts in our minds that *we didn't put there*! These keep us divided. It's also true, however, that as I get older I love seeing how we commune and come back together with strength and understanding. We are very, very dynamic and different people, and we have many different strengths, precisely because of our differences. ✹

22

FEEDING MIND, BODY, AND SPIRIT

Eric Adams

Sometimes it takes a crisis to bring to light what was always there but had been avoided for too many years. We are living this reality at the moment. But we all know out of crisis comes despair or opportunity; I choose the pathway of opportunity.

For me, a crisis manifested itself in my personal health in 2016, when I was fifty-six. I was experiencing abdominal pain, and the doctor diagnosed me with Type 2 diabetes. I had lost sight in my left eye, and the vision in my right was diminishing. My cholesterol levels were extremely elevated, and I had high blood pressure. I was also suffering from an ulcer and had permanent nerve damage in my hands and feet that my doctor told me was going to lead eventually to amputation. I was stunned.

Instead of sitting back and saying, "Woe is me!" I asked myself a question: "Why *not* me?" At that moment, I could have followed the all-too-usual pathway of those with my condition. They go on dialysis and they lose their sight from diabetes, which is the number one cause of blindness and the number one cause of non-trauma limb amputation. But that's not who I am as an individual. I firmly believe that you stay in the darkness until someone shows you the light. That was the case with my realization about how my fast food, junk-food, slave-food diet was poisoning my mental and physical state.

Now, when you receive that knowledge, you have to *choose* to move toward the light. I did some research and saw how a few doctors were suggesting that a whole foods, plant-based diet could not just medicate the diabetes but reverse it. So, I adopted this diet. What astonished me was the body's desire to heal itself, if it was just given the tools to do so. Within three months, I lost thirty pounds, my vision cleared up, my nerve damage went away, my ulcer vanished, and my blood pressure and cholesterol levels normalized. It was a complete reversal. I became more physically active, and even managed to persuade my mother to adopt this diet to help her own medical conditions. Because of the remarkable results I obtained, I recognized the need to make this information more widely available, which is why I began regular vegan meet-ups at Brooklyn Borough Hall for people to learn from one another and experts in business, health, and community organizing who were plant-based.

I consider myself to be a conscious Black man, and I don't believe you can be selective in conscious behavior. For me, Black pride is making a real examination of how just about everything we've done has been Europeanized, and not allowing ourselves to fall into the trap of fitting into someone else's definition of us. We define ourselves by knowing ourselves mentally, physically, and spiritually—and living that out every day. This entails not calling out names and not trying to fit into any style of dress or attire; instead, it means being Black from the inside out, and all that that identity stands for.

The vestiges of slavery, which include the food that African-Americans eat, are still very real. In 2019, I flew to Senegal in order to form a sister-city agreement between Gorée Island and Brooklyn. Brooklyn has one of the largest concentrations of Africans in the diaspora, and Gorée Island was one of the places in Africa from which slaves were shipped to the Americas. I visited Gorée Island to re-establish our relationship with our cousins, our uncles, and our distant relatives, both at home and abroad. I wanted, as other countries have done, to let folks go to their home of origin and use the strengths of America to create partnerships to help build those countries. Ghana has given dual citizenship to African-Americans, and Senegal and Ivory Coast are open to the idea of giving land. So, we need to be open to helping rebuild the continent and using our expertise to deal with some of the issues that slavery created.

That visit and that connection were very powerful for me. One of the disconnections fostered by slavery is between African-Americans and Africans elsewhere, so that Africans in America don't want to deal with Africans on the continent, and vice versa. In fact, I believe the European colonial powers deliberately brainwashed us to ensure we separated ourselves from one another: not only between Africans and the diaspora, but within the continent itself.

The mistrust and separation within the larger communities of people of African descent, fostered by colonialism and slavery, manifest themselves among African-Americans in other ways. We need to learn how to communicate with one another; we need to learn how to listen, and to do so deeply. We also have to take healing into our own hands. We're still experiencing the trauma of slavery and racism in our lives—at, I believe, an epigenetic and cellular level. That trauma manifests itself in broken relationships, violence, and self-hate. You cannot be a Black man or woman in a toxic society or environment and not in some way have been impacted by these realities.

The problem is we're not doing enough to reverse the impact. The real healing process can't be as periodic as visiting one's family during Thanksgiving and Christmas, or sitting in church and singing a hymn or two. We have to go to a deep place internally and learn the power of being still in order to reverse some of the mental disorder that's affecting us.

Connected to our healing has to be our health—and intrinsic to our health is the food we eat. Food is poisoning us, and it has a clear connection to slavery. For me, it is inconsistent to be walking around wearing a dashiki but carrying slave food in my hand. When we look at what this food is doing to our health, it should infuriate us all that the slave master is still winning by keeping us on a food plantation. If we're going to be free, let's *be* free. My discipline comes from wanting to practice what I preach. And it's about being healthy and taking care of myself, using the power of food.

Once you make the transition, you can no longer hide yourself from the realities. At some of the social gatherings that I attend, I see our grandmothers being wheeled away from the tables with arthritis or a heart condition. I hear people talking about their dialysis. We hold hands together around the meal table and pray for the health of our loved ones in the hospital. And yet we are consuming the foods that are causing these very tragedies. It's my mission to get every mosque, church, and temple to start talking about how we can stop feeding our crisis on the end of our forks.

This passion extends to my political career. As a very mission- and vision-driven person, I firmly think that with the right vision, it is possible to bring about real change—not just symbolic gestures that kick the can down the road. Unfortunately, we're missing that vision at all levels of government.

I started my professional life as a computer programmer, spent two decades in law enforcement, served for four terms in the New York State Senate, and since 2013 have been the Brooklyn Borough President. In each of my roles in public life I have seen how failed policies create an environment that forces people to stay in terrible conditions. One way to solve this reality is to change those policies to ones that improve the quality of life for many people. This is why I am running to be mayor of New York City in 2021.

POLICING

I believe I am uniquely qualified to meet the challenges of this moment—particularly on the issue of appropriate policing. When I joined the New York Police Department, homicides were at about two thousand a year, with almost a hundred thousand robberies and felonious assaults; there were shootings and rapes, and crack was running rampant. During the 1980s, Black grandmothers were trapped in their homes, so traumatized were they by crime. And, no matter where you place the blame or what you consider the causes, those crimes were taking place disproportionately in communities of color. So, I know the need to maintain law and order.

But I have also experienced victimization by the police; my brother and I were beaten up by cops when I was fifteen. Indeed, I came into the force (as a computer programmer) with a level of animosity toward policing. To this day, I don't know of a single Black person who doesn't have an issue with over-aggressive policing. In 1995, I was one of the cofounders of 100 Blacks in Law Enforcement Who Care, whose goal was to speak out against racial profiling and police brutality and advocate for diversity within the police department—from top to bottom.

Now, there are clearly a lot of things the police department must improve on as it continues to evolve—because people should not be afraid of the police. And we must continue the fight to take bias and brutality out of the department by making it more diverse, and better assessing officers' abilities and prejudices. But we cannot allow the public to reject the concept of policing outright; public safety is a prerequisite for prosperity. Since I joined the NYPD thirty-five years ago, there have been many things that *were* done right regarding policing, and because of those policies, thousands of New Yorkers are growing up not being traumatized on every corner with another mural dedicated to the life of someone who was killed prematurely. That's real. This city is safer than it was. I remember New York when we all had "no radio" signs in our cars and we created an entire industry out of not being safe. I know what it was like when we were living that way. In fact, as a computer programmer, I was part of the original team who looked at how we could reverse criminal activity in a way that was functional, and we were able to figure out how to deal successfully with some aspects of crime.

PROGRAMS

The COVID crisis has revealed major disparities and systemic flaws across the entire range of public services, including in public health. Throughout the COVID crisis, I spent all my time monitoring the coronavirus and its effects on the people of Brooklyn. That commitment reflected my leadership style. I think generals lead their troops into battle, and don't send them into battle and ask, "How is the war?" I'm on the ground. People will tell you that when I walk the streets, I will give someone my cell number so we can interact one-on-one. I'm clear that I'm not elected to *be* served, I'm elected *to* serve. I consider myself to be a servant leader. And I do not have a problem with understanding that that's my role.

Part of that servant leadership is not only to meet people literally on the street, but to do so conceptually: You have to meet them where they *are*, and then take them where they *ought* to be. I don't go to people as a vegan or a plant-based eater and say, "Listen, you need to get rid of all the meat that you're eating." That's just not a reality.

Meatless Monday is a great way to provide people with small, incremental steps that allow them to explore a meatless diet. The meatless day a week can extend to a meatless Monday, Wednesday, and Friday. When people start seeing the health benefits—when they stop feeling bloated, sick, and lethargic—they are going to evolve on their own, from poisoning themselves to *life*. Meatless Monday is, therefore, a way of engaging in a conversation with people on why they might consider reducing and then ending their meat consumption. We need to answer basic questions for people also, and that's what I believe Meatless Monday allows us to do. Meatless Monday responds to the urgent need for all of us to cut down on our meat consumption—for our health, for the state of the planet, and, of course, to reduce the number of animals raised and killed.

As I discovered with my own healing, we have an incredible opportunity to use food as medicine across the city. In 2019, I arranged with Bellevue, a public hospital in Manhattan, to start the **Plant-Based Lifestyle Medicine Program**. The aim is to treat the underlying causes of diseases through diet and lifestyle changes. Six hundred people signed up for the program, and 470 have now gone through the program. As they do so, we're finding individuals are reducing the amount of medicine they take, and even coming off it altogether; they are not just mitigating but reversing their diseases. It's my belief that this project is going to be the hallmark for how we practice medicine in the future—not just in New York City, but perhaps in the United States. This program is the first "lifestyle medicine clinic" in a major institution such as a public hospital.

Another initiative I'm very proud of is our program that encourages the practice of **meditation**. It's my belief that we have to start arming children with self-care. I have sent teachers away to learn how to meditate, so they can learn mindfulness and meditation to teach our children. Many of our children sit in school every day, and we try to ask them to learn how to multiply and divide. In reality, many children are effectively telling us, "Listen, we're divided; who's dealing with our pain? I just had someone in my life who was shot and killed. Who's talking to me?" Or "I am in a domestic violence situation: someone just tried to molest me. Who's dealing with my pain?"

So, we want to provide children with the power to deal with this trauma. This is because our spirit is like a sponge: if it's saturated with the madness of life that we experience every day, we can't take in anything healthy. Through the practice of meditation, children can learn how to wring out the despair they're saturated with so they can start to absorb what it is to have a healthy and beautiful life. I believe every child should start the school day with meditation and mindfulness, and that is what we're pushing for in New York City.

The fourth initiative I'm proud of is our **Zero to Three Project** on education and the development of a child's mind. Neurologists are telling us that a child's mind develops

80 percent within the first 900 days from conception, and yet we do not start formally educating children and families until the child is either 3K or pre-K: that's three or four years old. That is too late. So, we're following the science and starting a program in Brooklyn where we'll be empowering families with something that we call Brooklyn New Beginnings. The aim is to show families what they can do at that early stage in getting their child ready to learn how to start absorbing information during those crucial periods. Because if you lose a child at three years old—from zero to three—you'll never get them back. And we lose a countless number of children because no one is focusing on that area. Everyone says it's too difficult. I refuse to accept that. It's not something that we ought to do; it's something we *must* do.

NEW YORK CITY

Should I become mayor of New York City, there would be three major ways I would address how government creates our food crisis. The first would be to make the city function better and to stop creating crises across agencies. I'm reminded of a quotation from Archbishop Desmond Tutu, who said, "There comes a point where we need to stop just pulling people out of the river. We need to go upstream and find out why they're falling in." This is my mindset. The tragedy in New York, as in the cities across America, is that not only are we not going upstream to find out why people are falling in the river in the first place, but our agencies—the Department of Education, Department of Homeless Services, Department of Buildings, and so on—are pushing them in the river and creating the flow. Our aim should be to create some systemic functionality, so that we don't have departments that create crises for the other agencies to fix. I'm well qualified to address this, since I was part of an agency and organizational institution that went from being dysfunctional to functional.

The second plan is to put in place the necessary resources to stop literally feeding the healthcare crisis. In many cases, two out of the three meals a child receives a day come from the school, and that food is unhealthy. Then the child returns home and the food they eat at home is unhealthy. This unhealthy diet will lead to asthma, childhood obesity, and childhood diabetes, and we will continue to feed the crisis.

In City Harvest and other programs where the poor go to get food, we have to move away from caloric consumption to nutritional input. In 2019, I volunteered my time over the Thanksgiving season at a food pantry, and looked at the food we were giving people who were already going through a healthcare crisis; it was almost criminal. As we prepared the food, people were walking past the vegetables, to run over to the ham, turkey, and canned foods, because they didn't know how to cook the beets or collard greens.

We have to be bold enough to say, "If you're hungry, you're going to be ready to eat something that's going to make you healthy people." I understand it can be difficult to change. The first time I tried to move toward a plant-based lifestyle, the meals I prepared were probably horrendous. But I never gave up and continued to try. Out of that came some amazingly tasty dishes. My go-to meal is a black lentil soup with seven different varieties of beans; some fruit chopped in the soup with flaxseeds and nuts; lots of veggies (such as kale and peppers); and garlic and seasonings (such as cumin, paprika, pepper, and turmeric). The basis of the soup is black lentils liquefied with mushrooms and red lentil pasta. It's a very healthy and also a very filling meal.

This is just one example of the many dishes you can make. We need to start showing people how to eat healthily, and how it tastes good and is good for you—particularly on our dime. Senior centers must have healthy food. Jails: healthy food. Hospitals: healthy food. If we're feeding, and you're eating, on my dime, you're going to eat healthy foods. I'm not going to pay for your crisis. I'm going to pay for your health so you can live better.

Lastly, and probably most importantly, we have to revamp our educational system to teach our children better life habits, as well as provide a better overall education. We have to start early. We have to make sure we scale up success and create an environment that's conducive to developing the full personhood of children. And that's mind, body, and soul. We must feed them right, and we must educate them right. We must give them the proper amount of emotional stability. If we do that, we can change the course of this entire city. Because anything can happen when people are healthy, and healthy is not only what we consume in food, but also what we consume in what we hear, what we see, and what we feel.

Healthy at Last

In October 2020, I published *Healthy at Last: A Plant-Based Approach to Preventing and Reversing Diabetes and Other Chronic Illnesses.* The book goes into detail about what I have outlined here: my life story, my confrontation with my mortality, and how I used a plant-based diet to heal myself and how you can do the same. It explains how I began and continue my vegan journey, and how and why I have made it my mission to tackle chronic disease in the African-American community, and beyond. *Healthy at Last* is not my final word on the subject of the systemic problems around access to healthy food that Black people face. Instead, it is my first public declaration of what I aim to make a rallying call for all public figures and politicians: that justice, decency, public and private health and wellbeing, sound budgeting, and a whole range of other pressing issues that face us now and in the future will not be solved unless we make the switch to a diet that sustains us and the planet. ✿

23

THE REVOLUTION INSIDE

An Interview with Mutulu Olugbala a.k.a. M-1 of dead prez

Brotha Vegan: *Tell us your name and about your journey to health.*

M-1: My name is Mutulu Olugbala, also known as M-1 of the tell-it-like-it-is, everything-is-political hip hop duo dead prez. I am a changemaker, global force connector, conscious content creator, and propagandist. Yeah. I guess we'll start there.

My journey toward health began in 1991. I come from a relatively poor community whose practices around food and health have left us with a plethora of diseases and illnesses. I gained a little consciousness by reading Malcolm X and then from that, *How to Eat to Live* by Elijah Muhammad, which I directly referenced from Malcolm. At that point, I decided I was ready to not eat pork. Following pork came beef, with a little help from KRS-One, and then chicken.

In 1991, I moved to that kind of lifestyle, but it wasn't actually the most healthy. It was a step forward in consciousness, but I had no formal training on how to prepare meals so nutritionally I would be able to get what I needed to maintain a certain kind of health regimen. I began to work out—as a kind of revolutionary political theory in action. I worked out, and my health became optimal so I could be the best freedom fighter I could. This is still the perspective from which health emanates for me.

Since that time, I've come to grow and learn about different communities and different perspectives of health and the "why" of veganism, but I became vegan long before it was popular, or as popular as it is now. I continued down that road for many years, but then I became more conscious of sugars, and processed and pre-prepared foods, and learned about whole foods. I read Dr. Afrika's books. He helped me understand what foods were for what things in your body.

As I said, dead prez was a fighting, political organization. But we also were poets and rappers. As we grew as these, we began to talk about these issues. That journey was enhanced by watching my partner, Stic.man, become ill from gout. He turned to some of the healers in our community in Brooklyn. Queen Afua became one of the main healers that he went to. Then he started to entertain a raw diet, and did that for close to eighty days, which cured him of his illness. He introduced me to raw food, and I incorporated it into our diet.

From there, I began to incorporate whatever I needed to facilitate the lifestyle of a young activist-artist running around the world and not getting enough sleep or enough of a lot of things I needed to help my body. I began to see the issue holistically: that it wasn't just about eating healthily, but about a healthy lifestyle as a whole.

Around seventeen to twenty years later, I started incorporating fish into my diet. Why I wanted fish is a hard question to answer, but to each his own. I felt that I wanted protein and a certain kind of protein, and cheap. And I felt good. So, for me, veganism was not all about saving the animals; it was really about saving ourselves. And once I had a perspective on health, I knew how to maintain a healthy regimen. Even that worldview has shifted, as I became more conscious of fish and the ecology of the ocean. A few years later, I put down fish.

Today, I've maintained that kind of nutritional lifestyle for my family and my children, who eat from a plethora of foods in different ways. Some do not react well to gluten in the diet; for me, gluten doesn't have the adverse effects I've seen in my children. I've had to hold back some foods from them in order for them to grow and change. That has been my journey around health, in a nutshell. It's way more complicated than that, but this is the shortened version.

BV: *You've touched on your family's being vegan. Were your children born vegans?*
M-1: Yes, they are a result of my experiences. My children's mother is a vegan chef. When I met her, I had been studying Eastern medicine and holistic foods, and she was a raw chef at one point. She began to introduce the same regimen to our children. They were born in a vegan environment and have maintained it to this day. I have five girls, and they all

maintain a very healthy lifestyle. They even have a more strict diet than I do, because some things affect them differently.

BV: *How do you and your daughters live their lives as conscious vegans?*

M-1: Those of us who have children or are preparing to raise children want to guide our children in the best ways toward a lifestyle that is healthy. For me, it's about not only what you put inside their bodies, nutritionally, but what you feed their minds and what you feed the spirit. I've raised my children consciously around what we ingest: how much outside influence comes from media and television; about a family lifestyle of loving and being able to come back and huddle in and circle so we can sum up the outside world as it relates to how we live.

How we live is a lot different for my children when they go to school and open their lunch boxes and other kids see they have seaweed snacks and gluten-free alternatives to the regular snacks. Sometimes they get ostracized or talked about or put in the middle—or even have just a lot of eyes on them, which can be uncomfortable. So we need to explain those situations and how we are different.

A lot of times I forget that, even though I have been on this health journey, many people have not. Even some of us who are healthy are still learning. I'm not speaking as some sort of arrogant know-it-all; I'm learning every day. I tell my children that they can learn from other children's lifestyles. They can't eat the other foods, but they can learn about what makes them healthy and what doesn't. That has been the way I have raised my tribe. We consciously feed them less TV and more conscious music and a diversity of culture, so they can connect it to healthy lifestyle. We practice yoga and meditation and Eastern thought processes. We go to churches that widen and expand their cultural views. They know what's happening in Africa versus what's happening in Europe, India, South America, and Mexico—and how people eat—so they can associate lifestyle and culture with nutrition.

BV: *How does your wife work with you as a parent?*

M-1: Well, we have the same opinion about life. We move in unison. In the most loving way, we understand and see life. Things are constantly changing; every day there's a new scenario that we must determine how to navigate. She is—as, I hope, I can be to her—a balance: that kind of rock. It's not static: it's ongoing and changing, and each day we have to reassess how we feel and look and are. In that way, we balance each other and become better people.

The centerpiece of it is love. Love helps to control all other kinds of understanding of who we are. So she completes me in ways that I really at this time can't even explain. I have to mention that my children have two different mothers, so my children's mother—not my wife—is also a very special person. I mention her because she is integral to me generating the kind of balance and love and understanding that they need. Our balance is important as well, of course.

Those who have been through relationships understand this, but for many who haven't, it's important that we build families that endure and can be long-lasting. We want healthy bonds and bridges that are strong and don't fall down. That's my mantra throughout all my relationships. I'm mentioning my children's mother because she is the nourisher and feeder of our children's minds and we still maintain a common accord. People have to know this is possible and relationships don't have to be disjointed. When they are, it affects the mental, physical, and spiritual health of your whole unit. I have learned the good, the bad, and the ugly from that, as everybody should.

BV: *Could you tell how dead prez's song "Be Healthy" was supposed to impact the Black community?*
M-1: We wanted people to hear us and not *be* us, but to learn from our experiences. What we were learning from Dr. Afrika, Queen Afua, and the other teachers helped shape "Be Healthy." As we learned and grew from those experiences, we poured them into our music, which ultimately became the 2000 album *Let's Get Free*.

As I've said, health and wellness are a base formation for the structure, the foundation. "Be Healthy" was written to communicate to a community who, in general, has been unhealthy, raised on junk food, has lived in food deserts, and isn't privy to ruling-class health measures and standards. We wanted to speak in a way that was long lasting—like Fred Hampton of the Black Panther Party—in plain, proletarian English. We wanted to talk to the blunt smokers and the 40s drinkers. We wanted to talk to people who might look at who we are and what we did and say, "That's weird!" Then, instead of shunning it, say, "Well, let me try. Does that taste good?" Those kind of things. Through the years, many have come up after our performances and shows around the world and told us, "Hey, man—you guys showed me some stuff that I wasn't hip to, and I want to thank you for it." To me, that blessing doesn't belong to dead prez; it belongs to those who taught us. That was the reason why we made the song.

As for the album itself: We made *Let's Get Free* thinking, *What could we make that would impact our community?* We knew our radical ideas could be shut down, like those political prisoners who we were living and sacrificing for. *Let's Get Free* is the command and the directive that we wanted to start with. The album forms the contents page of our dead prez book. Songs like "We Want Freedom," "Be Healthy," "Propaganda," "Happiness," "Psychology," and "It's Bigger than Hip-Hop" are literally all chapters in that book. Even though we haven't finished writing the book, we have continued to write it. Maybe it will be completed by those we hand the baton to. I'm hoping. But that was the intention of *Let's Get Free*, the album.

BV: *What does Black liberation look like to you?*
M-1: Liberation is not a poetic term. It's a state of political and economic wellbeing for our people. It looks like independence and self-determination. In this country, we have been subjugated to oppression and we live in a subdued state still, in which we are affected by colonialism, capitalism, and the system that has been set in place to continue exploitation. That happens through food as well, which is why health is a part of that conversation, like I said. In order to be free, we have to be healthy. We have to be long, long-lasting fighters. Non-health is still pervasive in our community, which is the reason why diabetes, cancer, high blood pressure, and the rest are still rampant. This is how I understand liberation from Malcolm X's standpoint; from Marcus Garvey's; from the standpoint of liberation of Omali Yeshitela, founder of the Uhuru Movement; and from that of Chairman Fred Hampton of the Black Panther Party. This is what liberation is today. So, are we liberated? I think not. I think not.

BV: *Tell us about your background in organizing.*

M-1: I became kind of conscious of my situation in the world, and in reading and connecting with my partner, Stic.man, after I moved to Tallahassee, Florida, as a seventeen-year-old. I began hanging around a conscious Black bookstore and taking in lots of information. Not having the advantage of an organization that was a political structure that we could fold into and be active in, we made one for ourselves: the Black Survival Movement. We enticed our comrades and friends to join and study and be active.

That was my first try at being on the scene and doing something to save our people. It was done without a bunch of information but with wholeheartedness and a great attitude. It caught the attention of the Uhuru Movement and Omali Yeshitela, who does the intro to *Let's Get Free* and speaks on some songs, like "Police State." Through those teachings and teach-ins, and activism and growth and going through the community and meeting people, and leafleting and propagandizing, and learning how to sway the minds of people, I developed solid tools around being an organizer. I continued and that has made me who I am to this day.

BV: *Are there any campaigns you're concerned about or feel need more public support?*

M-1: Yes there are. The question of political prisoners is critical inside our community. A political prisoner is someone who has been jailed for their political beliefs. In the case of Black people and freedom-seeking Black people, those heroes and sheroes of the 1960s from Black political organizations sacrificed in a way that would leave them exiled and jailed. Ultimately, many of them were murdered for standing up for our rights to be free of capitalist exploitation and to live the kind of lifestyle that would allow us to be self-determining and independent, like Malcolm told us.

Political prisoners don't occur in a vacuum. They happen because there has been political organization and, more significantly, *effective* organization. The state doesn't want to lock up somebody who's not making a dent. They had to invent new laws, new infractions, kangaroo courts, and do all kind of tricky stuff so we wouldn't be able to navigate the system or have the kind of legal participation to unlock the cages.

The state's reaction to Black people's political organizing demonstrates that our movement is right and was right: that the things that African people in the U.S. and around the world need are related to our direct freedom—not only in terms of food, clothes, and shelter, but justice and equality and power. Even when you begin to talk about climate change and our community, you're talking about communities that have been riddled with lead poisoning, riddled with chemical warfare in the shape of pills that have been deployed inside our children to cause different kinds of reactions in our brains. We're talking about a plethora of issues that relate to climate change that are different for African people than what happens in communities that have lived and benefited from African exploitation. A lot of people talk about saving the whales and the rest, and that is true. But in order to save the whales, we have to save ourselves, and saving ourselves will save the whales. We'll clear up their environment.

One of my focuses now is on the need to protect our women and reproductive health. One of the things happening inside our community is the lack of understanding about the attack on the womb, from before our children are born, and what goes into the mortality rate of our children: because of who we are; because of our skin color. I have begun to create products that to me are revolutionary because they're non-toxic and organic, and are meant to bolster women's reproductive health in order for us to be able to talk about that in the best kind of way.

What we're saying here is, we have to get through the primary contradiction in order to get to the secondary contradictions. If you strike the middle of the spider's web, the whole web comes down. But if you just take down one of the pieces of the web from the side, the spider just rebuilds. That's the analogy I want to make, on the issues and causes that I think need to be highlighted—which are plenty and many.

Finally, I want to implore those who are reading this that we have to be revolutionaries inside our children. When they ask us, "What do we do?" we should say, "I'm a teacher, but I'm also a revolutionary"; or "I'm a chef, but I'm also a revolutionary." We need to implant this revolutionary ideology inside our children as babies in order to raise a future that will have the mindset and not have to come to consciousness the way I did. They will have a tradition and institutions of revolution from here on out. ☀

24

HIDDEN GEMS

Scott "Burnhard" Bernard

When I graduated school with a degree in business and marketing, I didn't see myself going into fitness, personal training, the health field, or motivational speaking. In fact, I didn't so much stumble into this career, as it stumbled into me. I'd always loved keeping fit, but I mainly understood the mechanics of the body and fitness through calisthenics learned in the street or the park, rather than anything formal in the gym. In fact, I turned any environment I could into a workout space, a place without limits. Perhaps because I was exercising in a public area, people started gravitating toward me, because they saw the physique I had developed, and they began to follow me on social media.

I've concentrated on body weight-training, because it gives you the same kind of flexibility as calisthenics. Some people feel that they have to go to a gym and use the machines to get a proper workout. Now, there's nothing wrong with the gym, and I work out there when I can. But gyms can be expensive and they're not open all the time, and I don't want either myself or my clients to skip a workout if the gym is closed. That's why calisthenics and body weight-training are so valuable: you can be innovative and flexible and use your own weight to strengthen and tone your body. Squats, dead weight, compound movements: these are all valuable. However, my love and passion for fitness came from and remain in body weight-training.

My vegan journey began in 2015. I was shooting a documentary film on calisthenics when I slipped and fell on my wrist. It seemed a minor injury at the time, but the next morning I found out how painful and detrimental to my ability to work out and train that injury was: I couldn't move my wrist at all. I waited for it to heal by itself, and when it hadn't after a week, I went to the doctor. He didn't say much and prescribed medication, which I took for about two months, without success: the wrist still didn't feel right. Not to be able to see any improvement in my wrist was depressing, because I'm an athlete and I am used to performing at my best. However, one thing the doctor did say during that visit kept ringing in my head: "Scott: You have inflammation."

This made me think. I started doing some research, and before long I discovered that meat is highly inflammatory. I was astonished. Both my parents are Jamaican, and I come from a West Indian/Caribbean culture and had been eating meat my whole life. I couldn't believe it: I was young and healthy . . . how could meat be causing me this problem? I had also fully bought into the idea that meat was essential if you were working out because it was a good source of protein. I also believed that the more meat you ate, the manlier you were. So, there I was, thinking, *If I give up meat, I'm going to lose all my muscles and the physique I've worked so hard for, because I'm not going to be getting enough protein.* I realize now that I was processing this knowledge not through health but through vanity.

However, I began to think about it and decided to keep an open mind. I knew I needed another option, because my wrist wasn't getting any better, and pharmaceuticals were not working for me. I decided to be realistic about my choices and conducted eight to nine months of research. In doing this, I stumbled upon the wisdom of our ancestors and elders, such as Dr. Sebi, Dr. Llaila Afrika, and Queen Afua. These three furthered my interest in continuing my journey to educate myself and absorb as much information as I could before making any decisions, because I had never changed my diet before. In March 2016, after spending Fashion Week in Paris, I felt I had enough information at that point to challenge myself to not eat meat for one week. (As I say, I had to be realistic with myself; I knew I couldn't just go cold turkey.)

This is the first important lesson, as far as I'm concerned. Some people put themselves into a position regarding dietary change that they cannot handle. They aren't realistic with themselves. Instead of conducting research into how to prepare meals or what nutrients they need and how to eat a balanced diet—or even starting slowly with Meatless Monday, and then adding Tuesday, or Wednesday, and so on—some people will simply remove meat and dairy from their diet. It's my belief that that is why they ultimately fail to transition to veganism or eating a plant-based diet.

In preparation for my meat-free week, I knew that the human body thrives on macronutrients, protein, fats, and carbohydrates, and that as long as I was incorporating these into my diet—especially a vegan or plant-based one—I would be fine. Sure enough, I survived my first seven days! In fact, that first week was perhaps one of the best weeks of my life. Within a matter of days, I found myself thinking more clearly; the blemishes and acne about which I'd always been self-conscious began to disappear, and I noticed that I was sleeping better and was more energized throughout the day. Above all, I felt rejuvenated, more in tune with myself. This dietary shift was, in essence, a detoxification. My body had been overworked in attempting to digest disgusting processed foods and meats.

Naturally, having felt so much better through the first week, I had no reservations about extending my meat-free diet for another seven days. This period I like to call, "The Week of Revelations." This was the week where my wrist began to heal and function properly. I returned to the gym and completed ten to fifteen pull-ups on the machine and felt none of the sharp pain that had accompanied the inflammation. When I'd done the pull-ups, I examined my wrist and felt nothing. I took the exercise up a notch, and started some muscle-ups, which are a very taxing, advanced move that require a lot of wrist flexion as you move from a pull-up into a dip. I completed five to seven of these successfully, which was not an easy task even before I hurt my wrist. I remember literally looking at my wrist and saying to myself, *I healed myself with food!* I never went back to that doctor again.

I was still being realistic with myself. I was, after all, breaking long-standing generational habits and traditions. I decided to go vegetarian. On that journey, I also learned the second piece of essential information: listen to your body. Within the first two weeks, I quit eggs because my body rejected them; it was as if it was telling me: *These are not for you.* I became more attuned to what my body was saying, and it began to talk to me about dairy. This was very difficult for me, but I started to quit dairy products one by one, taking each day as it came to see what happened. Finally, I felt what I will call synergy—being one—with my body. The next thing I knew, I was vegan.

Now, as is the case with many people who go vegan, it's often a challenge to explain your choices to your relatives. My family already knew I was health-conscious; however, it so happened that I went vegan when my grandmother was visiting from Jamaica. My grandma is a very good cook, and she expresses her skills and love for her family through her food. The last time she'd seen me, I had been eating curried chicken and oxtail, and so she decided to cook me curried chicken and white rice. When I said to her that I couldn't eat the meal, she was shocked and wondered out loud if there was something wrong with me. When I told her I'd become a vegan, she had never heard of the term. I broke it down for her: I was like a Rastafarian, except without the dreads!

My grandmother not only accepted the idea gracefully, but welcomed it, and made me traditional Jamaican meals without meat. The rest of my family were also very accepting of my new lifestyle. If anything, my mother became more interested in what I was doing because she began to see the changes in me.

This provided me with another essential lesson: We have to be examples for our family and friends. When they see that we are happy and fulfilled—as well as healthy—in our vegan lifestyle, they will begin to ask questions and become curious. They will notice how we are operating on a higher frequency. They will see that if we eat foods with life in them, we will display more life and vitality as well.

Since my transition to veganism, I've become a certified nutritionist and National Academy of Sports Medicine–qualified personal trainer. I've helped hundreds of people convert to a plant-based, vegetarian, or vegan diet, or simply enabled them to reduce their meat intake. In my coaching practice and my vegan advocacy, I have learned yet another lesson—beyond being realistic, educating yourself, listening to your body, and being a role model. It is: You need to find your reason. For me, it was needing to heal myself. For others, it may be something else. Finding your reason gives you the focus, passion, and discipline to see it through.

One transition that was particularly meaningful to me was with a good friend of mine named Blocka, a world-class dancer who has performed in many music videos. I remember the day when he was admitted to the hospital with an allergic reaction to some spicy shrimp he'd eaten. He was in very serious condition, and I introduced him to sea moss (red algae), bladderwrack (a kind of seaweed), and burdock root, and helped him on his vegan journey. Today, he is doing well and no longer has any allergies.

I've been incredibly honored and gratified by the response people have had to my advocacy. I created a video called *Vegan: What I Eat in a Day*, which went viral. I was in the process of shooting the next video, which involved me doing calisthenics in the park, when a woman came up to me and said, "Oh! You're the guy on YouTube that's talking about healthy fitness." I said that I was, and we hugged, and she began to talk to me.

"You don't understand how much of an influence you are in the Black community," she told me. "We need this." She confided in me that diabetes ran in her family.

I was shaken by that information, because it was not the first time I'd heard someone from the Black community talk to me about that—and not just about diabetes. I'd been told that cancer or high blood pressure, or some other condition, ran in the family or that some had a gene for this or that illness. It seemed impossible for me to believe that all of these chronic diseases were running through all our families. They were clearly holding us back, and yet in some way they presented us with an excuse not to take control of our health. *Who*, I thought, as this woman talked to me, *is going to be the one to break the chain?*

One way I believe it is possible to do exactly that is recognizing what our great ancestor Dr. Sebi says: "Disease cannot thrive in an alkaline body." The only way diseases can thrive, he says, is if you create an environment that is more acidic than alkaline. This is a body that is filled with processed, toxic, or acidic foods—ones that introduce mucus into the body.

I see this toxicity every day; in fact, I lived it. I was born in the Bronx, and I remember growing up eating some unhealthy Chinese food, Kentucky Fried Chicken, and pizza all day—to name just a few. In consuming these meals, we are glorifying the "-itis," whatever it may be, and ingesting what is detrimental to us. We have to reverse that trend.

And it's not just foreign or processed foods that are bad for us: certain traditions from within the African-American community are killing us, and we need to re-imagine these traditions and become the masters of our own narrative. For instance, it's Thanksgiving and you have a family get-together. You know Aunt Shirley has high blood pressure, but you put before her and the rest of the family high-caloric, acidic foods that promote high blood pressure, cancer, and disease. But you do it because it's "tradition." This is an oxymoron: you're gathering the family together to celebrate and yet you're doing harm to those you love!

The Bible (Hosea 4:6) says, "My people are destroyed for lack of knowledge." This is never more true than in inner-city neighborhoods, where there isn't a lot of information being presented about health, fitness, and wellness. If you don't know the alternatives, you will not thrive; if you *do* know, you have the *choice* to be better—to put in the effort and take control over your own body and life.

Now, I understand that this is hard. I understand there is a stigma associated with our food: that we have to eat fried chicken, pork, and beef, and love Soul Food and watermelons. But these are slave-master foods; they are not what our ancestors were eating. Our ancestors came from Kemet—the "Black land" that existed before the Arabized Egyptian state. They came from the great civilizations of Keme, Mali, Kush, and Timbuktu. Our peoples ate off the land and consumed ancient grains such as fonio and farro. To be sure, they also ate meat, but they did so minimally.

This is our older heritage, the one of free peoples, and we have a right to reclaim that heritage for veganism. To be Black and vegan is to reclaim our power and to break many stereotypes. One is that to be a vegan you have to be a skinny white person who does yoga and walks their dog in some tony neighborhood. Brothas like me are speaking a different narrative and breaking that stereotype.

We're also encouraging our brothas and sistahs to do what they can to break free of a medical system that over-medicates us and takes far too much of our wealth. If you can help your family members literally return to Mother Nature, and add more plant foods and more whole grains into your diet, you can reduce and even reverse chronic health problems, and save your family astronomical sums of money at the pharmacy. All it takes is discipline and wanting it badly enough. And that's the key: Anyone who is a plant-based physician, advocate, or fitness and wellness counselor can present you with the information and talk to you until they're blue in the face. But the solution is in your hands: What are you going to do with the valuable gems that you have in your hands?

Being Black and vegan isn't just about honoring a heritage, it's about power. This power is not about feeling superior to anyone else. I don't care if you are celebrity or a multi-millionaire; at the end of the day, we're all human beings. But being Black and vegan is about setting a powerful example in our neighborhoods and beyond. It's about being a source of information and inspiration, so that if you want more information about the lifestyle or even take that journey yourself, you can see someone who looks like you and who understands your reality. I'm not saying there's anything wrong with consulting with a white person, but there is a level of comfort and relatability that we have. We are the hidden gems in the neighborhood, because there aren't (yet) a lot of Black vegan brothas.

Being a Black vegan brotha also means we can be role models in our relationships and in our attitude toward life. I helped my current partner transition to a plant-based diet, and because of the knowledge that I have acquired through Dr. Sebi, Dr. Afrika, Queen Afua, and other healers, I am attuned to a holistic healing that helps our entire relationship thrive and grow.

I have also been inspired by the editor of this book, Omowale Adewale, who has been on the vegan, plant-based journey for years. From the moment I met him, he told me his experiences and showed me how he meets and conquers challenges. One form of inspiration is how in-shape he is as a man in his forties! As a mixed martial artist and boxer, he demonstrates every day how you can get all the protein you need to build muscle and maintain strength and definition. He explodes the notion that if you don't eat meat you won't get enough protein or build enough muscle. When you see brothas like Omowale or myself, you can see that anything is possible.

Another brotha I admire is the Nashville-based vegan trainer Tay Sweat (iamthevegantrainer.com). His life story is extraordinary: at the age of fourteen, he weighed over 300 pounds, and, as his website states, "he suffered from ailments such as eczema, heart & digestive issues, and was diagnosed as pre-diabetic." I know that he studied with Dr. Sebi and safely and responsibly lost a third of that body weight. He not only became an athlete but, as he says, "reversed all of his ailments due to the change in his diet." Last but not least, I look up to John Lewis, the Badass Vegan (badassvegan.com). This is a man who was a Division I college basketball player, and who looks younger than me (I'm twenty-seven; he's forty-one!).

These are three great Black men I look up to for inspiration and whom I relate to. They motivate me because they've been walking the talk for so long.

Finally, I think it's important to remember that you don't have to become a super-athlete to be a vegan, or vice versa. I do tailor my fitness regimens and diet suggestions for individuals who may have particular goals in mind, but I don't have a target audience when I talk about veganism, fitness, and wellness. All types of people, young and old, men and women, follow me, and that is something I'm very proud of. It also reflects a fundamental truth about this journey: Our health should be our natural heritage, as individuals and as a people. We should have the knowledge and the power to be able to *choose* to be healthy. ✸

25

KNOWING OUR FOREFATHERS

Lord Cannon

I am LordMurkEl, also known as Lord Cannon, born thirty years ago in Harlem, New York. I was raised by Spanish speakers from "Boriken," the word I was taught the indigenous people of the island known today as Puerto Rico knew it by. They lived in the South Bronx, and I consequently experienced various cultures on the streets and in my home. I was good at school, moved again, and when I was about sixteen, I began to study what I thought was Black history—the Black Panthers, Elijah Muhammad of the Nation of Islam, and the Black Muslim movement—finally finding Moorish Science at seventeen. I was really into the hip hop group The Diplomats, and this combination of music and revolutionary ideas caused me to want to be my own boss. Ten years later, I'm the owner of a vegan shop and deli called NatchaAkhz Hood Vegan Shop&Deli and Moor2Life Consulting, a service centered on Moorish nationality, citizenship, life coaching, research, and Spanish tutoring.

Hip hop and veganism are a huge part of my culture. Hip hop is Moorish-American culture made in the United States. All the lanes are based upon sounds that are American-made: the blues, R&B, and jazz. Hip hop is the manifestation of what I was doing thousands of years ago, a culture that ties me to the ancestral roots. For instance, the dancing looks just like Native American dancing, because our ancestors are one.

In my music, I rap about my life, about being a vegan, and still being in the street. I make vegan bars and vegan punch lines: I want people to know you can be vegan and still have fun. I've been writing every day since I was fifteen or sixteen, but I've taken it to the next level: writing, free-styling, and martial arts. I found a few open-mic scenes in Brooklyn and started to realize that people appreciated what I brought to them. For me, hip hop is a lifestyle and culture: the dialect, the being in the right place at the wrong time. I'm working on four albums, and I'm still learning more of the game.

I became vegan in November 2012, having just turned twenty-two. My curiosity and studies of Moorish Science sparked an entire awakening: of who my ancestors were and how and what they ate. I started questioning why I dressed and ate a certain way and how I interacted with people in my environment: other Asiatics like myself, the police, society as a whole. I also happened to have a friend who was vegan and very pretty. We were both raised in Harlem, both of us were Puerto Rican, and both of us were interested in Moorish Science. I recall reading *How to Eat to Live* by the Honorable Elijah Muhammad, in which he critiqued the eating of animal flesh, and I began to take my diet and fasting seriously. I also started to become more interested in Islam, or peace with God and my environment.

All praise is due to Allah: this was the beginning of my ongoing vegan journey. Veganism has nothing to do with being effeminate; it's about acknowledging your ancestors. If you do so, you'll be so powerful you won't have to be violent. I see people are conditioned and indoctrinated into slave mentality regarding eating. For me, veganism is a way of fighting slavery and that slave mentality. It extends to all the utensils we use in NatchaAkhz Hood Vegan. I've cared about the environment since a child; I have to maintain the planet while I'm doing this. That's real. I also don't wear fur: not only because it isn't inherently part of my culture, but because it is against the rules of Islam to kill a living creature simply to wear it. But I am *not* not going to wear fur because a European tells me. A European should be more worried about how many of my people he's imprisoning daily rather than how many animals he himself is killing.

I started NatchaAkhz Hood Vegan for a certain group of people: those who are referred to as Negro, Black, or Colored—who are *not* of Caribbean ancestry or Hispanic descent. I told myself: "I'm gonna make food that *we* want to eat. I'll make you a chop cheese sandwich, but I want to make it vegan. I don't want 'Sarah' or 'Sally' or 'Caroline' to make my vegan bacon egg and cheese, because they're not from where I'm from. Y'all don't even use seasoning." I said to myself: "Boom! I'm gonna show how we do it in the South

Bronx and Harlem, because we use seasoning. *Un poco Adoba aqui; un poco Achiote allá!* I start using the Sofrito. Mmm! Mmm! Mmm! I'm official!"

I tell people that I make Moorish-American food, because it's not Black food if you're not Black. Moorish people are not Negros, not Colored, not so-called African-Americans. Moors are Asiatics. Instead of arguing with someone who doesn't understand, I'm gonna call my food what it is, and you're gonna make the correlation for yourself. My energy is giving off peace, because the food I'm making is good. I'm not just giving people food but showing them the divine and a pathway to the ancestors. To have peace with Allah, you have to go deep within yourself, because Allah is all things in existence. Love is a skill that should be harnessed by and worked on by more people. I think that comes naturally to me because I was given a lot of affection as a child. I'm not too soft, but I'm also not too stern.

Some want to play with me. Because I'm Asiatic, and I have the appearance of a so-called Black man, they tell me, "I don't want to pay $20 for that," even though they'll go to a white restaurant and pay $20 every day. A few times, I've said, "Don't try to short me; short the white man. *Yo, porque tu?* Why you playing with me?" And he'll relax and buy the sandwich.

Now, if you ask me why my sandwiches cost $20, the answer is, *because I made them.* By ascribing value to what I feed people, I'm empowering them to think about what they feel their own food is worth, and to test me and force me to improve. They'll be inspired to think bigger and better, and we can start to become an economic powerhouse as a people. But we can't do that if we're not being the example that we want other people to see.

This was the example I was given by the Honorable Elijah Muhammad and Master Fard Muhammad, the founder of the Nation of Islam. This is the example I give with my food, as I would if I were teaching Moorish Science or practicing martial arts. Food is effective because it tastes amazing, activates nostalgia, and leaves you feeling satisfied.

Interesting story: A European once told me that my sandwiches were too expensive to sell in New Jersey. I thought: *Look at this European trying to tell an Asiatic how much to sell their stuff for!* I went right back to the hood—to one of the projects—and I sold out for three weeks. I've gotten invites to vend at world-class locations because people can see my drive.

Customers can spend $40 and say, "Man, I'm just coming back 'cause I like the energy." That's powerful. I inspire people to spend money. What's more Harlem than that?

The Challenges and Successes of Business

One challenge is a lack of capital to properly maintain and keep a business. Another is that New York City makes it very difficult because of the many regulations you have to deal with. Yet another is providing customers with food that's soy-free, gluten-free, or both.

A fourth challenge is becoming "official" and professional and not losing "street cred"—to conform and still be a hood vegan. It's like being an independent rapper for five years and then signing to a major label. People might think, *He don't sound hungry no more*. I recognize that issue. I need to acknowledge that, if I'm going to make my own way, be independent, and keep a job, sometimes I'm not going to have people's support, and at other times, that support is going to be overwhelming. Although the community can be tight, I've encountered some weird, other-side, colorism/racism, self-hating shit. Because of that competitiveness and attitude, some people have blown a chance to collaborate with me and draw attention and momentum to what they're doing.

In contrast with the challenges, however, the vegan community in New York can be very helpful and supportive. The vegan community right now is like the hip hop community in the early days. You can call somebody up and say, "Yo, I heard you *killed this* over here—that was hot! And I just wanted to let you know—I see you, my G!"

Everything else is pretty smooth. Allah makes everything come together.

Always Learning

I'm always learning and trying to grow. I started studying a form of Jujitsu in 2015. My teacher is Professor Dominick Brioché of Moorish-Haitian descent, and probably the most impressive woman I know, in every way—her manner of speech, dress, combat, and comportment. She and the style of martial arts I follow help me walk with my ancestors, because the founder of the system handed this system to a brother, and that brother gave the system to another brother, and that brother gave that system to a sister. There are plenty of vegans in my dojo as well. Grand Master Bill McCloud is a well-known vegan practitioner, and some in the upper-class were vegan when I joined the dojo and told me I was in the right place.

Aside from these teachings, I've taken it upon myself to learn the various studies of my ancestors—including astrology, divination, dancing. Eventually, I'm going to study law, so I can be a vegan rapper and a vegan lawyer and help bail people out! I'll get the necessary training to take people who owe us our just due to court. They can't give me the land, because they never owned it. But they *can* give me the money.

I want to make a better, brighter place for my daughter. I want NatchaAkhz to be operating in every state in the United States of America where there's an Asiatic presence by the year 2040. I want us to acquire real estate; I want to open up schools, establish temples, and found institutions of higher learning, community centers, and birthing centers. I'm constantly seeking out new disciplines I want to study—but all in the realm of Moorish Science. As a brother, I recognize that all the sciences belong to me and my people, and so it's just a matter of time before I embrace them all: all the cultures, religions, languages, and perspectives that make up the one great God.

The goal is to keep the Asiatics, and the sons and daughters of the Asiatic race, in North America so they learn love instead of hate, and know their higher and lower selves. I want to teach the human family the oneness of Allah and Man. I want to unite Asiatic nations who believe they are different due to the efforts of Europeans to teach us that we're different. I want to say to all the Moors and those who call themselves "African-Americans," Indians, and Asiatics that we come together as one people here, and can attain a unified presence, politically and socioeconomically.

One thing is certain: I don't want my daughter to have to do the things that I had to do. I want it to be easier for her. I want to teach her from a young age to do things for herself—just like in our ancestors' culture. I want to show her how to cook, to spell, to communicate, to run a business, to learn about money. Ultimately, the goal is moral and spiritual relief, which is desperately needed by our people, who are dying because they don't know their forefathers.

For more information on my journey, myself, and Moorish Science, check out www.moorishharlem.nyc and www.natchaakhz.com as well as my Instagram pages: @moorishharlem.nyc and @moor2lifeconsulting.

Peace and Love to the readers and the supporters of Omowale's great program. ☀

26

KNOW BETTER, DO BETTER (CLICHÉD, YET SO TRUE)

Michael Barber

My doctor casually informed me that my white blood cell count was low.

"What does that mean?" I asked him.

"Don't be alarmed, but it could be cancer . . . leukemia," he replied. "We will have to run tests."

Knowing what I know now, the O'Jays' song "For the Love of Money" comes to mind.

During this time, I was suffering from brain fog, chronic fatigue, dry mouth, skin irritation, and gastric issues when I consumed wheat, grains, red meat, dairy, eggs, coffee, alcohol, and fried foods. *Ok*, I thought to myself. *I'll let them run more tests. But why doesn't my doctor refer me to a nutritionist, allergist, an arthritis expert, or an oncologist?* Eventually, I asked my doctor about my diet. His response was customary: "I don't think that it has anything to do with the foods that you're consuming." I found this answer perplexing, considering that from my perspective there was a clear connection with the types of foods I was consuming and my physical state. Furthermore, why did he tell me to come back in four months if my symptoms persisted, which was the time that he projected he was going to be settled in at his new medical practice?

African-American males often have genetic markers that vary constitutionally, relative to their white contemporaries. I had to learn that rather significant bit of information from my friend and yoga instructor, whose brother had a similar scare with cancer when he was informed that his white blood cell count was low.

My primary doctor's default denial, along with the outright rejection by many other doctors (not healers) of the idea that a person's constitution and nutritional habits must be factored into their current and prospective state of wellness, is profoundly disturbing. It is especially troubling in light of all of the studies that clearly cite the adverse impact to people—no matter where they live on this planet—of consuming a standard American diet (SAD). This information, along with the failure to acknowledge the historic impact on people who have been injected with poisonous vaccines, as well as the targeting of certain racial groups that have experienced spikes in poorer health outcomes—such as autoimmune deficiencies—was enough for me to seek alternate methods of addressing my medical issues.

I started researching cancer and discovered a correlation between the consumption of meat, dairy, and inflammatory foods and increased rates of autoimmune diseases, cancer, and other health-related deficiencies. This led me to stop eating meat and dairy and to start consuming whole foods and drinking alkaline water. Further, I learned that many people have used holistic healing modalities to cure themselves of cancer and autoimmune problems. Based on my research, I started cleansing, detoxing, and consuming herbs and sea vegetables such as bladderwrack, burdock, ginger, Irish sea moss, Pau D'Arco, ginger, and turmeric to assist me on my journey to achieve optimal health.

Next, I began to attend vegan and vegetarian festivals throughout New York State and met vegans who understood my struggles, as many had faced their own health challenges and had overcome them, largely by adopting a vegan lifestyle. There were several points of no return for me, and one of them was attending an Alkaline Eclectic cooking demo, hosted by founders Crush Foster and Kelly Keelo, in Bushwick, Brooklyn. It felt awesome to be in a room full of people that looked like me and to learn how to use alkaline foods to create an environment ideal for cellular rejuvenation and the healing of my body. Around that time, I lost thirty-five pounds and felt empowered as my brain fog, inflammation, and other symptoms began to dissipate.

Several months later, I attended the Black VegFest in Brooklyn, which was a huge turning point for me. I visited the festival with my sixteen-year-old son on a rainy Saturday morning in August. It was uplifting and inspiring to converse with so many like-minded individuals that looked like me and discuss the tenets of healthy living and raising our cellular vibrations. That day, I was introduced to many wonderful folk who embraced all people—vegans and non-vegans alike—and I began to learn about the importance of creating spaces for intersectional discussions, and how to decolonize my body.

I thank the good brother Omowale Adewale for establishing a venue for people of color to learn about veganism, compassion, and humanity, as he unapologetically uses Black VegFest as a space to lift the voices of people who are often culturally marginalized by mainstream vegans—a majority of whom are, despite our common interests, too often hypocritical.

Through veganism, I not only healed myself, but also developed a greater understanding of the unsustainable environmental impact that breeding animals has on our planet. I comprehended that we are dying prematurely as a result of being in thrall to the trappings of a seemingly civilized and evolved society. I now see the fallacy of eating for pleasure to the detriment of our own livelihoods; and, most important, I realize the importance of raising our collective vibrations and evolving as a conscious people. I have learned there is no substitute for the enzymes, minerals, and other sources of life energy in the food and herbs I eat. As a result of this newfound wisdom and understanding of my body, my diet consists of very high-energy, nutrient-dense whole foods, and I keep processed foods to a minimum. My system tends not to digest products like seitan, soy, or gluten very well. Today, I feel like I have a new lease on life and there is no turning back!

We have been conditioned to believe everything our doctors, teachers, and others in authority tell us. They—specifically doctors—studied modern medicine and took an oath to treat people with a high standard of care. However, the medical system doesn't benefit from people's being cured, but rather thrives on our becoming patients. The system doesn't teach the power of positive thinking, nutrition, raising vibrations, or cellular development in a way that empowers us to not need the modern-day medical system, its treatments, or its medications. I had to take control of my health and realize that answers were out there, and it was my responsibility to find them and not rely on the system to help me find the solution to getting out of the maze that the system itself built or at the very least is the ultimate benefactor of! I started to change my vibrations.

A statement I believe is, "If you act the way you want to be, sooner or later you will be the way that you act." I stopped eating dead animals and saying I was "sick," and instead started eating fruits and vegetables and saying, "I'm in the process of healing." Eating dead animals is not a reflection of an evolved culture, nor is consuming poison because it tastes good, and blaming death on our family's genes.

Let's get and stay woke, good brothers: the struggle continues! ☀

27

WHY BLACK MEN SHOULD GO VEGAN

Kevin Jenkins

They say bad things come in threes, and I should have known this. However, I was too busy enjoying life to see this ominous sign, until I received a third phone call. You see, in 2018, I received three calls from three Black men who called me because they knew that I am a vegan and certified as a vegan lifestyle coach and educator. Each called stating they wanted help with the same problem. And what was this problem? They all had prostate cancer.

To say I was shocked is an understatement. One brother was a close relative, and the other two were associates of mine in my profession as a pastor. These men called me not only because I was their friend but also because they have been close observers of my lifestyle and, as one of them said, I was a cheerleader for avoiding the use of animals in eating and clothing. Two of these men had personally heard me pontificate about this subject for decades.

So, in order that other Black men do not experience this dreaded disease, which claims the lives of one in twenty-three men in our community and at a rate 2.4 times more than white men,[*] I'm going to suggest five reasons why there is a significant need for Black men to go vegan.

1. PROTEIN

When I am in dialogue with many brothers about the possibility of transitioning from meat eating to eating plants, the first question on a brother's mind is "Where do I get my protein?" This question is the result of the successful brainwashing by the meat and

---

[*] Lannis Hall, Arnold D. Bullock, et al. "Prostate Cancer Isn't Colorblind," *New York Times*, July 27, 2016, https://www.nytimes.com/2016/07/27/opinion/prostate-cancer-isnt-colorblind.html; and Boston Scientific. "Prostate Cancer: Patient Resources," n.d., https://www.spaceoar.com/patients/prostate-cancer-resources-and-articles/prostate-cancer-in-african-american-men/.

dairy industry emphasizing the falsehood that the highest source of protein you can get is from the consumption of animal products. But there is another reason why men ask this question: They fear the loss of muscle mass if they stop eating meat.

Let me assure you that you will not lose out on your protein source or muscle mass. Plants not only have protein, but the largest animals on Earth are plant eaters: oxen, gorillas, elephants, rhinos, horses, and giraffes, to name a few. Examine these creatures, and you will notice they have no diminished muscle mass. Furthermore, check out Black male vegan athletes like Omowale Adewale, Dominick Thompson, Torre Washington, Badass Vegan, and others for concrete proof that vegan men have muscle mass. For many in our society, protein deficiency is not the problem; it's fiber deficiency. And only plants contain fiber.

2. PASSION

The second reason to go vegan is sex. Now, if you fear the loss of protein, I am sure this next reason to go plant-strong will give you plenty of motivation. I don't know of any man, especially a Black man, who doesn't want the edge in the bedroom. How much this is desired is indicated by the amount of money that is spent annually on erectile dysfunction (ED) medication. According to Zion Market Research, the global ED drugs market will reach $7.10 billion by 2024.* ED is the result of blockage of the heart, which prevents blood flow to the penis. Heart blockage is the direct consequence of eating animals and raising bad cholesterol, which in turn has deleterious consequences on your "sex machine." If you want to sing like James Brown in the bedroom even in your old age—eat plants!

---

* Zion Market Research. "Global Erectile Dysfunction Drugs Market Will Reach USD 7.10 Billion by 2024: Zion Market Research," October 5, 2018, https://www.globenewswire.com/news-release/2018/10/05/1617442/0/en/Global-Erectile-Dysfunction-Drugs-Market-Will-Reach-USD-7-10-Billion-by-2024-Zion-Market-Research.html.

3. PROTECTION

Men are naturally protectors. We have a desire to prevent harm to our families and communities. Going vegan is another way that you can follow your natural instinct as a protector. What do I mean? Going vegan protects not just your health but also animals and the environment. Planet Earth is in the midst of climate change; global warming is the topic of the day. Numerous studies confirm that one of the best ways to help the environment is to reduce the intake of animal food and/or eliminate it altogether. It is as simple as substituting beans for beef.* Men were made to be protectors, and going vegan will fulfill part of this mission.

4. PROTEST

Coupled with protection is protest. Veganism is a social justice movement. You don't necessarily have to march in the streets with picket signs decrying the social evils of the day. You can protest this by simply adopting a vegan lifestyle, which includes watching what you eat and what you wear. Here's what you protest when you go vegan:

- More than 200 million land animals killed daily
- 72 billion land animals killed per year
- Over 1.2 trillion aquatic animals killed for food annually[†]

And this is just for food, not counting killing animals for fashion. Remember: Going vegan is a protest against the use of animals for food *and* clothing. You not only protest animal abuse and slaughter by your dietary and fashion choices, but you say, "Black Lives Matter!" Because you're taking care of your health.

---

* Susan Levin. "How You Can Help Save the Planet—and Yourself—Simply by Substituting Beans for Beef," *Salon*, June 11, 2017, https://www.salon.com/2017/06/10/how-you-can-help-save-the-planet-and-yourself-simply-by-substituting-beans-for-beef_partner/.

† Matthew Zampa. "How Many Animals Are Killed for Food Every Day?" *Sentient Media*, September 16, 2018, https://sentientmedia.org/how-many-animals-are-killed-for-food-every-day/.

For example, did you know that in 2011, CVD (cardiovascular disease) caused the deaths of 46,081 Black men and 47,130 Black women?* In his book *How Not To Die*,† Dr. Michael Greger lists the fifteen leading causes of death caused by sickness and tells us all of them can be avoided if we eat more plants! By going vegan you wage a protest against a healthcare system that is not focused on healthcare but rather on disease care.

You protest animal slaughter and disease, but also fast food genocide. When I was a child, one of my great cartoon heroes was Popeye. Popeye got strong because he ate spinach. He was the first vegan superhero. But Popeye must be rolling in his grave because so many chicken fast food places are using his name.

I always say you can get away with murder when you put murder in food. Just take a look in our neighborhoods, and you can see fast food places and liquor stores. And what is the result? Our community is burdened with obesity, diabetes, and cancer. As Black men we can combat these medical problems by not only going vegan but also establishing farmers markets where people can have access to more fruits and vegetables.

5. POWER

The fifth and final reason why Black men should go vegan is intriguing. It's intriguing because in our history there is a consistent attempt to deny Black men power—whether it's politically, educationally, or professionally. So how does going vegan help a Black man secure power?

In a way, I hope I have secured this argument in my previous points. However, let me add two more reasons under the umbrella of power: energy and anti-aging. I'm not telling you something that I have not experienced. I have been plant-based for over forty-four years, starting with becoming vegetarian when I was nineteen and vegan forty years later.

---

* American Heart Association/American Stroke Association. "African-Americans & Cardiovascular Diseases: Statistical Fact Sheet 2015 Update." https://www.heart.org/idc/groups/heart-public/@wcm/@sop/@smd/documents/downloadable/ucm_472910.pdf.

† Michael Greger, M.D. *How Not to Die: Discover the Foods Scientifically Proven to Prevent and Reverse Disease* (New York: Flatiron Books, 2015).

My energy levels are off the charts because I haven't eaten animals who are killed in slaughterhouses, hearing the screams of their fellow creatures and smelling the blood of the dying. When you are eating animals, you are placing that energy inside of you. This is confirmed by studies that suggest a connection between mental illness and diet.[*]

Eating plants energizes you because they also contain anti-aging properties. I always love the shock on people's faces when I tell them how old I am! Before I give the big reveal, I always ask them to guess my age. And I always get ten to twenty years younger. This is the result of a combination of spirituality, a positive attitude, consistent exercise, and a vegan lifestyle.

Black men: You are destined for glory and greatness. What you do for your health will impact our communities. It's time to consider going vegan. Going vegan will empower you to fight against the unrelenting challenges we face daily in a society designed to disempower us.

Becoming stronger mentally, physically, and spiritually starts with what's on your plate. And we if start this journey, we can chant like actor Derek Luke in the movie *Antwone Fisher*: "I'm still standing. I'm still strong." ❀

---

[*] James Ponder. "School of Public Health Study Links Unhealthy Diet to Mental Illness in California Adults," Loma Linda University Health, February 20, 2019, https://news.llu.edu/research/school-of-public-health-study-links-unhealthy-diet-mental-illness-california-adults.

BIOGRAPHIES

Eric Adams has been Brooklyn Borough President since 2013, and has served the City of New York as a police officer, legislative leader, activist, and coalition builder. In 1995, he cofounded 100 Blacks in Law Enforcement Who Care, and was elected to the New York State Senate in 2006, representing parts of Brooklyn. He is the author of *Healthy at Last: A Plant-Based Approach to Preventing and Reversing Diabetes and Other Chronic Diseases* (Carlsbad, CA: Hay House, 2020). In 2020, he announced he was running to be mayor of New York City.

Omowale Adewale is an activist and organizer, and the founder of Black VegFest, a network of African-American festivals celebrating veganism, wellness, social justice, and resilience throughout the United States. A former athlete in bodybuilding and track and field, he is certified both in plant-based nutrition and as a USA boxing coach. He lives in upstate New York. His website is omowale.org.

Baba Brother-D B. Aammaa Nubyahn is a retired community health worker, continuously involved in Pan-African Nationalist and related political work since 1971. He is best known for the hip hop era's first radical rap, "How We Gonna Make the Black Nation Rise." You can view a number of his thought-provoking videos on his YouTube channel: www.youtube.com/user/TheNuashe.

Michael Barber is a diversity and inclusion professional, vegan, human rights advocate, and former Black VegFest organizer. Through his work, he seeks to dismantle systems of oppression, diversify and empower people within those systems to reach organizational potential, and increase awareness of the benefits of holistic living. Toward that end, he recently completed the Plant-Based Nutrition Certificate Program through the T. Colin Campbell Center for Nutrition Studies at Cornell University, and is currently enrolled in the Diversity and Inclusion Certificate Program at Cornell. Veganism has helped him to increase the quality of his health, connection with Mother Earth, and his level of compassion for all living beings.

Scott "Burnhard" Bernard is a fitness model, holistic fitness coach (both online and offline), motivational speaker, fitness enthusiast, community activist, and forever a student for LIFE. He lives in New York City.

Ra-leek Born is a high school student and boxer at Eastern Queens Boxing Club. Originally from Norfolk, Virginia, he lives in Queens, New York. At the age of ten he won the Metro Junior Olympic Championship, and in 2019 was the New York State Silver Gloves Champion.

Lord Cannon (a.k.a. LordMurkEl) is a rapper, activist, and the founder of NatchaAkhz, a hood vegan shop and deli in Harlem, New York. For more information on his journey, his life, and Moorish Science, check out www.moorishharlem.nyc and www.natchaakhz.com as well as his Instagram pages: @moorishharlem.nyc and @moor2lifeconsulting.

Anthony Carr is a Ph.D. candidate at the University of South Carolina in counselor education and supervision. He has been a vegan for twelve years.

Fred "Doc" Beasley II is founder and chapter leader of New York City's Hip Hop Is Green, a plant-based multimedia company developed to introduce inner-city youth to the benefits of living a healthy, balanced lifestyle in flavorful and digestible ways. He is a global youth culture architect and lifelong creative who has traveled the world doing interactive workshops and lectures designed to empower the disenfranchised. He produced the award-winning documentary *Raise Up: The World Is Our Gym* (2016), and is currently working on his first children's book. He resides on Roosevelt Island in New York City with his wife and four children.

Jae Yahkèl Estes, XVX is ineffable. A radical revolutionary rational realist. A parent, a partner, a poet, and a prophet. A musician, a muse, a mage, and a monk. An artist, an activist, an anarchist, and an alliteratist. Visit leafcakelife.com.

A. Breeze Harper has a Ph.D. in critical food geographies and is the founder of the Sistah Vegan Project. She started The Sistah Vegan Project as an online forum that focuses on how plant-based consumptive lifestyle is affected by factors of race, racisms, sexism, heterosexism, classism, and other social injustices within the lives of black females. From this forum, she developed *Sistah Vegan: Black Women Speak on Food, Identity, Health, and Society*, which in 2020 celebrated its tenth anniversary with a new foreword by Breeze Harper. Breeze lives in the Bay Area of California. Her website is www.abreezeharper.com.

Khnum "Stic" Ibomu is a rapper known for his work in the political hip hop duo dead prez. Stic is also a runner, author, and social justice activist who promotes a healthy lifestyle through veganism. In his book *Eat Plants, Lift Iron*, Stic chronicles his effort, as a slim runner, to gain weight on a high-performance plant-based diet. The book includes contributions from certified personal trainer and strength coach Scott Shetler as well as holistic nutritionist and plant-based chef Afya Ibomu. Stic views health advocacy as a "revolutionary act."

Kevin Jenkins, D.Min., VLCE, CPT is pastor of the Genesis Seventh-Day Adventist Church in Plainfield, New Jersey; host of THE COOL Vegan Radio Show on Blogtalk Radio; and a vegan lifestyle coach and educator.

Malcolm Jones (malc) is a recent graduate from Towson University. He's going to run his own movie studio in the future. He would like to recognize his family, friends, teachers, and peers. If you would like to reach out to Malcolm, you can do so through Instagram: @27malcolm.

Charles McCoy, a.k.a. PlantHero, is community nutritionist at Wonderful Life Adult Day Care, LLC, and Paradise Adult Day Care Center, both in Brooklyn, New York. He is also senior culinary specialist at Public School 150 and a part-time brand ambassador for Beyond Meat. He is the founding director and CEO of Plant Harmony Health Center

& Plant Health Care Inc., which is devoted to integrating recent scientific findings with already proven health facts around the plant-based diet.

Kezekial McWhinney-StLouis is a Black queer and nonbinary vegan who connects with veganism through their various identities. Kez is outspoken about the many injustices in the world and works with organizations like the Rockland Pride Center and Woodstock Animal Sanctuary to spread awareness about human and animal rights issues that need attention. They recently moved from Pennsylvania to live with their brother, Travis, who is also a Black vegan, in New Jersey.

Milton Mills, M.D. practices urgent care medicine in the Washington, DC area, and has served previously as associate director of preventive medicine and as a member of the National Advisory Board for Physicians Committee for Responsible Medicine (PCRM). He has been a major contributor to position papers presented by PCRM to the United States Department of Agriculture regardingdietary guidelines for Americans, and has been the lead plaintiff in PCRM's class-action lawsuit that asks for warning labels on milk. Dr. Mills earned his medical degree at Stanford University School of Medicine and completed an internal medicine residency at Georgetown University Hospital. He has published several research journal articles dealing with racial bias in federal nutrition policy. He frequently donates his time via practicing at free medical clinics, and travels widely, speaking at hospitals, churches, and community centers throughout the country. He was featured in the documentary films *What the Health* and *The Silent Vegan*.

Stewart Devon Mitchell is the author of *Liberation Summer*, *#greatestwrapperalive: A Memoir Recipe Book Through the Power of Conscious Hip Hop Lyrics*, *There Is Beauty in the Darkness*, and *Kayla the Vegan*. He lives in Brooklyn, New York.

Brandon Morton is currently in his final year studying at Bronx Community College in partnership with the New York Botanical Garden for a degree in horticulture.

Mutulu Olugbala, a.k.a. M-1 of dead prez, is a rapper, activist, and author from Brooklyn, New York. His albums with dead prez include *Let's Get Free* (2000), *Revolutionary But Gangsta* (2004), *Live in San Francisco* (2008), and *Information Age* (2012). In 2006, he produced a solo album, *Confidential* (2006).

Donald Peebles is a writer, author, and soap opera lover who is working on a book project on Black soap opera history. He is an adult librarian at the Brooklyn Public Library.

Kimatni Rawlins founded Fit Fathers to inspire other men to lead the charge in prioritizing healthier eating and exercise to enhance the lives of themselves and their families. After losing fifty pounds, he created the educational website FitFathers.com to help other dads do the same. Rawlins is a certified fitness trainer, graduate of the Plant-Based Nutrition Certificate, and the founder of Automotive Rhythms Communications, LLC, a lifestyle automotive media and marketing portal consisting of Internet, network television, online video, print, radio, and event properties. In the ten years of its existence, Automotive Rhythms has positively educated millions of automotive buyers on how they view and purchase new and used vehicles. He is the proud father of two young girls. He lives in Silver Spring, Maryland.

Anteneh Roba, M.D. is a board certified anti-aging and obesity medicine physician. He is president and cofounder of the International Fund for Africa (IFA), a non-profit organization and a registered non-governmental organization in Ethiopia dedicated to helping both human and nonhuman animals in Africa. Through IFA, Dr. Roba has been involved in improving healthcare for children in Ethiopia as well as feeding hungry schoolchildren, and has worked to make medical care accessible to the people of rural Ethiopia. He is the co-editor with Rainer Ebert of *Africa and Her Animals: Philosophical and Practical Applications* (Pretoria: UNISA Press, 2018), and has contributed chapters to two books, *Circles of Compassion: Essays Connecting Issues of Justice* (Boston: Vegan Publishers, 2015) and *Rethink Food: 100+ Doctors Can't Be Wrong* (Houston: Two Skirts Productions, 2014).

Dr. Roba frequently lectures on the health and societal benefits of a plant-based diet and related issues affecting Africa. He lives in Fairfax, Virginia.

Richard W. Rogers Jr. has since 2017 been the director of the Philadelphia VegFest, a festival celebrating vegan and whole-food, plant-based lifestyles and featuring vendors and exhibitors of related foods, goods, services, and activities, as well as musicians, performers, presenters, and speakers versed in the lifestyle. He is the owner of Plant Based Human, a vegan café in Ambler, Pennsylvania.

Bryant Terry is an award-winning chef, educator, speaker, author, vegan, and activist with a mission to "create a healthy, just, and sustainable food system." Terry is the chef-in-residence at the Museum of the African Diaspora in San Francisco and the host and co-creator of the web series *Urban Organic*. In 2002, Terry founded b-healthy (Build Healthy Eating and Lifestyles to Help Youth), a New York City-based initiative created to empower youth to fight for a just food system. Terry continues to partner with schools and communities nationwide to inspire young people to get involved in the food justice movement. His latest book, *Afro Vegan*, was nominated for an NAACP Image Award in the Outstanding Literary Work category.

Donald Vincent ("Mr. Hip") is a writer and creative director living and working in Los Angeles. He is the author of *Convenient Amnesia* (Frankfort, KY: Broadstone Books, 2020) as well the album *Vegan Paradise*, a cruelty-free hip hop poetry project created in 2018. He lives in Los Angeles, California.

Dr. Ietef "DJ Cavem" Vita is chief executive officer at Plant Based Records, a record label dedicated to culinary climate action and making music fresh again by dropping organic, compostable, and plantable items. He is the co-owner of Vita Earth, LLC, an environmental work and plant-based culinary action for a healthy body and planet, and the CEO of Eco-Cultivator. He earned a Ph.D. in urban ecology from the Denver Institute of Urban Studies in 2017. He is based in Denver, Colorado.

Torre Washington, vegan since 1998, is a five-time bodybuilding champion. Born in Alabama, Washington spent part of his childhood in Jamaica and views his veganism as an extension of his Jamaican heritage; the Rastafarian Ital way of life is nutritionally similar to the vegan diet. In addition to his bodybuilding goals, Washington aims to help to grow the vegan community. He plans to launch a website to promote veganism for the animals and the planet; create a documentary on veganism; and develop an event that will focus on vegan fitness. ✺

ABOUT THE EDITORS

Omowale Adewale is an activist and organizer, and the founder of Black VegFest, a network of African-American festivals celebrating veganism, wellness, social justice, and resilience throughout the United States. A former athlete in bodybuilding and track and field, he is certified both in plant-based nutrition and as a USA boxing coach. He lives in upstate New York. His website is omowale.org.

A. Breeze Harper has a Ph.D. in critical food geographies and is the founder of the Sistah Vegan Project. She started The Sistah Vegan Project as an online forum that focuses on how plant-based consumptive lifestyle is affected by factors of race, racisms, sexism, heterosexism, classism, and other social injustices within the lives of black females. From this forum, she developed *Sistah Vegan: Black Women Speak on Food, Identity, Health, and Society*, which in 2020 celebrated its tenth anniversary with a new foreword by Breeze Harper. Breeze lives in the Bay Area of California. Her website is www.abreezeharper.com.

ABOUT THE PUBLISHER

Lantern Publishing & Media was founded in 2020 to follow and expand on the legacy of Lantern Books—a publishing company started in 1999 on the principles of living with a greater depth and commitment to the preservation of the natural world. Like its predecessor, Lantern Publishing & Media produces books on animal advocacy, veganism, religion, social justice, and psychology and family therapy. Lantern is dedicated to printing in the United States on recycled paper and saving resources in our day-to-day operations. Our titles are also available as e-books and audiobooks.

To catch up on Lantern's publishing program, visit us at www. lanternpm.org.

facebook.com/lanternpm
twitter.com/lanternpm
instagram.com/lanternpm